Saad Elkhadem

# THE
# YORK DICTIONARY

## OF

English — French — German — Spanish

# LITERARY TERMS

and

their Origin

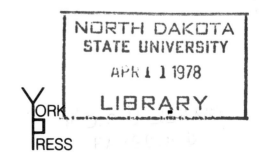

York
Press

## Acknowledgment

I wish to express my sincere gratitude to Professors

> Franz Eppert,
> Nela Hidalgo,
> Elisabeth McIntyre,
> Roger Moore, and
> Fernando Poyatos

for their valuable assistance and advice.

I am deeply indebted to Françoise Vandervennet-Elkhadem for reviewing the French terms and suggesting others I have overlooked.

S.E.

## The York Dictionary of English-French-German-Spanish Literary Terms and their Origin

Copyright © 1976, York Press
P.O. Box 1172
Fredericton, N.B.
E3B 5C8 CANADA
ISBN 0-919966-04-7 Cloth bound ed.
0-919966-01-2 Paper bound ed.

> "Si quid novisti rectius istis,
> Candidus imperti; si non, his utere mecum!"

Horace

Linguists and literary historians seem to agree that defining literary terms is not only a difficult task, but also a risky and thankless one. More toilsome and less rewarding is the attempt to find the equivalent of a literary term in another language, simply because often there is none, or because other literatures sometimes use the same term to label a different phenomenon. I recommend, therefore, that the *translations* of English terms not be used uncritically.

In spite of these reservations, I have undertaken this task because I believe that students of literature, especially those of comparative literature, will be able to use these definitions and translations as a *springboard* for their own research. (The French, German, and Spanish indexes at the end of the book should assist in the search for more precise equivalents.) I hope also that by giving the reader an idea about the origin of a term and offering him other words similar or relevant to it, he will better understand its nature and significance.

Since a dictionary of this nature cannot be regarded as definitive, I should be grateful for any advice or suggestion I may receive.

S. E.

# List of Signs and Abbreviations

| | |
|---|---|
| * | : see |
| ** | : compare |
| ◡ | : unstressed (or short) syllable |
| — | : stressed (or long) syllable |
| ◡‿ | : either stressed (long) or unstressed (short) syllable |
| / / | : caesura or diaeresis |
| Ar. | : Arabic |
| dim. | : diminutive |
| F. | : French |
| G. | : German |
| Gael. | : Gaelic |
| Gk. | : Greek |
| Ir. | : Irish |
| It. | : Italian |
| Jap. | : Japanese |
| L. | : Latin |
| ME | : Middle English |
| ML | : Medieval Latin |
| OE | : Old English |
| OF | : Old French |
| OHG | : Old High German |
| Prov. | : Provençal |
| Rep. | : representatives |
| S. | : Spanish |

# A

**abecedarian** [L. of the alphabet]; (F. acrostiche alphabétique; G. Abecedarius, Abecedarien; S. acróstico): an *acrostic based on the alphabetical order of the initial words of successive lines. A poem written in this manner is called an abecedarius. (**acronym.)

**abecedarius:** *abecedarian.

**abstract** [L. drawn away]; (F. abstrait; G. abstrakt; S. abstracto): (1) subjective, ideal, insufficiently factual, and lacking in representation; as opposed to *concrete; (2)=*brief. (**abstract poetry; epitome; objectivity.)

**abstract poetry** [*abstract]; (F. poésie abstraite; G. abstrakte Dichtung; S. poesía abstracta): a type of poetry that does not reflect personal experience, deal with actual events, or represent concrete objects. (**abstract; concrete; objectivity; vorticism.)

**absurd** [L. incongruous]; (F. absurde; G. absurd; S. absurdo): *theater of the absurd.

**acatalectic** [Gk. not stopping]; (F. vers acatalectique; G. akatalektisch; S. acataléctico): a verse ending with a complete and undefective metrical foot. (**brachycatalectic; catalectic; hypermetric.)

**accent** [L. song added to speech]; (F. accent, ictus; G. Akzent, Betonung; S. acento)=*stress.

**accented syllable** [*accent, *syllable]; (F. syllabe accentuée; G. betonte Silbe; S. sílaba acentuada): a stressed syllable. (**beat; scansion; stress; syllable.)

**accentual verse** [*accent, *verse]; (F. vers rythmique; G. akzentuierender Vers; S. verso rítmico): a verse whose meter is based on stressed and unstressed syllables rather than on the length of time it takes to pronounce the syllables. (**alternate verse; atonic; quantitative verse; short syllable; thesis; tonic.)

**acephalous** [Gk. headless]; (F. acéphale; G. Akephal; S. acéfalo): a verse that does not adhere to the metrical pattern because its first syllable is missing. (**aphaeresis; brachycatalexis; catalectic; headless line; reizianum.)

**acmeism** [Gk. completion]; (F. acmeisme; G. Akmeismus, Adamismus; S. acmeísmo): a neoclassical literary movement in Russia in the second decade of the twentieth century opposing *symbolism. Rep. N. Gumilyov, S. Gorodetsky. (**classic(3); classicism(2); constructivism; formalism(2); socialist realism.)

**acronym** [Gk. tip of name]; (F. sigle; G. Akronym; S. sigla): a word that consists of the initial letters of other words. (**acrostic.)

**acrostic** [Gk. verse's tip]; (F. acrostiche; G. Akrostichon; S. acróstico): this occurs when the initial letters of lines or chapters form a word or a phrase. (**abecedarian; acronym; acroteleutic; anagram; cryptogram; mesostich; telestich.)

**acroteleutic** [Gk. extreme end]; (F. acroteleuton; G. Akroteleuton; S. acroteléutico): a combination of *acrostic and *telestich in the same line, stanza, or paragraph. (**mesostich.)

**act** [L. action]; (F. acte; G. Akt, Aufzug, Auftritt; S. acto): one of the main extrinsic as well as intrinsic divisions of a drama. The number of acts depends upon the developing and unfolding of the *plot. An act can be divided into smaller units known as scenes; the number of these depends upon (1) backgrounds needed; (2) frequency of appearance of new characters. (**drama; dramatic techniques; mise-en-scène.)

**acting time**= *fable time.

**action** [L. performance]; (F. action; G. Handlung; S. acción): the manner in which the events of a narrative or dramatic work unfold. (**argument; dramatic techniques; fable(2); plot; story; unities.)

**adage** [L. proverb]; (F. proverbe, adage; G. Spruch, Sprichwort; S. adagio): a saying or a *proverb. (**aphorism; apophthegm; epigram; maxim; paroemiac; sentence.)

**Adonic verse; Adoneus** [named after Adonis, a figure in Greek mythology]; (F. adonique; G. adonischer Vers, Adonius; S. verso adónico): a classical verse that consists of two metrical feet; e.g. the fourth and last line of the *Sapphic stanza.

**adventure novel** (F. roman d'aventures; G. Abenteuerroman; S. novela de aventuras): a novel that stresses the adventurous and uncommon aspects of life without considering the inwardness of the characters or the Zeitgeist. (**event-novel; novel.)

**adynaton** [Gk. impossibility]; (F. adynaton; G. Adynaton; S. adynaton): a rhetorical figure in which the word "never" is replaced by a series of impossibilities.

**aestheticism** [Gk. to perceive by the senses]; **aesthetic movement** (F. esthétisme; G. Ästhetizismus; S. movimiento estético): a French literary and artistic movement in the first half of the nineteenth century which demanded that art be freed from any obligation toward society and that its sole aim be a purely aesthetic one ("l'art pour l'art," art for art's sake). (**Tachtigers.)

**affective fallacy** (F. critique par l'effet, critique impressioniste; G. affektiver Trugschluß; S.—): an error in evaluating the poetic merit of a poem which results from stressing the importance of its effect on the reader instead of considering its intrinsic and extrinsic qualities. (**analysis; intentional fallacy; impressionistic criticism.)

**age of reason:** *Enlightenment.

**agit-prop; agitprop** [agit(ation)+prop (aganda)]: a literary work noted for its rhetorical style and demagogic content. (**epic drama; living newspaper.)

**agon** [Gk. gathering, contest]; (F. agon; G. Agon; S. agono): the third and most important part of ancient Greek comedy (prologue, parodos, and agon). (**parabasis.)

**air**= *aria.

**alba**= *aubade.

**Alcaic strophe; Alcaic stanza** [named after the Greek poet Alcaeus, circa 600 B.C.]; (F. strophe alcaïque; G. alkäische Strophe; S. estrofa alcaica): a *strophe of four lines; the first and second lines have eleven syllables each, the third has nine, and the fourth has ten. (**Asclepiadic strophe; choriamb; Sapphic.)

**Alexandrine** [F. of Alexander; so called because of its use in the Old French epic on Alexander the Great]; (F. alexandrin; G. Alexandriner; S. alejandrino): a line that usually consists of six *iambics with a *diaeresis after the third stress: ⏑＿⏑＿⏑＿ // ⏑＿⏑＿⏑＿.

**allegory** [Gk. speak figuratively]; (F. allégorie; G. Allegorie; S. alegoría): the presentation of actions, characters, and abstract ideas through symbolic fictional figures. (**anthropomorphism; apologue; chiffre; dolce stil nuovo; dream allegory; image; morality play; parable; rebus.)

**alliteration** [L. to the letter]; (F. allitération, rime sénées; G. Alliteration, Stabreim, Anfangsreim; S. aliteración): (1) repetition of initial sounds, usually consonants, in two or more words; also known as true alliteration, initial rhyme, or head rhyme; (2) repetition of non-initial consonant sounds in two or more words; also known as hidden alliteration. (**mālahāttr; rhyme.)

**allusion** [L. playing with]; (F. allusion; G. Anspielung, Andeutung; S. alusión): an implied indication or direct reference to persons, things, or events, whether real or fictitious, which call up relevant associations. (**anticipation; digression; innuendo; key novel; suspense.)

**almanac** [Ar. calendar]; (F. almanach; G. Almanach, Kalender; S. almanaque): a form of folk literature which includes interesting facts, statistics of all sorts, jokes, fiction, and poetry; very popular during the seventeenth and eighteenth centuries. (**annals.)

**altar poem** (F. poème idéogrammatique en forme d'autel; G. Figurengedicht; S. poema ideográfico en forma de cruz): a poem printed to form the design of an altar or cross, which is also the *central motif of the poem; a form of the *carmen figuratum.

**alternate rhyme** (F. rimes alternées, rimes croisées; G. Kreuzreim; S. rima alternada): the rhyming of lines according to the scheme abab. (**rhyme.)

**alternate verse** (F. vers cadencé; G. alternierender Vers; S. verso cadencioso, verso alternado): a verse in which stressed and unstressed syllables alternate: ⏑＿⏑＿⏑＿ . . . (**accentual verse; quantitative verse.)

**ambiguity** [L. double sense]; (F. ambiguïté; G. Ambiguität; S. ambigiedad): the capability of suggesting more than one meaning or of saying something that may be understood in two or more possible senses; it is an important element in poetry. (**amphibology; double entendre.)

**Amerind literature** [Amer(ican)-Ind(ian)]; (F. littérature amérindienne; G. Literatur der Indianer; S. literatura indigenista): literature of the native people of the Americas.

**amoebean verse** [Gk. interchanging, answering]; (F. poème amébée, vers stichomythiques; G. Amoibaion, Amoibaia; S. amebeo): a poem in dialogue form. (**débat; flyting;

Fescennine verses; partimen; tenzone.)

**amphibology; amphiboly** [Gk. ambiguity]; (F. amphibologie; G. Amphibolie; S. anfibología): *ambiguity caused by deviation from the usual rules of *syntax. (**anastrophe; double entendre; hypallage; hyperbaton; inversion.)

**amphibrach** [Gk. short on both sides]; (F. amphibraque; G. Amphibrachus, Amphibrachys; S. anfíbraco): a metrical foot that consists of a long (or stressed) syllable between two short (or unstressed) ones: ◡_◡. (**amphimacer; rocking rhythm.)

**amphimacer** [Gk. long on both sides]; (F. amphimace; G. Amphimacer, Amphimacus; S. crético): a metrical foot that consists of one short (or unstressed) syllable between two long (or stressed) ones: _◡_ . (**amphibrach; cretic; dochmius.)

**amplification** [L. extending, enlarging]; (F. amplification; G. Amplifikation; S. amplificación): a rhetorical device based on the expansion of a statement by means of rhetorical figures such as *hyperbole, *antithesis, *sententia, etc.

**ana** [L. of, or belonging to]; (F. ana; G. Ana; S. ana, anecdotario): a collection of *anecdotes. **analects.

**anachronism** [Gk. going backwards in time]; (F. anachronisme; G. Anachronismus; S. anacronismo): the intentional or unintentional chronological misplacing of persons, objects, or events within a literary work. (**hysteron proteron; prochronism.)

**anaclasis** [Gk. bending back]; (F. anaclase; G. Anaklasis; S. anaclasis):

(1) deviation of one foot from the metrical pattern of the verse; (2) a rhetorical figure which occurs when one speaker repeats a word that has just been spoken by someone else in order to stress its meaning or importance. (**anadiplosis; incremental repetition; repetend.)

**anacoluthon** [Gk. without continuation]; (F. anacoluthe; G. Anakoluth; S. anacoluto): the sudden discontinuation of a sentence in order to begin a new one; it expresses the excitement or the confusion of the speaker. (**aposiopesis; correctio; ellipsis; syllepsis.)

**anacreontic poetry** [named after the Greek poet Anacreon, 580-495 B.C.]; (F. anacréontique; G. Anakreontik; S. anacreóntica): convivial and cheerful lyric poetry with motifs such as feasting, drinking, love, and good company; popular in the seventeenth and eighteenth centuries. (**carpe diem; drinking song; light verse; rococo; vers de société; wine song.)

**anacrusis** [Gk. beginning of a song, prelude]; (F. anacrouse; G. Auftakt, Anakrusis; S. anacrusis): one or more unstressed syllables at the beginning of a verse; these syllables are not part of the metrical pattern. (**hypermetric.)

**anadiplosis** [Gk. doubling]; (F. anadiplose; G. Anadiplose; S. anadíplosis): a rhetorical figure used to increase the effect of sound by repeating the last word of a sentence or a verse at the beginning of the following one. (**anaclasis (2); anaphora; complexio; conduplicatio; echo; epanadiplosis; epanalepsis; epiphora; palilogy; ploce; symploce.)

**anagnorisis** [Gk. recognition]; **discovery; disclosure; recognition** (F. anagnorisis; G. Anagnorisis; S. anagnórisis): the tragic hero's recognition of his real nature and factual capacities or his discovery of the circumstances surrounding him; the term was used by Aristotle in his *Poetics*. (\*\*catharsis; dramatic irony; dramatic techniques; hamartia; hybris; nemesis: peripeteia; tragic.)

**anagoge; anagogy** [Gk. lead up]; (F. anagogie; G. Anagogie; S. anagogía): \*interpretation of a text from a mystical point of view. (\*\*analysis.)

**anagram** [Gk. reversal of letters]; (F. anagramme; G. Anagramm; S. anagrama): the formation of new words by rearranging the letters of other words. (\*\*cryptogram; logogriph; logomachy.)

**analects** [Gk. things collected]; (F. analecta, analectes; G. Analekten, Analekton; S. analectas): a collection of texts or quotations from more than one writer. (\*\*ana; anthology; cento; chrestomathy; collage; montage.)

**analogy** [Gk. proportion, correspondence]; (F. analogie; G. Analogie; S. analogía): resemblance without direct relationship. (\*\*tertium comparationis.)

**analysis** [Gk. break up, dissolve]; (F. analyse; G. Analyse; S. análisis): separating a literary work into its intrinsic and extrinsic components and examining the relation of each part to the others and to the whole. (\*\*anagoge; apparatus criticus; critique; exegesis; explication; extrinsic structure; impressionistic criticism; intentional fal-lacy; interpretation; intrinsic structure; new criticism; paraphrase.)

**analyzed rhyme** (F. rime apophonique; G. apophonischer Reim; S. rima apofónica): the use of \*assonance and \*consonance in a line or a group of lines. (\*\*rhyme.)

**anapaest; anapest** [Gk. pushed up]; (F. anapeste; G. Anapäst; S. anapesto): a metrical foot that consists of two unstressed (or short) syllables followed by one stressed (or long) syllable: ◡◡— . (\*\*dactyl; prosodiac; rising meter.)

**anaphora** [Gk. carrying back]; (F. anaphore; G. Anapher, Anaphora; S. anáfora): a rhetorical figure in which one or more words are repeated at the beginning of successive verses or sentences; opposite of \*epiphora. (\*\*anadiplosis; complexio; conduplicatio; palilogy; ploce; symploce.)

**anastrophe** [Gk. a turning back]; (F. anastrophe; G. Anastrophe; S. anástrofe): a rhetorical figure: inverting the usual syntactical order of words. (\*\*amphibology; hypallage; hyperbaton; inversion; palindrome; syntax.)

**anecdote** [Gk. unpublished]; (F. anecdote; G. Anekdote; S. anécdota): a short story that discloses, usually in a witty fashion, specific characteristics of a well-known personality; it can also reveal the peculiarity of a certain historical situation. (\*\*ana; apophthegm; exemplum; narrative poetry.)

**Angry Young Men:** a group of post World War II English playwrights noted for their revolt against the social norms and moral attitudes of the late forties and fifties; rep. J. Osborne, Sh. Delaney.

**animal poetry** (F. poésie animale; G. Tierdichtung; S. bestiario): a literary work in which animals play the major role. (**beast epic; bestiary; fable(1).)

**annals** [L. yearly]; (F. annales; G. Annalen; S. anales): a record of historical events arranged in their chronological order. (**almanac; chronicle.)

**annominatio:** *paronomasia(2).

**anonymous** [Gk. without a name]; (F. anonyme; G. anonym; S. anónimo): a literary work of unknown authorship. Folk poetry, such as folk ballads, folk epics, folk plays, folk songs, folk tales, are characterized, amongst other things, by the anonymity of their authors. (**pseudonym.)

**antagonist** [Gk. contender]; (F. antagoniste; G. Antagonist, Gegenspieler; S. antagonista): one who opposes the leading character in dramas and narratives; also called counterplayer or villain. (**character; deuteragonist; foil; protagonist; tritagonist.)

**antanaclasis** [Gk. to reflect, bend back]; (F. antanaclase; G. Antanaklasis; S. antanaclasis): = *anaclasis(2).

**antemasque** = *antimasque.

**antepenult** [L. before the next to last]; (F. antépénultième; G. Antepänultima; S. antepenúltimo): the third syllable counting from the end of the word. (**penult.)

**anthology** [Gk. flower gathering]; (F. anthologie; G. Anthologie; S. antología): whereas in a *chrestom-

athy the texts are selected at random, in an anthology they are related to each other, either intrinsically or extrinsically. (**analects; cento; collage.)

**anthropomorphism** [Gk. of human form]; (F. anthropomorphisme; G. Anthropomorphismus, Vermenschlichung; S. antropomorfismo): the attribution of human characteristics to nonhuman things and creatures. (**allegory; apostrophe; empathy; poetic fallacy; personification; prosopopoeia.)

**antibacchius** [Gk. opposite of *bacchius]; (F. antibacchée; G. Antibacchius; S. antibaquio): a classical metrical foot that consists of two long syllables followed by a short one: $\_\_\smile$. (**bacchius.)

**anticipation** [L. before+to take]; **foreshadowing** (F. anticipation; G. Antizipation, Vorausdeutung, Vordeutung; S. anticipación): a narrative device used either to intensify the *suspense, increase the plausibility, or to present the narrative world as a whole and consistent unit by means of anticipating or visualizing future events and developments. (**allusion; innuendo; procatalepsis.)

**anticlimax** [Gk. opposite of ladder]; (F. anticlimax; G. Antiklimax, Abfall; S. anticlímax): (1) a rhetorical figure: arranging words or phrases in descending order according to their rhetorical intensity—often used for attaining a comic effect; (2) the weak ending of a highly dramatic *action. (**bathos (2); climax.)

**antihero** (F. anti-héros; G. Antiheld; S. antihéroe): a *protagonist who does not possess any heroic features or admirable characteristics. (**character.)

antimask=*antimasque.

antimasque [opposed to *masque]; antimask; antemasque (F. antimasque; G. Antimasque; S. antimascarada): a short play dealing with comical themes and grotesque situations, as opposed to the dignified masque. Antimasques preceded the main masques—therefore also known as antemasques—and were performed by professional actors. (**masque; drama.)

antinovel (F. antiroman; G. Antiroman; S. antinovela): a term used by Jean-Paul Sartre in his preface to the 1956 edition of Nathalie Sarraute's novel *Portrait d'un Inconnu*. The antinovel is noted for its illogical action, obscure motivations, extremely subjective attitude, and experimental style. (**chosisme; experimental novel; heterodox novel; novel; tropisme.)

antiphon [Gk. opposite voice]; responsive verse (F. antienne; G. Antiphon, Antiphonie, Wechselgesang; S. antífona): (1) a verse or a stanza sung alternately by two singers or two groups of singers; (2) responsive alternation between two singers or two groups of singers, also known as antiphony.

antiphony=*antiphon(2).

antispast [Gk. opposing]; (F. antispaste; G. Antispast; S. antispasto): a classical metrical foot that consists of one iamb and one trochee: ∪_ _∪.

antistrophe [Gk. turning back]; (F. antistrophe; G. Antistrophe, Gegenstrophe; S. antístrofa): (1) the second part of the triadically constructed Pindaric stanza (strophe, antistrophe, epode); (2) *strophe(1). (**mesode; Pindaric ode; triad.)

antithesis [Gk. opposition]; contrast (F. antithèse, contraste; G. Antithese, Kontrast; S. antítesis): a stylistic device based on opposition of terms, statements, motifs, or themes. (**amplification; antonym; chiasmus; correlative verse; enallage; oxymoron; paradox; parallelism; Petrarchism.)

antonomasia [Gk. in place of the name]; (F. antonamase; G. Antonomasie, Begriffstausch; S. antonomasia): the use of a characterizing designation (*epithet, title, or a descriptive phrase) in place of a proper name, usually to avoid repetition. (**circumlocution; metalepsis; metonymy; periphrasis; synecdoche.)

antonym [Gk. opposing name]; (F. antonyme; G. Antonym, Gegenbegriff; S. antónimo): a rhetorical figure in which words of opposite meanings are used within a sentence. (**antithesis; oxymoron; paradox.)

aphaeresis [Gk. taking away]; (F. aphérèse; G. Aphärese; S. aféresis): the omission of a vowel or a whole syllable at the beginning of a word. (**acephalous.)

aphorism [Gk. definition]; (F. aphorisme; G. Aphorismus; S. aforismo): a short, witty, and ingenious statement in prose. (**apophthegm; epigram; gnomic poetry; maxim; sentence.)

apocalyptic [Gk. revelation]; (F. apocalyptique; G. apokalyptisch; S.

apocalíptico): a literary work whose theme is a cosmic cataclysm which leads to the final destruction of evil.

**apocopated rhyme** [*apocope]; (F. rime apocopée; G. apokopierter Reim; S. rima apocopada): the rhyming of two words, one of which is shortened by *apocope.

**apocope** [Gk. to cut off]; (F. apocope; G. Apokope; S. apócope): the intentional omission of the last letter or the last syllable of a word. (**aphaeresis; apocopated rhyme; crasis; elision; syncope.)

**apocrypha** [Gk. hidden]; (F. apocryphe; G. Apokryphen; S. apócrifo): (1) literary works of dubious authenticity; (2) Apocrypha; early Christian writings, e.g. books of Septuagint and Vulgate, which are not included in the Bible. (**canon.)

**Apollonian** [resembling Apollo; in Greek mythology: the god of light and beauty]; (F. apollinien; G. apollinisch; S. apolíneo): an intrinsically and extrinsically exalted poetic creation which reflects a rational and harmonious experience; often associated with classicism. (**balance; classic(3); decorum; Dionysian; organic form.)

**apologue** [Gk. tale]; (F. apologue; G. Apolog; S. apólogo): a didactic fable or an instructive story; usually dependent on symbolic and allegorical figures. (**allegory.)

**apology** [Gk. justification]; (F. apologie; G. Apologie, Verteidigung; S. apología): a speech or a text which defends a person or a thing, admits errors, or justifies mistakes.

**apophthegm; apothegm** [Gk. saying]; (F. apophthegme; G. Apophthegma; S. apotegma): a terse *aphorism, usually attributed to a historical person. (**anecdote; epigram; gnomic poetry; maxim; sentence.)

**aposiopesis** [Gk. to stop speaking]; (F. aposiopèse; G. Aposiopese; S. aposiopesis): a rhetorical figure which leaves a statement incomplete; usually used to express excitement or confusion. (**anacoluthon; correctio; ellipsis.)

**apostrophe** [Gk. turn away]; (F. apostrophe; G. Apostrophe, Ausruf, Anrufung, Anrede; S. apóstrofe): a rhetorical figure: addressing personified things, absent persons, or gods. (**anthropomorphism; empathy; invocation; personification; poetic fallacy.)

**apothegm**=*apophthegm.

**apparatus criticus; critical apparatus** (F. appareil critique; G. kritischer Apparat; S. aparato crítico): all bibliographical and biographical data used in a critical study of a text. (**analysis; definitive edition; interpretation; primary source; recension; secondary sources; strategy.)

**apprenticeship novel; Bildungsroman** (F. roman d'apprentissage; G. Bildungsroman, Individualroman; S. novela de apprendizaje): a term coined by Wilhelm Dilthey in 1906 and used in Germany to describe a type of novel which deals with the positive and negative experiences of a person who is trying to reach a certain intellectual ideal or achieve a specific educational level. (**man-novel; novel; novel of development; novel of educational formation; novel of the artist.)

approximate rhyme=*imperfect rhyme.

**Arcadia** (F. Arcadie; G. Arkadien; S. Arcadia): a mountainous district of ancient Greece; often used as setting for *pastoral poetry. (**bucolic poetry.)

**archaism** [Gk. antiquated]; (F. archaïsme; G. Archaismus; S. arcaísmo): the use of obsolete words and the imitation of outmoded styles in order to reproduce the atmosphere of a past era. (**epigonism; imitation.)

**archetype** [Gk. old type]; (F. archétype; G. Archetyp, Archetypus; S. arquetipo): a typically human experience, a conventional theme, a traditional motif, or a stereotyped character. (**flat character; stock character; stock situation.)

**architectonics** [Gk. of a master builder]; (F. architectonique; G. Architektonik, künstlerischer Aufbau; S. arquitectónico): the extrinsic qualities and structural design of literary products and artistic creations. (**extrinsic structure; structure; texture.)

**argument** [L. what is shown]; (F. argument; G. Inhalt; S. argumento): summary or plot outline. (**action; content; fable(2); meaning; message; plot; story; tone.)

**aria** [It. air]; (F. aria; G. Arie; S. aria): part of a *musical drama sung by one person.

**arsis** [Gk. raising the voice]; (F. arsis; G. Arsis, Hebung, Betonung; S. arsis): in Gk. prosody: the shorter part of a metrical foot; in modern prosody: the accented part of a metrical foot. (**atonic; pentarsic; thesis; tonic.)

**art ballad; literary ballad** (F. ballade littéraire; G. Kunstballade; S. romance artístico): a *ballad noted for its ornate style and artistic form; it differs from the *folk ballad in that its author is known. (**ballad; ballad stanza.)

**art epic; literary epic; artificial epic; secondary epic** (F. épopée savante; G. Kunstepos; S. épica artística): a stately narrative poem whose authorship is known; it is usually in the form of a book which will be read by the literate. Art epics can be divided into different subgenres such as *courtly epics, *historic epics, *Christian epics, etc. (**epics; folk epic; narrative poetry.)

**art for art's sake:** *aestheticism.

**arte mayor** [S. major art]: Spanish verse forms that consist of nine or more syllables, usually twelve, divided into two *hemistichs with a *caesura. (**arte menor; copla de arte mayor.)

**arte menor** [S. minor art]: Spanish verse forms that consist of eight syllables or less. (**arte mayor.)

**Arthurian romance** (F. cycle d'Arthur, roman arthurien, roman de la table ronde; G. Artusroman; S. libro del ciclo artúrico): adventure stories about King Arthur, the semilegendary king of the Britons (sixth century) and his knights. (**chivalric romance; courtly epic; heroic epic.)

**artificial comedy:** *comedy of manners.

**artificial epic**=*art epic.

**art nouveau:** *Jugendstil.

**ascending rhythm** (F. rythme ascendant; G. aufsteigender Rhythmus; S. ritmo ascendente): *rhythm.

**Asclepiadic strophe** [named after the Greek poet Asclepiad, 300 B.C.]; (F. strophe asclépiade; G. asklepiadeische Strophe; S. estrofa asclepiádica): a *strophe of four lines; the first two lines usually have six syllables each, the third has three, and the fourth has four. (**Alcaic strophe; Sapphic.)

**aside; duplex method** (F. aparté; G. Beiseitesprechen; S. aparte): a word or a sentence spoken by an actor and heard by the audience, but supposedly not by other characters on the stage. (**dramatic monologue; parabasis; soliloquy.)

**assonance** [L. to begin to sound]; (F. assonance; G. Assonanz; S. asonancia): occurs when two words have the same vowels but different consonants; also called vowel rhyme. (**analyzed rhyme; consonance; imperfect rhyme; rhyme.)

**astrophic composition** (F. composition stichique; G. astrophische Komposition; S. serie indeterminada de versos): a poem or a group of verses not divided into *strophes or stanzas.

**asyndeton** [Gk. unconnected]; (F. asyndète; G. Asyndeton; S. asíndeton): a rhetorical figure: stringing related words together without conjunctions; opposite of polysyndeton. (**parataxis; pleonasm; tautology.)

**Atellan fables** [named after the ancient Italian city of Atella]; (F. atellanes, fabula atellana; G. Atellanen, fabula atellana; S. fábula atelana): coarse and uncouth slapsticks; popular in Latin literature in the first century B.C. (**low comedy.)

**atmosphere; mood** (F. atmosphére; G. Stimmung, Atmosphäre; S. ambiente): the overall effect of a literary work on the reader's mood. (**content; meaning; message; tone.)

**atonic** [Gk. without tone]; (F. atone; G. atonisch; S. átono): an unstressed syllable. (**arsis; thesis; tonic.)

**attitude** (F. attitude; G. Einstellung, Attitüde; S. actitud): *tone.

**aubade** [Prov. dawn]; **dawn song; alba** (F. aubade, poésie de l'aube; G. Tagelied; S. alborada): a song or poem of lovers parting at dawn. (**serenade.)

**Augustan period: Augustan age** [named after the Roman emperor Augustus, 63 B.C. — 14 A.D.]; (F. le siècle d'Auguste, époque de la reine Anne; G. der englische Neuklassizismus; S. neoclasicismo inglés, época de Augusto): refers to the neoclassical movement in English literature during the eighteenth century; writers such as Swift and Pope admired the Roman writers who lived during the reign of Augustus (Ovid, Horace, Vergil) and held their works as models of excellence. (**classicism.)

**autobiography** [Gk. write own life]; (F. autobiographie; G. Autobiographie, Selbstbiographie; S. autobiografía): the history of a person's life written by himself. (**biography; diary; memoirs; open form.)

**autotelic** [Gk. an end in itself]; (F. manifeste littéraire; G. autonom, eigengesetzlich; S. libro de tesis): a literary work created only to demonstrate certain artistic rules or to convey a specific message.

(**epideictic speech; esoteric; light verse.)

**avant-garde** [F. vanguard]; (F. avant-garde; G. Avantgarde; S. vanguardia): any literary or artistic movement which rejects orthodox and traditional approaches in favor of new and experimental ideas.

**ayre:** *aria.

# B

**bacchius** [Gk. of Bacchus, the god of wine]; (F. bachique; G. Bacchius; S. baquio): a classical metrical foot that consists of one short syllable followed by two long ones: ᴗ— —. (**antibacchius.)

**background** (F. cadre; G. Hintergrund; S. fondo): the scenery, the setting, or the circumstances relevant to a situation represented in a literary work. (**dramatic techniques.)

**Bajazzo:** *harlequinade.

**balance** [L. a pair of scales]; (F. équilibre; G. Balance, Ausgewogenheit; S. equilibrio): harmony between the different intrinsic and extrinsic elements of a literary work. (**Apollonian; classic(3); decorum; organic form.)

**ballad** [Prov. song sung while dancing]; (F. ballade; G. Ballade; S. balada): a short narrative poem in stanzas; often with lyrical and dramatic elements. (**art ballad; ballad stanza; broadside ballad; chapbook; folk ballad; minstrel; narrative poetry; scop.)

**ballade** [*ballad]: an Old French verse form that consists of three eight-line stanzas and an envoi of four lines; rhyme scheme: ababbcbC bcbC (C=refrain). (**canzone.)

**ballad meter:** *ballad stanza.

**ballad opera** (F. opérette, comédie musicale; G. Singspiel; S. opereta): a popular play marked by funny situations and melodious songs. (**cantata; musical drama; opera; operetta.)

**ballad stanza** (F. strophe de ballade; G. Balladenstrophe; S. estrofa de balada): a *stanza of four lines; the first and third lines—which usually rhyme—are iambic tetrameters; the second and fourth are iambic trimeters.

**barbarism** [Gk. the use of foreign words and styles]; (F. barbarisme; G. Barbarismus; S. barbarismo): violation of linguistic and stylistic rules. (**modulation; poetic licence; solecism; vernacularism; vulgarism.)

**bard** [Old Celtic poet-singer]; (F. barde; G. Barde; S. bardo): a Celtic *minstrel. (**rhapsodist; scop; skald.)

**baroque** [derived from the Portuguese word "barroco"=irregular pearl, or from the Italian painter Federigo Barocci, 1535-1612, who was known for his religious and colorful pictures]; (F. baroque; G. Barock; S. barroco): a seventeenth-century European literary and artistic movement noted for its complex forms, ornate styles, and antithetical attitudes. It may be placed chronologically between the *Renaissance and the *Enlightenment. (**bombast; culteranism; cultism; estilo culto; euphuism; Gongorism; logorrhoea; Marinism; orotund.)

**barzelletta:** *frottola.

**bathos** [Gk. depth]; (F. pathos outrancier; G. lächerlich übertriebenes Pathos; S. anticlímax(2)): (1) an overdone and therefore ludicrous *pathos; (2) a sudden drop from the elevated and dignified to the banal and crude. (**anticlimax.)

**beast epic** (F. épopée animale; G. Tierepos; S. bestiario): a long, allegorical narrative about animals. (**animal poetry; bestiary; fable(1).)

**beast fable:** *fable(1).

**beat** (F. ictus; G. Metrum, Maß; S. ritmo, compás): a term sometimes used instead of metrical *stress.

**Beat generation:** *Beat poets.

**Beatniks** [OHG+Yiddish: beat+a person connected with]: *Beat poets.

**Beat poets; Beat generation; Beatniks:** a group of American nonconformist poets in the late fifties, centered in San Francisco and New York.

**beginning rhyme:** *alliteration.

**belles lettres:** *belletristic literature.

**belletristic literature; belles lettres** [F. beautiful letters]; (F. belles lettres; G. Belletristik, schöne Literatur; S. bellas letras): *literature that is created mainly for enjoyment and entertainment without being overly didactic, pedagogical, or informative. (**didactic literature; esoteric; exoteric; trivial literature.)

**bestiary** [L. of beasts]; (F. bestiaire; G. Bestiarium; S. bestiario): a long didactic narrative about animals. (**animal poetry; beast epic; fable(1).)

**best seller** (F. best-seller; G. Bestseller; S. best seller): a book that sells a large number of copies within a short time. If such a work remains on the list of best-selling books for a long time, it is known as a steady seller.

**bibliography** [Gk. book writing]; (F. bibliographie; G. Bibliographie; S. bibliografía): (1) the classification and registration of all information pertinent to a publication (author, publisher, place of publication, date of publication, edition, number of copies printed, number of pages); (2) a catalog of bibliographical information or a list of books consulted by an author. (**apparatus criticus; primary source; secondary sources.)

**Biedermeier poets:** a term coined by Ludwig Eichrodt in 1850, and used later in connection with a group of German and Austrian authors who were contemporaries of the Young German writers (*Junges Deutschland); these poets were noted for their admiration of conservative ideals and for their glorification of the bourgeois way of life. Rep. Grillparzer, Stifter, Raimund, Mörike, Droste-Hülshoff.

**Bildungsroman:** *apprenticeship novel.

**billingsgate** [a fish market in London]; **billingsgate language** (F. langage des halles; G. Pöbelsprache; S. argot): the crude, trite, and abusive language of the low classes. (**barbarism; diatribe; lampoon; persiflage; philippic; vernacularism; vulgarism.)

**biography** [Gk. write a life]; (F. biographie; G. Biographie; S. biografía): a history of a person's life written by someone else. (**autobiography; hagiography; legend.)

**blank verse** [OHG: shining verse]; (F. vers blancs; G. Blankvers; S. verso blanco): unrhymed *iambic *pentameter: ◡—◡—◡—◡—◡—. (**heroic couplet.)

**blend; portmanteau word** (F. mot télescopé; G. Portmanteau Wort, Kontraktion; S. compuesto elíptico, creacionismo, neologismo): a word consisting of two words or parts of two words. (**tmesis.)

**blind motif** (F. motif retardateur; G. blindes Motiv; S. motivo ciego): a *motif which does not influence the action in any way but only causes an abnormal slowness in the development of the plot. (**leitmotif; retardation.)

**Bloomsbury Group:** an informal group of English poets and intellectuals who lived in Bloomsbury, a district of London. Famous among them are Virginia and Leonard Woolf, Lytton Strachey, and E. M. Forster.

**Blue Book** (F. livre blanc; G. das Weißbuch; S. libro oficial): a government publication which deals with a certain topic or justifies a specific policy.

**blues:** an American folk song usually in three-line stanzas expressing melancholy and despair. (**spirituals.)

**bombast** [Gk. silk garment]; (F. style ampoulé, pindarisme; G. Bombast, Redeschwulst; S. estilo bombástico): an inflated style; also a literary work marked for its pompous and pretentious style. (**baroque; culteranism; cultism; euphuism; Gongorism; logorrhoea; Marinism; orotund.)

**bon mot** [F. good word]; (F. bon mot; G. Bonmot; S. agudeza): a witty remark or a clever observation. (**proverb; wit.)

**book of etiquette:** *book of manners.

**book of manners; book of etiquette** (F. manuel de savoir-vivre; G. Anstandsbuch; S. libro de etiqueta): a book that prescribes rules for social occasions.

**boulevard drama** (F. théâtre de boulevard; G. Boulevardstück; S. comedia de los bulevars): trivial plays noted for their popular themes, witty dialogues, and limited intellectual content (the plays of S. Guitry or N. Coward). (**drama.)

**bourgeois drama** (F. drame bourgeois; G. bürgerliches Drama; S. comedia burguesa): a play that deals with the problems of the townsman or reflects the mediocrity of the social middle class. (**comedy of tears; drama.)

**bourgeois tragedy** (F. tragédie bourgeoise; G. bürgerliches Trauerspiel; S. tragedia burguesa): a *bourgeois drama that deals with a tragic situation or has a pathetic ending. (**comedy of tears; drama.)

**bowdlerize** [after the famous English editor Thomas Bowdler, 1754-1825]; (F. expurger, censurer; G. reinigen, verharmlosen; S. censurar): to edit a publication by cutting out offensive or morally objectionable parts. (**index(2).)

**brachycatalectic** [Gk. short omission]; (F. brachycatalectique; G. brachykatalektisch; S. verso braquicataléctico): a verse which lacks two syllables at the end. (\*\*acatalectic; acephalous; catalectic.)

brachycatalexis [Gk. short omission]; (F. brachycatalexe; G. Brachykatalexe; S.—): omission of two syllables at the end of a verse. (\*\*brachycatalectic; catalexis.)

break; pause (F. césure, pause, coupe; G. Pause; S. pausa rítmica): an interruption in the rhythmic flow of a verse (\*caesura, \*diaeresis) or a pause at the end of a line. (\*\*compensation; end-stopped line; enjambment; feminine caesura; rest; rhythm.)

brief; synopsis; abstract (F. résumé, synopsis; G. Zusammenfassung, Abstrakt, Synopsis; S. sinopsis): a concise article or an outline. (\*\*epitome; essay.)

broadside ballad (F. chanson populaire; G. Moritat; S. romance publicado en pliego suelto): a \*ballad or a folk song printed on a large sheet and offered for sale on the streets; popular in England in the sixteenth century.

broken rhyme (F. rime brisée; G. Reimbrechung; S. rima quebrada): the division of the last word in a verse so that its first part produces the rhyme while the second part starts the following line. (\*\*mosaic rhyme; rhyme.)

bucolic poetry [Gk. herdsman]; (F. poésie bucolique; G. bukolische Dichtung; S. poesía bucólica): poetry that idealizes rural life and depicts it as being pleasant and enchanting. (\*\*Arcadia; eclogue; georgic; idyll; pastoral poetry.)

burden [L. humming]; (F. refrain; G. Refrain; S. estribillo): (1) \*refrain or \*chorus; (2) the \*central motif of a poem. (\*\*carmen figuratum; incremental repetition; repetend.)

burlesque [It. comic, funny]; (F. burlesque; G. Burleske; S. burlesco): (1) a literary work which wittingly ridicules certain social situations or scornfully imitates specific literary products; (2) a satirical play with music and songs; (3) a variety show that consists of different short acts. (\*\*droll; extravaganza; farce; low comedy; parody; pastiche; persiflage; revue; satire; travesty; vaudeville.)

burletta [It. farce]; (F. burletta; G. Burletta; S. Farsa):=\*burlesque(3).

Burns meter: \*Burns stanza.

Burns stanza [named after the Scottish poet Robert Burns, 1759-1796]: a stanza of six lines; the first, second, third, and fifth are tetrameters; the fourth and sixth are dimeters; rhyme scheme: aaabab. (\*\*stanza.)

Byronic [from the English poet Lord Byron, 1788-1824]; (F. byronien; G. Byronismus; S. byroniano): heroic and romantic, but necessarily melancholic, self-centered, and ironic. (\*\*irony; romantic irony; Satanic school.)

# C

cacophony [Gk. bad sound]; (F. cacophonie; G. Kakophonie; S. cacofonía): dissonant and harsh-sounding combinations of words. (\*\*dissonance; euphony; incantation; jingle; onomatopoeia.)

**cadence** [L. fall]; (F. cadence; G. Kadenz; S. cadencia): (1) the metrical pattern at the end of a verse; (2) the rhythmical flow of a group of sounds. (\*\*rhythm.)

**caesura** [L. cut]; (F. césure; G. Zäsur; S. cesura): a slight pause within a verse. (\*\*break; chanson de geste; compensation; diaeresis(2); feminine caesura; hephthemimeral; hexameter; masculine caesura; medial caesura; penthemimeral; rest; trithemimeral.)

**calypso** [after Calypso, island nymph in Gk. mythology]: an improvised satirical \*ballad of the West Indies.

**canción** [S. literary song]: a Spanish lyric poem that consists of identical \*strophes.

**canon** [Gk. rule, measure]; (F. canon; G. Kanon; S. canon): (1) the authentic works of an author; (2) a list of books accepted as holy, authentic, and exemplary. (\*\*apocrypha; index(2).)

**cant** [L. sing]; (F. jargon; G. Jargon, Rotwelsch; S. germanía): \*jargon; also religious \*phraseology.

**cantar** [S. to sing]; (F. romancero; G. Cantar, spanisches Heldenepos; S. cantar, cantar de gesta): a Spanish epic poem; it corresponds to the French \*chanson de geste.

**cantata** [It. song]; (F. cantate; G. Kantate; S. cantata): a short \*musical drama for solo and chorus; popular in the seventeenth century. (\*\*ballad opera; opera; operetta.)

**canticle** [L. little song]; (F. cantique; G. Kirchenlied; S. cántico): a liturgical song. (\*\*carol(1).)

**canticum** [L. song]; (F. canticum; G. Canticum; S. cántico): part of the Roman drama which was recited or sung to flute accompaniment, as opposed to the spoken part known as \*diverbium.

**canto** [It. song]; (F. chant; G. Gesang; S. canto): a subdivision of an \*epic; it corresponds to the act of a play and the chapter of a book in prose.

**canzone** [It. song]; (F. canzone; G. Kanzone, Canzone; S. canción): a lyric poem that consists of several (five to ten) identical stanzas (usually of thirteen lines). The concluding stanza, known as the envoi, is shorter than the others and includes a dedication, a farewell note, or a commendatory remark. (\*\*courtly song.)

**capa y espada:** \*comedia de capa y espada.

**capitolo** [It. chapter]: an Italian poem in \*terza rima, mostly of a satirical or didactic nature.

**caricature** [It. exaggerate]; (F. caricature; G. Karikatur; S. caricatura): a ludicrously exaggerated representation of certain characteristics attributed to a person, a thing, or a situation. (\*\*comics; irony; sarcasm; satire.)

**carmen** [L. poem]; (F. carmen; G. Carmen; S. carmen): a lyric poem or a \*song.

**carmen figuratum** [L. shaped poem]; **pattern poetry; shaped poetry** (F. idéogramme lyrique, poème idéogrammatique; G. Bilderlyrik, Figurenlyrik, Figurengedicht, Bilderreim, Technopägnion; S. poema ideográfico): a poem printed to form a design which represents or symbolizes its \*central motif. (\*\*altar poem; burden(2).)

**carmina:** plural of *carmen.

**carnival comedy; Shrovetide play** (F. piéce de mardi gras, comédie carnavalesque; G. Fastnachtsspiel; S. comedia burlesca): a popular comedy which deals with religious, political, or social subject matter; it usually contains coarse jokes and uncouth language. (**drama.)

**carol** [L. choral song]; (F. chant de noël, carol; G. Weihnachtslied; S. villancico): (1) a song of religious joy (a Christmas song); (2) a round dance accompanied by songs. (**canticle.)

**Caroline period:** the reign of Charles I of England; the period between 1625-1642. (**Augustan period; Cavalier poets; Edwardian; Elizabethan age; Georgian poets; Jacobean; Restoration; Victorian.)

**carpe diem** [L. pluck the day]: a *motif in lyric poetry which praises momentary delights; it advises the enjoyment of earthly pleasures. The phrase was coined by Horace (65-8 B.C.) in his odes. (**anacreontic poetry; drinking song; Goliardic verse; ubi sunt motif; wine song.)

**catabasis** [Gk. descent]; (F. catabase; G. Katabasis; S. catábasis): the part of the *action that follows the *catastrophe. (**catastasis; climax(2); dramatic techniques; epitasis; Freytag's pyramid; peripeteia; protasis.)

**catachresis** [Gk. misuse]; (F. catachrèse; G. Katachrese; S. catacresis): a forced and improper combination of words or images. (**oxymoron.)

**catalectic** [Gk. incomplete]; (F. vers catalectique; G. katalektisch; S. cataléctico): a verse lacking one syllable or ending with an incomplete metrical foot. (**acatalectic; acephalous; brachycatalectic; catalexis; headless line; hemiepes; paragoge.)

**catalexis** [Gk. leave off]; (F. catalexe; G. Katalexe; S. catalecto): incompleteness in the last metrical foot. (**catalectic.)

**catastasis** [Gk. arrangement, formation]; (F. catastase; G. Katastase, Katastasis; S. catástasis): the last stage of the dramatic entanglement which leads to the *climax and the resolution of the conflict. (**catabasis; catastrophe; dramatic techniques; epitasis; Freytag's pyramid; peripetia; protasis.)

**catastrophe** [Gk. to overturn]; (F. catastrophe; G. Katastrophe; S. catástrofe): the untying of the dramatic knot and the solution of the conflict; also known as the resolution or the denouement. (**catabasis; catastasis; climax(2); dramatic techniques; epitasis; Freytag's pyramid; peripetia; protasis; suspense.)

**catharsis** [Gk. purification]; (F. catharsis; G. Katharsis; S. catarsis): an undefined term used by Aristotle in his *Poetics* with reference to tragedy; it could mean purgation of passions and emotions by means of fear and pity. (**anagnorisis; dramatic irony; dramatic techniques; hamartia; hybris; nemesis; tragic.)

**cauda; coda** [L. tail]; (F. strophe couée, rhythmus tripertitus caudatus; G. Schweifreim, Zwischenreim; S. coda): in a stanza that has the following rhyme scheme: aab ccb, the third and sixth lines are known as coudae. (**rhyme.)

**cautionary tale** (F. conte moral; G. lehrhafte Erzählung; S. cuento moral): an instructive *tale or a story with a didactic purpose. (**exemplum; fable(1); narrative poetry; parable.)

**Cavalier poets:** a group of English *Caroline poets known for their graceful and witty poetry. The Cavalier poets (Richard Lovelace, Sir John Suckling) supported King Charles I against the Puritans. (**Augustan period; Edwardian; Elizabethan age; Georgian poets; Jacobean; Restoration; Victorian.)

**Celtic Renaissance; Irish Literary Renaissance** (F. renaissance celtique, renaissance irlandaise; G. keltische Renaissance, irische Renaissance; S. Renacimiento céltico): a literary movement in Ireland in the nineteenth and twentieth centuries which attempted to revive old folk poetry and create a literature relevant to, and indicative of, the Irish way of life. Rep. D. Hyde, W. B. Yeats, S. O'Casey.

**cento** [L. patchwork]; (F. centon; G. Cento; S. centón): a literary work that consists of passages, quotations, and images selected from well-known authors of the past. (**analects; anthology; chrestomathy; collage; montage.)

**central motif** (F. motif central, motif récurrent; G. Zentralmotiv, Dingsymbol, Leitsymbol; S. motivo principal, motivo central): a *motif or a *symbol which runs through a poem. (**blind motif; burden; leitmotif; objective correlative; serenade.)

**chain rhyme** (F. rimes annexées, rimes concaténées, rimes fratrisées, rimes enchaînées; G. Kettenreim; S. rima encadenada): occurs when the last syllable of a verse is repeated at the beginning of the line immediately following; it also designates the rhyme scheme: aba bcb cdc . . . (**rhyme.)

**chanson** [F. song]; (F. chanson; G. Chanson; S. canción): a stanzaic poem intended for singing; it usually has mundane themes. (**chanson de geste; song.)

**chanson baladée** [F. *virelai.

**chanson de geste** [F. song of deeds]; (F. chanson de geste; G. Chanson de geste; S. canción de gesta): an Old French medieval *courtly epic. *La Chanson de Roland* is one of the most famous chansons de geste. These epics are divided into strophes (laisses) of different lengths; the lines, which have vowel rhymes, consist of ten syllables with a *caesura after the fourth syllable. (**cantar; chanson de toile; trouvère.)

**chanson de toile** [F. song of linen, weavers' song]; (F. chanson de toile; G. Chanson de toile, altfranzösische Romanze; S. chanson de toile): a medieval French narrative folk song which deals with love and adventure. (**chanson de geste; chant-fable.)

**chant** [L. sing]; (F. chant mélopée; G. Singsang; S. canto): a poem written to be recited in a monotonous, repetitive tone rather than to be sung or read.

**chantey; chanty:** *shanty.

**chant-fable** [F. sing-fable]: a popular French prose narrative of the twelfth and thirteenth centuries with certain parts in melodious verses. (**chanson de toile.)

chant royal [F. royal song]: a poem that consists of five stanzas of eleven lines each rhyming: ab ab cc dd edE and an envoi of five lines rhyming: ddedE (E=*refrain).

chapbook (F. livre de colportage; G. Volksbuch; S. pliego suelto): an anonymous book, sold by chapmen and hawkers, which contained folk tales, ballads, and songs.(**jestbook.)

chapter [L. little head]; (F. chapitre; G. Kapitel; S. capítulo): the main division of a book in prose; it corresponds to the *act of a play and the *canto of an epic.

character [Gk. to engrave]; (F. personnage; G. Charakter; S. personaje): (1) a person who plays a role in a dramatic or narrative creation—also known as figure or *persona; characters can be divided into major, minor, and marginal according to their degree of involvement in the plot. They may also be described as *flat or *round characters. (2) a short literary *sketch in prose or in verse. (**antagonist; archetype; characterization; confidant; deuteragonist; foil; protagonist; stock character; tritagonist; villain.)

characterization [*character]; (F. présentation, caractérisation; G. Charakterisierung; S. caracterización): the presentation and description of the figures involved in a narrative or play; this could be done directly by means of information supplied by the narrator or other characters, or indirectly as the *character reveals himself through his actions and reactions. (**motivation.)

charade [Prov. chat]; (F. charade; G. Scharade, Silbenrätsel, Rätsel; S. charada): a word represented by means of a gesture, a picture, or a *riddle.

charm [L. incantation]; spell (F. charme; G. Zauberspruch; S. encanto, hechizo): a magic spell chanted or recited to attract good luck or to expel evil; like riddles, gnomes, adages, proverbs, myths, legends, and traditions, it is one of the earliest forms of literature. (**incantation.)

Chaucerian stanza: *rhyme royal.

Chevy-Chase stanza [after a sixteenth-century English folk ballad]: a stanza that consists of four lines, the first and third lines are unrhymed and each has four metrical feet; the second and the fourth are rhymed and have three metrical feet; it is often used in English folk ballads.

chiasmus; chiasm [Gk. diagonal, in the form of a cross]; (F. chiasme, chiasma; G. Chiasmus; S. quiasmo): a rhetorical figure: the criss-cross placing of sentences or parts of sentences within a statement. (**antithesis; correlative verse; parallelism.)

chiffre [F. figure]; (F. image tangentielle; G. Chiffre; S. cifra): an incomplete *symbol or a deficient *image which suggests rather than specifies; frequently used in modern poetry. (**metaphor.)

children's song; nursery rhyme (F. chanson enfantine; G. Kinderlied; S. naná, cuento de niños): a poem to be sung; noted for its short lines and simple rhymes which deal with children and their world without being didactic or instructive.

chivalric romance; courtly romance; courtly novel (F. roman chevaleresque, roman courtois; G. Ritterroman, höfischer Roman, heroischgalanter Roman; S. novela de caballería): a medieval novel which deals with romantic and adventurous motifs and reflects courtly norms and ethics; also popular in the sixteenth and seventeenth centuries. (\*\*Arthurian romance; courtly epic; metrical romance; heroic epic.)

choliamb; choliambus [Gk. limping iamb]; (F. choliambe; G. Choliambus; S. coliambo, escazonte): a verse that consists of five iambs and a final trochee instead of six iambs as originally planned; also known as scazon: ◡‒◡‒◡‒◡‒ ‒◡.

choriamb [Gk. of one trochee and one iamb]; (F. choriambe; G. Choriambus; S. coriambo): a metrical foot that consists of one trochee and one iamb; often used by Sappho and Alceaus: ‒◡◡‒ .(\*\*Alcaic strophe; Sapphic.)

chorus [Gk. dance]; (F. choeur; G. Chor; S. coro): a performer or a group of performers who sometimes participate in the \*action; usually they comment on it or help create a specific atmosphere. (\*\*burden(1); commus; episode; exodus; parabasis; parodos; stasimon.)

chosisme [F. thing]: a narrative technique based upon an objective and detailed description of the things that surround the characters, regardless of their relevance to the situation depicted (A. Robbe-Grillet's *Instantanés*, 1962). (\*\*antinovel; digression; narrative techniques; slice-of-life; tropisme.)

chrestomathy [Gk. useful for learning]; (F. chrestomathie; G. Chrestomathie; S. crestomatía): a collection of texts, often in prose, usually compiled for pedagogical reasons. (\*\*analects; anthology; cento; collage.)

Christian epic (F. épopée chrétienne; G. christliches Epos; S. épica cristiana): a stately narrative which tells of the Christian doctrine or which glorifies Christ, his disciples, or his followers. (\*\*art epic; folk epic; liturgical drama; narrative poetry.)

chronicle [Gk. concerning time]; (F. chronique; G. Chronik; S. crónica): an objective historical account of events arranged according to their time sequence and not according to their relevance or importance. (\*\*annals; chronicle play.)

chronicle play (F. piéce historique; G. historisches Drama; S. comedia histórica): a play that supplies the audience with an objective and detailed account of certain historical events without analyzing them or commenting on their human relevance. (\*\*drama; historical play.)

chronogram [Gk. writing of time]; (F. chronogramme; G. Chronogramm; S. cronograma): a text in which certain letters stand for Roman numerals from which the date of the text may be established. (\*\*cryptogram.)

cinquain [F. of five lines]; (F. cinquain; G. Cinquain; S. quintilla): a short, precise, and elegant stanza of five lines; the first and fifth lines have two syllables each, the second four, the third six, and the fourth eight;

introduced by the American poetess Adelaide Crapsey (*Verse*, 1915).

**circumlocution** [L. speech]; (F. circonlocution; G. Weitschweifigkeit; S. circunlocución): a wordy, long-winded, and verbose style. (\*\*antonomasia; euphemism; euphuism; metalepsis.)

**citation** [L. summon]: \*quotation.

**classic** [L. of the first class]; (F. classique; G. klassisch; S. clásico): (1) belonging to ancient Greece or Rome; (2) a universal and enduring literary work; (3) a poetic creation noted for its harmony, simplicity, and adherence to strict intrinsic and extrinsic rules. (\*\*Apollonian; balance; decorum; organic form; universality.)

**classicism** [\*classic]; (F. classicisme; G. Klassik; S. época clásica): (1) art and literature of ancient Greece (the reign of Pericles, 500 - 429 B.C.) and Rome (the reign of Augustus, 63 B.C - 14 A.D.); (2) designation of different literary movements in Europe noted for their adherence to the literary models of ancient Greece and Rome; also known as neoclassicism. (\*\*Augustan period; Humanism; Pléiade; Renaissance.)

**clerihew** [after the English writer Edmond Clerihew Bentley, 1875 - 1956]; (F. clerihew; G. Clerihew, Spottgedicht; S.—): a humorous anecdotal poem of two couplets. (\*\*light verse; limerick; occasional verse.)

**cliché** [F. stereotype]; (F. cliché; G. Klischee; S. cliché, clisé): an overused phrase, expression, or image; therefore judged dull and unimaginative. (\*\*dead metaphor; formula; hackneyed expression.)

**climax** [Gk. ladder]; (F. climax; G. Klimax, Höhepunkt; S. clímax): (1) a rhetorical figure: arranging words or phrases in ascending order according to their rhetorical forcefulness; (2) the highest point in the development of a dramatic action. (\*\*anticlimax; catabasis; catastasis; catastrophe; dramatic techniques; epitasis; Freytag's pyramid; peripetia.)

**cloak-and-sword**: \*comedia de capa y espada.

**closed couplet** (F. distique épigrammatique; G.—; S. pareado): a rhymed \*couplet of epigrammatic nature. (\*\*epigram.)

**closet drama** (F. théâtre pour la lecture; G. Lesedrama, Buchdrama; S. teatro de cámara): a drama which, due to certain poetic (e.g. highly intellectual content) or technical (e.g. extreme length) characteristics, could not be performed on a public stage. (\*\*drama.)

**cobla** [Prov. stanza]: a \*stanza in Old Provençal lyric poetry. (\*\*troubadour.)

**cobla esparsa** [Prov. isolated stanza]: an Old Provençal instructive poem of one stanza.

**cock-and-bull story** [probably referring to a fantastic tale by the same name]; (F. histoire de pure invention; G. Münchhauseniade; S. cuento exagerado): a highly exaggerated, self-glorifying story. (\*\*fairy tale; fantasy fiction; tall tale; yarn.)

**Cockney School of Poetry**: a name applied in the early nineteenth century to a group of London poets (Keats, J. Hunt, and others). Their humble origins and preoccupation with social problems and political issues afforded them a certain amount of derision. (**Satanic school.)

**coda:** *cauda.

**cola:** plural of *colon.

**collage** [F. pasting]; (F. collage; G. Collage; S. centón): a literary text which depends to a great extent on quotations and *fragments of other works. (**analects; cento; Dadaism; montage.)

**colon** [Gk. limb]; (F. côlon; G. Kolon; S. colon): in verse as in prose, a rhythmical unit which lies between two stops or two pauses; a colon can be divided into smaller units with no independent meaning called commas. (**period(1); rhythm.)

**Columbina:** *harlequinade.

**comedia de capa y espada** [S. named after the costume worn by the upper class in Spain; cloak: capa, and sword: espada]: a Spanish play of intrigue that involves people from the upper class (caballeros). (**comedy of intrigue.)

**comedy** [Gk. processional song]; **high comedy** (F. comédie; G. Komödie; S. comedia): a play in which a real dramatic conflict based on reason and free will is resolved to the satisfaction of the protagonist. As opposed to *low comedy (farces, slapstick), genuine comedy depends on the *comic rather than on jokes, preposterous situations, and ludicrous or farcical events. (**drama.)

**comedy of character** (F. comédie de caractère; G. Charakterkomödie; S. comedia de figurón): a *comedy in which the distinguishing qualities of a person or persons, rather than events or incidents, are the main source of comicality. (**comedy of situation; drama.)

**comedy of humors** = *comedy of character.

**comedy of intrigue** (F. comédie d'intrigue; G. Intrigenstück; S. comedia de enredo): a *comedy based on secretive intrigues and tricky situations. (**drama.)

**comedy of manners; artificial comedy** (F. comédie de moeurs; G. Sittenkomödie, Sittenstück; S. comedia de costumbres): a *comedy which humorously and satirically criticizes the social and moral norms of society. (**drama.)

**comedy of situation** (F. comédie d'intrigue; G. Situationskomödie, Handlungskomödie; S. comedia de enredo): a *comedy based on dramatically entangled situations rather than on the traits of the characters. (**comedy of character; comedy of intrigue; drama.)

**comedy of tears** (F. comédie larmoyante; G. Rührstück, weinerliches Lustspiel; S. comedia sentimental, comedia lacrimosa): a play which deals with tragic bourgeois situations but which ends happily due to a very naive and oversentimental formula (*poetic justice). (**bourgeois drama; bourgeois tragedy; drama; drame.)

**comic** [Gk. festivity]; (F. comique, catastase référentielle; G. Komik; S. cómico): a cheerfulness caused by the sudden discovery of a discrepancy between how people and things actually are and the way they claim or seem to be, i.e. a discrepancy between appearance and being. (\*\*comedy; dramatic techniques; humor; incongruity; irony.)

**comic relief** (F. détente comique; G. komische Entspannung; S. interpolación cómica): comic scenes or humorous episodes incorporated into a play—usually a tragedy—in order to lessen the dramatic impact on the audience temporarily before it resumes its intensity. (\*\*dramatic techniques; tragicomedy(2).)

**comics; comic strip** (F. bande dessinée, bande illustrée; G. Bildergeschichten, Karikaturstreifen, Bilderbogen-Geschichten; S. comics, tiras cómicas): a narrative sequence achieved by means of drawings and words.

**comic strip:** \*comics.

**comma** [Gk. segment]; (F. comma; G. Komma; S. coma): \*colon.

**commedia dell'arte** [It. comedy of art]: unlike the Italian Renaissance comedy of character or situation (known as commedia erudita), the commedia dell'arte had no fixed text but instead a plot outline; professional actors, who represented popular stereotypes, had to improvise while performing. (\*\*repartee; stock character.)

**commedia erudita** [It. learned comedy]: \*commedia dell'arte.

**common measure:** \*common meter.

**common meter; common measure** (F. quatrain hymnique; G. Hymnenstrophe; S. estrofa de himno): a verse form usually used in hymns (also known as hymnal stanza) and which consists of four lines; the

first and third have four iambs each, the second and fourth three iambs; the rhyme scheme is abab or axay.

**common rhythm:** \*running rhythm.

**commus** [Gk. to hit]; (F. kommos; G. Kommos; S. komos): an elegiac and highly emotional song sung by the chorus in ancient Greek drama. (\*\*elegy.)

**comparison:** \*simile.

**compensation** [L. counter balance, exchange]; (F. compensation; G. Ersatz, Kompensation; S. compensación): the correction or adjustment of an irregular metrical unit by means of pauses or extra syllables. (\*\*break; caesura; rest.)

**complaint** [L. beat the breast]; (F. complainte; G. Klage, Elegie, Klagelied; S. lamento): a sad lyrical monologue in which the poet expresses his sorrows and seeks consolation and relief. (\*\*commus; dirge; elegy; epicedium; lament.)

**complexio** [L. combination]; (F. complexion, épistrophe; G. Complexio; S. complexión): a rhetorical figure: a combination of \*anaphora and \*epiphora.

**conceit** [L. thought]; (F. concetti; G. Konzetti; S. concepto): a strained comparison or a farfetched \*metaphor. (\*\*image; metaphysical conceit; Petrarchan conceits; simile.)

**conceptism** [L. thought]; (F. conceptisme; G. Konzeptismus; S. conceptismo): a literary style used in Spain in the seventeenth century which is noted for its obscure allusions and farfetched metaphors. (\*\*culteranism; cultism.)

**concrete** [L. created together]; (F. concret; G. konkret; S. concreto):

complex, unique, and based on personal experience and actual events, as opposed to *abstract. (**objectivity.)

concretism [*concrete]; (F. concretisme; G. Konkretismus; S. concretismo): a movement in modern lyric poetry which stresses the optical and acoustic characteristics of words rather than their denotative or connotative meaning. (**Dadaism; letterism.)

conduplicatio [L. repetition]; (F. conduplication; G.—; S. conduplicación): a rhetorical figure used for emphasis; a word or a group of words are repeated in succeeding clauses. (**anadiplosis; anaphora; complexio; epiphora.)

confidant; confidante [L. trustworthy]; (F. confident, confidente; G. Vertrauter, Vertraute; S. confidente): a minor or marginal *character (a friend, a maid, a servant, etc.) to whom another character, usually the protagonist, confides his secrets.

connotation [L. conjoined observation]; (F. connotation; G. Konnotation, Nebenbedeutung; S. connotación): the different suggestions and associations over and above the denotative meaning evoked by a word. (**denotation; figurative; literal meaning; poetic diction; synonym.)

consonance [L. harmony]; (F. consonance; G. Konsonanz; S. consonancia): partly or totally identical consonant-sounds in words whose vowel-sounds differ. (**analyzed rhyme; assonance; imperfect rhyme.)

constructivism (F. constructivisme; G. Konstruktivismus; S. constructivismo): a literary movement in the USSR between 1924 and 1930; its theoretician K. L. Zelinski decreed that all intrinsic and extrinsic elements of a literary work should be "constructed" according to and in conformity with its theme or central motif, which was usually a patriotic one. Rep. I. Selvinski, V. Inber, E. G. Bagricki. (**acmeism; formalism(2); socialist realism.)

content [L. contained]; (F. contenu; G. Inhalt; S. contenido): as opposed to form (*intrinsic structure; extrinsic structure), content is the summary of the events depicted and of the ideas expressed in a literary work. (**argument; atmosphere; fable(2); meaning; message; plot; story; subject matter; theme.)

contrafacture; contrafact; contrafactum [L. counterfeit]; (F. contrefaçon; G. Kontrafaktur; S. canción a lo divino): a religious song based on the melody of a popular, secular song; very seldom the other way around.

contrast: *antithesis.

conundrum [origin unknown]; (F. charade; G. Scharade; S. adivinanza): a riddle based on a *pun. (**charade; homograph; homonyms; homophones.)

convention [L. come together]; (F. convention; G. Konvention; S. convención): certain artistic devices such as *rhyme, *aside, *teichoscopy, which, although they do not conform to reality, have been tolerated by the public through the years.

conversation piece (F. pièce de salon; G. Konversationsstück; S.—): (1) a serious though unpretentious poem;

(2) a play that deals with every-day themes and motifs; noted for its witty and amusing dialogues (A. Dumas, O. Wilde, S. Guitry). (\*\*drama.)

**copla** [S. little song]: a popular short song which usually consists of four \*octosyllabic lines of which the second and fourth are linked by \*assonance or rhyme.

**copla de arte mayor** [\*copla; \*arte mayor]: a stanza of eight twelve-syllabic lines which rhyme abbaacca or abbaacac.

**copyright;©** (F. copyright, droit d'au-teur, propriété littéraire; G. Verlagsrecht, Nachbildungsrecht; S. propiedad literaria): the legal right to publish or reproduce a literary work for a certain period of time (in the U.S.A., twenty-eight years renewable for another twenty-eight years; in Canada, for a period of fifty years after the author's death).

**coronach** [Ir. Gael. weeping together]: an Irish or a Scottish \*dirge.

**Corpus Christi play** [L. body of Christ]; (F. mystère, Passion; G. Passionsspiel; S. auto sacramental): a popular religious play of the Middle Ages which deals with the suffering and death of Jesus Christ. (\*\*drama; liturgical drama; passion play.)

**correctio** [L. correction]; (F. correc-tion; G. Correctio; S. corrección): a rhetorical figure: making a state-ment, withdrawing it, and replacing it by a stronger one. (\*\*anacolu-thon; aposiopesis; palinode.)

**correlative verse** (F. vers rapportés; G. korrelativer Vers; S. verso cor-relativo): verses that include two or more groups of words in which the words of the first group are systematically and reciprocally re-lated to the words of the following group or groups. (\*\*antithesis; chiasmus; enallage; parallelism.)

**counterplayer:** \*antagonist.

**counterpoint rhythm** (F. contrepoint; G. kontrapunktischer Rhythmus; S. ritmo de contrapunto): a complex rhythm caused by a frequent depar-ture from the original metrical pattern so that two rhythmical pat-terns exist in the same poem. (\*\*descort; rhythm.)

**counterplot:** \*subplot.

**counterturn** = \*antistrophe.

**couplet** [F. little couple]; (F. distique; G. Paarreim, Reimpaar, Couplet, zweizeilige Strophe; S. dístico): a \*stanza of two lines. (\*\*heroic coup-let; octosyllabic couplet; open couplet.)

**courtesy book:** \*book of manners.

**courtly epic** (F. épopée courtoise; G. höfisches Epos; S. novela de caball-ería): a stately narrative which re-flects conventionalized codes of the court and glorifies knightly ideals. (\*\*art epic; chanson de geste; chivalric romance; courtly love; folk epic; metrical romance; pastourelle.)

**courtly love** (F. amour courtois; G. Frauendienst, Minne, Minnedienst; S. amor cortés): a noble passion depicted in the \*courtly epics, \*chivalric romances, and love songs of the Middle Ages; influenced by the lyrics of the Provençal \*trouba-dours, love-making adhered to feudal moral codes and chivalric social conventions; recurring motifs are: idealized womanhood, the ennobling power of love, humility, selflessness, and the complete devotion of a courageous lover. (\*\*dolce stil nuovo; erotic poetry; ghazel; lai; minnesong; rispetto.)

**courtly novel:** \*chivalric romance.

**courtly romance:** \*chivalric romance.

**courtly song; courtly love song** (F. chanson de trouvère, lai, chanson de troubadour; G. Troubadourlyrik, Trouverelyrik; S. canción trobadoresca, cantiga): songs of the Provençal \*troubadours, usually in the form of a \*sestina, \*canzone, or \*sirventes, which dealt with certain recurring themes (\*courtly love) and motifs (idealized womanhood, lover's selflessness and humility).

**crasis** [Gk. mixing]; (F. crase; G. Krasis; S. crasis): the fusion of two separate vowels into one; it usually takes place in order to adhere to the metrical pattern. (\*\*apocope; diaeresis(1); elision; hiatus; synaeresis; synaloepha.)

**Creacionismo** [S. creation]; **creationism:** a short-lived Spanish literary and aesthetic movement established by the Chilean poet Vicente Huidobro during the First World War which later blended with \*Ultraismo; the representatives of this movement (Gerardo Diego, Juan Larrera) attempted to create a new pure poetry by freeing it from reality.

**cretic** [Gk. Cretan]; (F. crétique; G. Kretikus; S. crético)=\*amphimacer.

**crisis** [Gk. decision, outcome]; (F. crise; G. Krise, Handlungshöhepunkt; S. crisis)=climax(2).

**critical apparatus:** \*apparatus criticus.

**critique** [Gk. judge]; (F. critique; G. Kritik; S. crítica): a critical study of a literary text. (\*\*analysis; apparatus criticus; impressionistic criticism; interpretation; strategy.)

**cross rhyme** (F. rimes croisées; G. Kreuzreim; S. rima alternante): the rhyme scheme abab cdcd efef . . . (\*\*rhyme.)

**crown of sonnets** (F. couronne de sonnets; G. Sonettenkranz; S. corona de sonetos, ciclo de sonetos): a lyrical unit of seven \*sonnets joined together by repeating the last line of each sonnet at the beginning of the following one; the last line of the seventh sonnet is the first line of the first sonnet. (\*\*sonnet cycle.)

**cryptogram** [Gk. hidden writing]; (F. cryptogramme; G. Kryptogramm; S. criptograma): a statement hidden behind a certain arrangement of letters or words. (\*\*acronym; acrostic; acroteleutic; anagram; chronogram; logograph; logomachy; mesostich; palindrome; telestich.)

**cubism** (F. cubisme; G. Kubismus; S. cubismo): a school of art in early twentieth-century Paris (Cézanne, Picasso, Braque) which presented objects by means of geometric shapes and patterns; inspired by this new kind of painting, cubist poets (Apollinaire, Reverdy) attempted to project the inner substance of their objects by reducing the extrinsic structure to a minimum. (\*\*futurism; vorticism.)

**culteranism** (F. cultéranisme; G. Kulteranismus; S. culteranismo): a European literary style of the sixteenth and seventeenth centuries characterized by its use of farfetched metaphors, obscure allusions, hyperbaton, and latinized syntax. It is sometimes known as *Gongorism, *Marinism, *preciosity, or *euphuism. (**baroque; conceptism; orotund.)

cultism (F. cultisme; G. Kultismus; S. cultismo): the extensive use of foreign words (usually Latin or Greek) in a literary text; often associated with the literary movements of *conceptism, *culteranism, and *Gongorism.

curtain raiser; curtain lifter (F. lever de rideau; G. Vorspiel; S. paso): a short independent play presented before the main play. (**drama.)

curtal [L. shortened] sonnet (F. sonnet écourté; G. Kurzsonett; S. soneto inconcluso): a *sonnet of eleven lines only and rhyming: abcabc dcbdc.

cynicism [Gk. doglike]; (F. cynisme; G. Zynismus; S. cinismo): *satire.

# D

dactyl [Gk. finger]; (F. dactyle; G. Daktylus; S. dáctilo): in *quantitative verse: a metrical foot of one long syllable followed by two short ones; in *accentual verse: a metrical foot of one stressed syllable followed by two unstressed ones: _ᴜᴜ. (**anapaest.)

Dadaism [derived from the stammering sounds "da da" of baby talk; French word for hobby horse]; (F. dadaïsme; G. Dadaismus; S. dadaísmo): a rebellious literary and artistic movement that was started in Zurich in 1916 by Tristan Tzara and Hans Arp with the revue theater "Voltaire" as their meeting place. In 1918 it spread to Berlin and in 1919 to Paris. Disenchanted with everything around them, the Dadaists attacked bourgeois values and established norms; they favored primitive manifestations of feeling and simultaneous association of ideas. Before blending with *surrealism in 1921, the movement produced many senseless sound poems and various literary collages which appeared in the journal *Dada*. (**futurism.)

dawn song: *aubade.

dead metaphor (F. métaphore vieillie, cliché; G. verblaßte Metapher, Ex-Metapher, konventionalisierte Sprachbilder; S. metáfora léxica, metáfora fósil): a *metaphor which has been used so often that it has lost its figurative value and become a mere expression. (**catachresis; cliché; formula; hackneyed expression.)

débat [F. debate]; poetic debate (F. débat; G. Streitgespräch, Streitgedicht, Debatte; S. debate): a medieval literary form in which two persons—often allegorical—dispute a topic or discuss a controversial issue. (**amoebean verse; dialogue; enthymeme; flyting; syllogism.)

decadence [L. to fall]; (F. décadence; G. Dekadenzdichtung; S. decadentismo): a literary movement in Europe at the end of the nineteenth century (also known as fin de siècle), noted for its negative attitude towards established values and its pessimistic interpretation of the epoch. In their search for novelty, writers and poets of this movement (Nietzsche, Schnitzler, Baudelaire, Oscar Wilde, Chekhov, and many others) wrote about perversity, corruption, material and moral decay, mental depression, and apathy (*Weltschmerz). (**Hermeticism; Jung-Wien.)

**decastich** [Gk. ten verses]; (F. dizain; G. Dekastichon; S. décima): a poem or a *stanza of ten lines.

**decasyllable** [Gk. ten syllables]; (F. décasyllabe; G. Dekasyllabus, Zehnsilber; S. decasílabo): an iambic line of ten syllables; often with a *caesura after the fourth syllable: ◡—◡— // ◡—◡—◡— .

**decorum** [L. grace]; (F. bienséance; G. Angemessenheit; S. decoro): coherence and congruity of the intrinsic and extrinsic aspects of a literary work. (**Apollonian; balance; classic(3); organic form.)

**definitive edition** (F. édition ne varietur; G. Ausgabe letzter Hand; S. edición definitiva): (1) the final version of a text as approved by the author himself; (2) the most authoritative and reliable edition. (**apparatus criticus; recension.)

**denotation** [L. designate]; (F. dénotation; G. Denotation; S. denotación): the thing that a word explicitly means, names, describes, or signifies. (**connotation; figurative; literal meaning; poetic diction; synonym.)

**denouement** [F. untying]; (F. dénouement; G. Lösung; S. desenlace): *catastrophe.

**descending rhythm** (F. rythme descendant; G. fallender Rhythmus, absteigender Rhythmus; S. ritmo descendente): *rhythm.

**descort** [F. discord]: a Provençal song in different stanza forms and various metrical patterns; it is sometimes written in more than one language. (**counterpoint rhythm; macaronic poetry.)

**detective story** (F. roman policier; G. Detektivroman, Detektivgeschichte; S. novela policíaca): a story or a novel which deals with a detective investigating a crime. (**penny dreadful; thriller; whodunit.)

**deus ex machina** [L. god from the machine]: a person in a drama who suddenly appears from nowhere and becomes involved in the later stages of the action in order to resolve the conflict. Also any unmotivated action or improbable dramatic device which leads to the rewarding of the virtuous characters and the punishment of the evil ones (*poetic justice). (**dramatic techniques; machinery.)

**deuteragonist** [Gk. the second actor]; (F. deutéragoniste; G. Deuteragonist; S. deuteragonista): *protagonist.

**development novel:** *novel of development.

**diaeresis; dieresis** [Gk. separation]; (F. diérèse; G. Diärese; S. diéresis): (1) the separation of two successive vowels so that they will not be pronounced as a diphthong; (2) a slight pause within a verse which coincides with the end of a word as well as with the end of a metrical foot. (**Alexandrine; break; caesura; hemistich; hiatus; rest.)

**dialect:** *vernacularism.

**dialogue** [Gk. conversation]; (F. dialogue; G. Dialog; S. diálogo): a conversation between two or more persons. Dialogues are indispensable to dramatic works, and often appear in narrative and lyric poetry. Dialogues are sometimes treated as an independent literary genre (when an author—in his attempt to appear objective and impartial—lets two or more imaginary speakers examine a subject from different points of view). (**amoebean verse; débat; duologue; eclogue; Fescennine verses; flyting; open form; stichomythia; syllogism.)

**diamb:** *diiamb.

**diary** [L. daily allowance]; (F. journal intime, journal particulier; G. Tagebuch; S. diario): a daily record of observations and personal activities. (**autobiography; memoirs; open form.)

**diatribe** [Gk. discord, occupation, philosophical conversation]; (F. diatribe; G. Diatribe; S. diatriba): a literary genre in the form of a speech, sermon, or lecture which is noted for its uncouth language, satirical remarks, and ironic statements. (**folly literature; lampoon; philippic; skit.)

**dibrach** = *pyrrhic.

**diction** = *poetic diction.

**didactic** [Gk. to teach] **literature** (F. littérature didactique; G. didaktische Dichtung, Lehrdichtung; S. literatura didáctica): literature which is mainly instructive or explicitly informative. (**belletristic literature; dit; epic drama; esoteric; exoteric; morality play; trivial literature.)

**dieresis:** *diaeresis.

**digression** [L. departure]; (F. digression; G. Digression, Abschweifung; S. digresión): a literary device used frequently in narrative poetry. One distinguishes: (1) relevant digression, i.e. the narration of insignificant incidents which are of minor relevance to the main plot, the very detailed description of motifs and leitmotifs, the elaborate explanation of specific situations or motivations, the elucidation of a special feeling or idea. (2) Irrelevant digression, i.e. long description of objects or the discussion of ideas and issues which are of no relevance to the progression of incidents nor of any significance to the characters, setting, or Zeitgeist of the story. (**allusion; chosisme; narrative techniques.)

**diiamb; diamb** [Gk. double iamb]; (F. diïambe; G. Diiambus; S. diyambo): a *dipody of two iambs: ◡__◡__ . (**ditrochee.)

**dime novel:** *penny dreadful.

**dimeter** [Gk. of two measures]; (F. dimètre; G. Dimeter; S. dímetro): (1) a classical verse of two identical measures; (2) a metrical unit of two feet or two *dipodies. (**tetrapody.)

**Dinggedicht** [G. a thing poem]; (F. poésie objet; G. Dinggedicht; S.—): an objective and detached poetic description of the substance and the intrinsic virtues of an object as seen from within. (**empathy.)

**Dionysian** [resembling Dionysius, the god of wine]; (F. dionysiaque; G. dionysisch; S. dionisiaco): a literary work that deals with a sensuous and frenzied experience in an unorganized manner; often associated with *Romanticism. (**Apollonian; dithyramb; spasmodic school.)

**dipody** [Gk. double foot]; (F. dipodie; G. Dipodie; S. dipodia): a single measure of two metrical feet. (**diiamb; dimeter; ditrochee; monopody; syzygy; tetrapody; tripody.)

**direct interior monologue:** *interior monologue.

**dirge** [L. to direct]; (F. chant funèbre; G. Trauergesang, Klagelied; S. canto fúnebre): a solemn and mournful short poem sung at funerals. (**commus; complaint; coronach; elegy; lament; monody; requiem.)

**disclosure:** *anagnorisis.

**discovery:** *anagnorisis.

**dispondee** [Gk. double *spondee]; (F. dispondée; G. Dispondeus, Dispondäus; S. dispondeo): a single measure of two *spondees: _ _ _ _. (*proceleusmatic; pyrrhic.)

**dissonance** [L. sounding in opposite ways]; (F. dissonance; G. Dissonanz; S. disonancia): the combination of harsh sounds (*cacophony), or the clashing of discordant extrinsic qualities. (**euphony; incantation.)

**distich** [Gk. double verse]; (F. distique; G. Distichon; S. dístico elegíaco): a *couplet that consists of a *hexameter and a *pentameter; often used in elegies (elegiac distich). (**epigram; fatras; monostich.)

**distichomythia** [Gk. dialogue in *distichs]; (F. distichomythie; G. Distichomythie; S. diálogo en dísticos): *stichomythia.

**distributed stress; hovering accent; resolved stress** (F. accent mobile, accent affectif; G. schwebende Betonung; S. acento afectivo, acento móvil): the formation of a spondee (i.e. two long or two stressed syllables) for rhetorical reasons. (**enclitic; logical stress; proclitic; recessive accent; syllaba anceps.)

**disyllabic; dissylabic** [Gk. of two syllables]; (F. dissyllabique; G. zweisilbig; S. disilábico): consisting of two syllables. (**monosyllabic; polysyllabic.)

**dit** [L. speech]; (F. dit; G. Dit; S. dicho): a short, instructive, and satirical poem in couplets or stanzas. (**ditty; folly literature; satire.)

**dithyramb** [Gk. a sobriquet of Bacchus, the god of wine; song in honor of Dionysius]; (F. dithyrambe; G. Dithyrambe, Dithyrambus, Dithyrambos; S. ditirambo): a wild, ecstatic, and emotional song which does not conform to any specific metrical pattern; also any *Dionysian literary product. (**Apollonian; spasmodic school.)

**ditrochee** [Gk. double trochee]; (F. ditrochée; G. Ditrochäus; S. ditroqueo): a metrical unit that consists of two *trochees: _ u _ u. (**diiamb; dipody.)

**ditty; dittie** [*dit]; (F. chansonnette; G. Liedchen; S. cantilena): a short poem usually put to music. (**dit; song.)

**diverbium** [L. dialogue in a drama]: the spoken part of the Roman drama, as opposed to the recited or sung part known as *canticum.

**dixain:** *dizain.

**dizain; dixain** [F. of ten lines]; (F. dizain; G. Dizain, Dixain; S. dizain): a poem or a *stanza of ten lines.

**dochmius; dochmiac** [Gk. oblique, slanting]; (F. dochmiaque; G. Dochmius; S. pie docmio): a metrical foot that consists of one *iamb and one *amphimacer: ᴗ__ __ᴗ__ .

**doggerel; doggrel** [origin unknown]; (F. vers de mirliton, vers de méchants; G. Doggerel; S. versos burlescos): a defective verse usually used for comic effects. (**folly literature.)

**dolce stil nuovo** [It. sweet new style]: North-Italian lyric poetry of the thirteenth century noted for its allegorical-mythical interpretation of earthly love and for its tender and melodious verses. Rep. Guitone d'Arrezzo, Guido Cavalcanti, Dante. (**courtly love; erotic poetry; minnesong.)

**domestic tragedy**=*bourgeois tragedy.

**double decker:** a novel in two volumes.

**double entendre** [F. double meaning]; (F. double entente; G. Doppelsinn, Zweideutigkeit; S. doble sentido): an ambiguous word or a phrase capable of two interpretations. (**ambiguity; amphibology.)

**double rhyme** (F. rime léonine, rime double; G. Doppelreim, zweisilbiger Endreim; S. rima doble): occurs when the rhyming parts consist of two syllables. (**feminine rhyme; rhyme.)

**down beat** (F. tonique; G. tonisch; S. tónico): a term sometimes used instead of *tonic.

**drama** [Gk. deed, action]; (F. drame; G. Drama; S. drama, comedia): a literary composition written for presentation on the stage by means of words and gestures. Dramas can be divided according to different extrinsical or intrinsical aspects such as the number of acts (one, three, or five-act plays), number of actors (mono drama, duo drama), the degree of dependence on music (opera, operetta, musical, burlesque . . .), the nature of the plot (tragedy, comedy, tragicomedy . . .), the subject matter (historical, bourgeois, liturgical . . .), the intellectual content (comedy of manners, conversation piece, farce, morality play . . .), the cause of the conflict (comedy of character, comedy of intrigue, miracle play . . .). (**antimasque; boulevard drama; carnival comedy; chronicle play; closet drama; comedy of situation; curtain raiser; drame; dramatic techniques; drama of the absurd; droll; dumb show; epic drama; folk play; harlequinade; living newspaper; low comedy; masque; melodrama; mime; mummery; mystery play; pantomime; passion play; problem play; radio play; revue; satyr play; television play; variety show; vaudeville; virgin play.)

**drama of the absurd** (F. théâtre de l'absurde; G. absurdes Theater, absurdes Drama; S. teatro del absurdo): a modern dramatic form which does not adhere to traditional dramatic norms nor to conventional dramaturgical devices. It relies upon *grotesque situations, illogical actions, and experimental structure. Rep. Beckett, Ionesco. (**drama; dramatic techniques.)

**dramatic** [*drama]; (F. dramatique; G. dramatisch; S. dramático): relating to drama; also contrasting or tense.

**dramatic irony; tragic irony; Sophoclean irony** (F. ironie tragique; G. tragische Ironie; S. ironía dramática): a confident or frolicsome statement made by someone who—due to oversight (*hamartia) or superciliousness (*hybris)—is not aware of the sad things that await him. (\*\*dramatic techniques; irony; irony of fate; romantic irony; Socratic irony.)

**dramatic monologue** (F. monologue dramatique; G. Rollengedicht; S. monólogo): a literary work or a part of a literary work in which a character—historical or fictional—reveals his personality or expresses his feelings. (\*\*aside; monodrama; monologue; parabasis; soliloquy.)

**dramatic poetry** (F. poésie dramatique; G. dramatische Dichtung; S. poesía dramática): one of the three main categories of poetry; the other two are lyric poetry and narrative poetry; it encompasses dramatic genres such as comedy, tragedy, tragicomedy. (\*\*drama; dramatic techniques.)

**dramatics** (F. dramaturgie; G. Dramatik; S. dramática): art and technique of dramatic composition. (\*\*drama; dramatic techniques.)

**dramatic techniques:** \*\*act; action; anticlimax(2); background; bathos; catabasis; catastasis; catastrophe; character; characterization; comic; comic relief; deus ex machina; drama; dramatic irony; dramatic monologue; dramaturgy; epic drama; epitasis; fable; falling action; Freytag's pyramid; grotesque; hamartia; humor; hybris; initial incident; interlude; mise-en-scène; pathos; play within a play; plot; protasis; radio play; retardation; scene; setting; soliloquy;; stichomythia; tableau; teichoscopy; television play; tetralogy; theater of the absurd; tragic; trilogy; unities.

**dramatic unities:** \*unities, the three.

**dramaturgy** [Gk. dramatic composition and performance]; (F. dramaturgie; G. Dramaturgie; S. dramaturgia): theories and techniques of theatrical representation. (\*\*drama; dramatic techniques.)

**drame** [\*drama]; (F. drame, mélodrame; G. Schauspiel, Rührstück, Problemstück; S. melodrama): a sad and pathetic play noted for its exciting plot, obvious superficiality, and exaggerated emotionality. (\*\*comedy of tears; drama; melodrama.)

**dreadful:** \*penny dreadful.

**dream allegory; vision** (F. songe, vision allégorique; G. Traumallegorie, Traumdichtung; S. visión alegórica): a literary form in which the author depicts an alleged vision, describes fantastic landscapes, and interprets the many symbolic events and allegorical figures which he pretends to encounter. (\*\*allegory.)

**drinking song** (F. chanson à boire; G. Trinklied; S. canción anacreóntica): a song that praises the drinking of alcoholic beverages and glorifies the atmosphere created by alcohol. (\*\*anacreontic poetry; carpe diem; wine song.)

**droll** [F. jester, rascal]; (F. farce; G. Posse; S. entremés): a short farcical play. (\*\*burlesque(2); drama; low comedy.)

**dumb show** (F. pantomime; G. Pantomime; S. pantomima): a \*drama or a part of a drama which is communicated only by means of signs and gestures. (\*\*masque; mummery; pantomime.)

**duodrama:** \*drama.

**duologue** [Gk. two speeches]; (F. dialogue, duodrame; G. Zwiegespräch; S. diálogo): a *dialogue or a duodrama. (**drama.)

**duple meter** [L. double measure]; (F. mètre binaire; G. zweisilbiges Metrum; S. bimembre): a meter that consists of two-syllabic feet. (**duple rhythm.)

**duple rhythm** [L. double]; (F. rythme binaire; G.—; S.—): a rhythmical unit that consists of one two-syllabic metrical foot. (**rhythm.)

**duplex method:** *aside.

**duration** [L. length of time]; (F. durée; G. Dauer; S. duración): the length of time needed to pronounce a syllable; also the length of a vowel; it is one of the factors which determine the *rhythm of a line or a stanza.

# E

**ecclesiastical drama**=*liturgical drama.

**echo** [Gk. sound]; (F. écho; G. Echo; S. eco): a rhetorical figure achieved by repeating a syllable, a word, or a group of words. (**anaclasis(2); anadiplosis; anaphora; complexio; conduplicatio; echo verse; epanadiplosis; epanalepsis; epiphora; palilogy; ploce; symploce.)

**echoic word**=*onomatopoeia.

**echo verse** (F. écho; G. Echo; S. eco): a line or a poem in which one or more *echos take place. (**epanalepsis.)

**eclogue** [Gk. choice, selection]; (F. églogue; G. Ekloge; S. égloga): a short *pastoral poem in a *dialogue form. (**Arcadia; bucolic; idyll; georgic.)

**Edwardian:** relating to the age of Edward VII of England (reigned 1901 - 10); this era was noted for its political stability, material security, and socially critical attitude. (**Caroline period; Cavalier poets; Elizabethan age; Georgian poets; Jacobean; Restoration; Victorian.)

**educational novel**=*novel of educational formation.

**Einfühlung** [G. insight, empathy]: *empathy.

**elegiac distich:** *distich.

**elegiac quatrain**=*elegiac stanza.

**elegiac stanza; elegiac quatrain** (F. strophe élégiaque; G. elegische Strophe; S. estrofa elegíaca): a *stanza of four iambic pentameters ($\cup\_\cup\_\cup\_\cup\_\cup\_$) rhyming abab. (**endecha.)

**elegy** [Gk. mourning song]; (F. élégie; G. Elegie, Klagelied; S. elegía): a lyric poem in which the poet laments the death of someone dear to him. (**complaint; commus; dirge; distich; elegiac stanza; endecha; epicedium; epitaph; lament; monody.)

**elision** [L. push away]; (F. élision; G. Elision; S. elisión): the intentional omission of an unstressed vowel or syllable within or at the end of a word in order to conform to the metrical pattern of a verse. (**apocope; hiatus; synaeresis; synaloepha; syncope.)

**Elizabethan age** (F. période élisabéthaine; G. Elisabethanisches Zeitalter; S. época isabelina): the reign of Queen Elizabeth I of England (1558 - 1603); it is regarded as one of the most fruitful periods in English literature (Shakespeare, Spenser, Jonson . . .). (**Caroline period; Cavalier poets; Edwardian; Georgian poets; Jacobean; Restoration; Victorian; University Wits.)

**ellipsis; ellipse** [Gk. omission, lacking]; (F. ellipse; G. Ellipse; S. elipsis): a rhetorical figure: omitting a word or words from a sentence. These words are necessary for a correct grammatical construction, but their omission does not obscure the meaning of the sentence. (**anacoluthon; aposiopesis; syllepsis.)

**elocution:** *eloquence.

**eloquence** [L. talent for speaking]; (F. éloquence; G. Eloquenz, Redegewandtheit, Beredsamkeit; S. elocuencia): the practical mastery of forceful and persuasive oral expressiveness, as opposed to theoretical *rhetoric.

**emblem** [Gk. inlaid work serving as model]; (F. emblème; G. Emblem; S. emblema): a picture or a sign symbolizing a certain idea with a very short text, usually of a didactic nature, explaining it or commenting on it. (**allegory; rebus; symbol.)

**embracing rhyme** (F. rimes embrassées; G. umarmender Reim, umschlie- $\beta$ender Reim, umschlungener Reim; S. rima abrazada): the rhyme scheme abba cddc . . . (**enclosing rhyme; redondilla; rhyme.)

**embryonic rhyme:** *imperfect rhyme.

**empathy** [Gk. emotion, passion]; (F. incarnation; G. Einfühlung; S. personificación, animización): the personification of an object by infusing one's own feelings into it, as opposed to a rational understanding of the object. (**allegory; anthropomorphism; apostrophe; Dinggedicht; personification; poetic fallacy.)

**emphasis** [Gk. demonstration, exposition]; (F. accent emphatique, accent d'insistance; G. Emphase, Nachdruck; S. énfasis): stressing a certain syllable or a specific word in order to give it greater importance or special impressiveness. (**anaclasis (2); anadiplosis.)

**Empfindsamkeit** [G. sensibility, sentimentality]: a German term used in connection with the sentimental novels of Fielding, Sterne, and Goldsmith whose works had a great impact on German writers like Gellert, Jacobi, and Goethe. (**sensibility, sentimentality.)

**enallage** [Gk. interchange]; (F. énallage; G. Enallage; S. enálage): relating certain words to each other although they do not logically or grammatically fit together. (**antithesis; chiasmus; correlative verse; parallelism.)

**enclitic** [Gk. to lean on]; (F. enclitique; G. enklitisch, Enklise; S. enclítico): the pronunciation of a word which has no independent accent as part of the preceding word. (**distributed stress; proclitic; recessive accent.)

**enclosing rhyme; enclosed rhyme** (F. rimes embrassées; G. umarmender Reim, umschlie$\beta$ender Reim; S. rima abrazada): a stanza or a poem of four lines with the rhyme scheme abba. (**embracing rhyme; palinodic, redondilla, rhyme.)

**encomiastic** [Gk. praise]= *panegyric.

encomium [Gk. praise]; (F. encomion; G. Enkomion; S. encomio): *panegyric.

endecasillabo=*hendecasyllable.

endecha [S. lament]: a mournful Spanish song in stanzas of four lines, each line has five, six, or seven syllables; assonance is used in the second and fourth lines of the stanzas. (**elegiac stanza; elegy.)

end rhyme; terminal rhyme (F. rime finale; G. Endreim; S. rima final): is produced when the rhyming words of two or more lines are placed at the end of these lines. (**rhyme.)

end-stopped line (F. rhèse; G. Zeilenstil; S. esticomitia): a line which is a complete syntactical and metrical unit with a distinct pause at its end, as opposed to the run-on line. (**break; enjambment.)

English sonnet: *sonnet.

enjambment; enjambement [F. running over]; run-on line (F. enjambement; G. Enjambement, Versbrechung, Zeilensprung; S. encabalgamiento): the running over of a sentence from one line of a poem into another without any pause. (**break; end-stopped line; open couplet.)

Enlightenment (F. siècle des lumières; G. Aufklärung; S. ilustración): a philosophical movement in Europe during the eighteenth century (Descartes, Hume, Locke, Leibniz, Kant), which demanded the free use of reason in questioning and examining traditional values and ideals; it had a great influence on the European literature of the epoch. (**Göttinger Hain; irrationalism; Preromanticism; rationalism; Scholasticism; Sturm und Drang.)

enoplius; enoplion=*prosodiac.

ensenhamen [Prov. instruction]: a Provençal didactic and instructive poem.

enthymeme [Gk. consider]; (F. enthymème; G. Enthymem; S. entimema): a *syllogism based mainly on rhetorical elements. (**débat; epideictic speech; flyting; harangue; homiletics; polemic; tenzone; tirade.)

Entwicklungsroman: *novel of development.

enveloping structure (F. récit à tiroir; G. Rahmenstruktur; S. narración dentro de un marco): occurs when a line, a stanza, or a story encloses other lines, stanzas, or stories. (**episode; episodic structure; frame story; narrative techniques; play within a play.)

envoi; envoy [F. send]; (F. envoi; G. Geleit, Schluβstrophe; S. tornada): *canzone.

epanadiplosis [Gk. doubling]; (F. épanadiplose; G. Epanadiplose; S. epanadiplosis): a rhetorical figure: repeating at the end of a clause or sentence the word with which that clause or sentence began. (**anadiplosis; anaphora; complexio; conduplicatio; echo; epanalepsis; epiphora; palilogy; ploce; symploce.)

epanalepsis [Gk. resumption]; (F. épanalepse; G. Epanalepse; S. epanalepsis): a rhetorical figure used for increasing the elocutionary effect by repeating a word or a group of words within a phrase. (**anadiplosis; epanadiplosis; hendiadys; pleonasm; tautology.)

epanodos [Gk. return]; (F. épanode; G. Epanodos; S. epanodos): a *ploce or *complexio.

epanorthosis [Gk. correction]=*correctio.

**epic** [Gk. word, narrative poem]; (F. épopée; G. Epos; S. épica): a stately narrative poem of extended length; epics are usually divided into *folk epics and *art epics. (**canto; narrative poetry; narrative techniques.)

**epic drama** (F. drame épique; G. episches Theater; S. drama épico): a new form of drama introduced by Bertold Brecht (1898 - 1956) which differs from the traditional forms in that the illusion of the audience is continuously neutralized by means of the so-called estrangement effects (Verfremdungseffekt), i.e. songs, narrative interludes, comments, reports, etc., so that the audience can form an objective and unbiased opinion about the political or social issues presented in the play. (**agit-prop; living newspaper.)

**epicedium** [Gk. funeral song]; (F. épicédion; G. Epikedeion, Epicedium; S. epicedio): a mournful short poem sung at the graveside; usually in the form of a *distich. (**commus; dirge; elegy; epitaph.)

**epic poetry**= *narrative poetry.

**epideictic speech** [Gk. to show, to display]; (F. discours épidéictique; G. Epideiktik; S. epideíctico): a speech that has no practical purposes (as opposed to legal or political speeches); the orator, who usually praises or blames persons and objects, is mainly interested in demonstrating his rhetorical abilities. (**autotelic; eloquence; enthymeme; harangue; homiletics; invective; oration; panegyric; tirade.)

**epigonism** [Gk. born after]; (F. epigones; G. Epigonentum; S. epígono): inferior imitation of a dis-

tinguished writer by a later generation. (**archaism; imitation; Münchner Dichterkreis; neo-humanism; neoromanticism; Parnassians.)

**epigram** [Gk. inscription]; (F. épigramme; G. Epigramm; S. epigrama): a short, witty, and ingenious statement in verse; usually in the form of a *distich. (**aphorism; apophthegm; closed couplet; gnomic poetry; maxim; sentence; triolet.)

**epigraph** [Gk. inscription]; (F. épigraphe; G. Epigraph; S. epígrafe): a short text at the beginning of a book or chapter of a book suggesting a specific theme or referring to a certain motif. (**exordium; invocation; prologue.)

**epilogue** [Gk. after speech]; (F. épilogue; G. Epilog, Nachwort, Schlußrede; S. epílogo): the concluding part of a literary work or the final speech which an actor addresses to the audience; as opposed to *prologue. (**peroration.)

**epinicion:** *panegyric.

**epiphany** [Gk. appearance]; (F. manifestation, révélation; G. Offenbarung; S. epifanía): the revelation of a mood by means of suggestive words or the sudden manifestation of a condition by way of gestures.

**epiphora** [Gk. addition]; (F. épiphore; G. Epiphora; S. epífora): a rhetorical figure: repeating one or more words at the end of successive verses or sentences; opposite of *anaphora. (**anadiplosis; complexio; conduplicatio; palilogy; ploce; symploce.)

**epirrhema** [Gk. the added speech]; (F. épirrhème; G. Epirrhema; S. epirrema): the spoken part which follows a song in ancient Greek comedy; usually of a satirical nature. (**episode(1); stasimon.)

**episode** [Gk. inserted in]; (F. episode; G. Episode; S. episodio): (1) the spoken part between two songs in ancient Greek tragedy; (2) a coherent and independent plot which forms an integral part of a narrative or dramatic work. (**enveloping structure; episodic structure; frame story; stasimon.)

**episodic structure** (F. oeuvre à tiroirs; G. episodische Struktur; S. estructura episódica): the form of a narrative or dramatic work which consists of coherent and independent stories or scenes that have a common intrinsical factor (theme, motif, characters, settings, etc.). (**enveloping structure; frame story; narrative techniques; picaresque.)

**epistle** [Gk. letter]; (F. épître; G. Epistel, Briefgedicht; S. epístola): a lyric or narrative poem in the form of a letter; often of a didactic and instructive nature.

**epistolary novel** [*epistle]; (F. roman épistolaire; G. Briefroman; S. novela epistolar): a novel that consists, entirely or partly, of fictitious letters. (**narrative techniques; novel.)

**epistrophe**= *epiphora.

**epitaph** [Gk. belonging to a funeral or a grave]; (F. épitaphe; G. Epitaph; S. epitafio): a short literary work in which a deceased person is commemorated; also the inscription on a gravestone. (**dirge; elegy; epicedium; lament.)

**epitasis** [Gk. intensity]; (F. épitase; G. Epitasis, ansteigende Handlung; S. epítasis): the part of the drama in which the nature of the plot is revealed and the dramatic entanglement begins. (**catabasis; catastasis; catastrophe; climax(2); dramatic techniques; Freytag's pyramid; initial incident; peripeteia; protasis.)

**epithalamium** [Gk. bridal song]; (F. épithalame, poème nuptial; G. Epithalamium, Hochzeitslied; S. epitalamio): a joyous song in praise of marriage. (**panegyric.)

**epithet** [Gk. addition]; (F. épithète; G. Epitheton; S. epíteto): a characterizing word or phrase; an appropriate adjective; when used repeatedly in a literary work, it is called a stock epithet. (**antonomasia; hypallage.)

**epitome** [Gk. cut, section]; (F. épitomé; G. Epitome, Zusammenfassung; S. epítome): a summary, a *brief, or a typical representation. (**essay.)

**epitrite** [Gk. one and one third]; (F. épitrite; G. Epitrit, Epitritus; S. pie epítrito): a Greek metrical foot of three long syllables and a short one; according to the position of the short syllable, the epitrite is designated as primus ($\cup$ _ _ _), secundus (_ $\cup$ _ _), tertius (_ _ $\cup$ _), or quartus (_ _ _ $\cup$). (**paeon.)

**epizeuxis** [Gk. liaison]; (F. épizeuxe; G. Epizeuxis; S. epizeuxis)= *epanalepsis

**epode** [Gk. sung after]; (F. épode; G. Epode, Abgesang; S. epodo): (1) the third and last part of the Pindaric stanza; (2) a short verse which follows a longer one; (3) a lyric poem in which a shorter verse always follows a longer one. (**triad.)

**epopee** [Gk. writing epics]; (F. épopée; G. Epopöe; S. epopeya): an epic or a narrative poem.

**epos** [Gk. narrative poem]; (F. épopée; G. Epos; S. epopeya): an epic or a narrative poem.

**epyllion** [Gk. little epic]; (F. poème alexandrin; G. Epyllion; S. poema épico al estilo alejandrino): a short sophisticated epic with mythological themes created by the Alexandrian writers of the third century B.C.; it was later imitated by other intellectual writers, the so-called poeta doctus.

**equivalence** [L. of equal value]; (F. équivalence; G. Equivalenz, Gleichwertigkeit; S. equivalencia): metrical equality reached by substituting one metrical foot for another. (**substitution.)

**equivoque; equivoke** [F. equivocal]= *ambiguity.

**ermetismo:** *Hermeticism.

**erotic** [Gk. sexual love] **poetry** (F. poésie érotique; G. erotische Literatur; S. poesia erótica): as opposed to love poetry (which describes feelings and sentiments and avoids sex) or pornography (which tends to arouse sexual desire), erotic poetry deals poetically with sensual love.

**Erziehungsroman:** *novel of educational formation.

**escape literature:** *trivial literature.

**esoteric** [Gk. from within]; (F. ésotérique; G. esoterisch; S. esotérico): a literary work, often in verse, which can be appreciated only by highly sophisticated readers; opposite of *exoteric. (**autotelic; belletristic literature; trivial literature.)

**essay** [F. trial, experiment]; (F. essai; G. Essay; S. ensayo): a subjective and stimulating treatise. (**brief; Festschrift; review; sketch; tract; vignette.)

**estilo culto**=*Gongorism.

**estrangement effect** (F. aliénation; G. Verfremdungseffekt; S. alienación): *epic drama.

**estribillo** [S. stirrup]: a *refrain of one or more lines. (**letrilla.)

**etiquette book**=*book of manners.

**eulogy** [Gk. praise, blessing]; (F. éloge; G. Eulogie, Lobgedicht; S. panegírico): a literary work written in commendation of a person or a thing. (**panegyric.)

**euphemism** [Gk. using words of good omen]; (F. euphémisme; G. Euphemismus; S. eufemismo): replacing an unpleasant expression by an agreeable one; alluding to distasteful things by tasteful words; paraphrasing of offensive texts. (**circumlocution.)

**euphony** [Gk. pleasant sound]; (F. euphonie; G. Euphonie; S. eufonía): agreeable and pleasant combination of sounds; opposite of *cacophony. (**dissonance; incantation; jingle; onomatapoeia.)

**euphuism** [for John Lyly's novel *Euphues*, 1579]; (F. euphuisme; G. Euphuismus; S. eufuismo): an affected and pretentious style marked for antithesis, alliteration, parallel grammatical structure, and allusions to mythological figures and historical events. (**baroque; bombast; culteranism; cultism; Gongorism; logorrhoea; Marinism; orotund; verbosity.)

**event-novel** (F. roman d'action; G. Ereignis-Roman; S. novela de acontecimientos): adventure stories which do not consider the inwardness of the characters; in this category one can include the adventure novel, Gothic novel, mystery story, crime story, detective fiction, and other similar types. (\*\*novel; penny dreadful; thriller; Western; whodunit.)

**excursus** [L. digression]; (F. excursus; G. Exkurs; S. digresión):=\*digression.

**exegesis** [Gk. exposition, explanation]; (F. exégèse; G. Exegese; S. exégesis): a critical explanation of a text, especially of the Scriptures. (\*\*analysis; explication.)

**exemplum** [L. model, example]; (F. exemplum; G. Exempel; S. ejemplo): a moralizing tale or an illustrative anecdote often used in speeches and sermons. (\*\*cautionary tale; narrative poetry; parable.)

**existentialism** (F. existentialisme; G. Existentialismus; S. existencialismo): a philosophical movement (Kierkegaard, Heidegger, Sartre) which deals with human existence and man's freedom in a purposeless world; it has had a great influence on the literature of the twentieth century, especially after the Second World War.

**exodus; exodos** [Gk. departure]; (F. exodos, exode; G. Exodos; S.éxodo): the final scene; the part that follows the last song of the chorus in Greek drama; opposite of \*parodos.

**exordium** [L. beginning]; (F. exorde; G. Exordium; S. exordio): the introductory part of a speech or an epic which draws the attention of the audience. (\*\*epigraph; invocation; prelude; prologue.)

**exoteric** [Gk. external]; (F. exotérique; G. exoterisch; S. exotérico): a literary work which is accessible and intelligible to the unsophisticated or unspecialized public; opposite of \*esoteric. (\*\*belletristic literature; trivial literature.)

**exoticism** [Gk. foreign]; (F. exotisme; G. Exotismus; S. exotismo): the persistent tendency toward what is outlandish, strange, or untried.

**experimental novel** (F. nouveau roman; G. Experimental-Roman; S. novela experimental): any novel that does not conform to conventional norms or deal with traditional themes. (\*\*antinovel; heterodox novel; narrative poetry; novel.)

**expletive** [L. filling out]; (F. explétif; G. Expletiv, Füllwort; S. expletivo): a syllable, word, or group of words inserted to fill a gap without adding to the general meaning of the sentence.

**explication** [L. unfolding]; (F. explication; G. Explikation, Erläuterung, Erklärung; S. explicación): a detailed \*analysis and systematic interpretation of the intrinsic and extrinsic characteristics of a literary work. (\*\*interpolation; interpretation; paraphrase.)

**exposition** [L. explanation]; (F. exposition; G. Exposition; S. exposición) =\*protasis.

**expressionism** (F. expressionisme; G. Expressionismus; S. expresionismo): a literary and artistic movement in the early twentieth century which attempted to project moods, emotions, and inner experiences by using nonnaturalistic devices such as distortion and abstraction. (**impressionism; Neue Sachlichkeit.)

**expurgate**=*bowdlerize.

**extravaganza** [It. extravagant]; (F. oeuvre fantaisiste, histoire abracadabrante; G. phantastisches Werk; S. disparate): a literary work noted for its fantastic themes, bizarre style, and parodical elements. (**burlesque(1); parody.)

**extrinsic structure** (F. structure extrinsèque; G. äußere Form; S. estructura extrínsica): the outer form of a literary work, i.e. all characteristics related to length, divisions, and style; opposite to *intrinsic structure. (**architectonics; structure; texture.)

**eye rhyme** (F. rime pour l'oeil; G. unreiner Reim; S. rima visual): occurs when the rhyming words are similar in spelling but different in pronunciation. (**rhyme.)

# F

**fable** [L. tale]; (F. fable; G. Fabel; S. fábula): (1) a satirical tale in verse or in prose about animals and plants; (2) plot outline of a narrative or dramatic work. (**action; allegory; anthropomorphism; apologue; argument; cautionary tale; fable time; personification; plot; story.)

**fable time; acting time** (F. moment de l'action; G. erzählte Zeit; S. tiempo de la obra literaria): the time of the play's action or the story's plot measured according to the information supplied by the playwright or the narrator. (**action; narrative techniques; narrative time; plot; story.)

**fabliau** [F. short tale]; (F. fabliau; G. Fablel, Schwank; S. fabliau, trova, romance satírico): a coarse, comic, satirical, and often obscene *tale in verse. (**narrative poetry.)

**fabula atellana**=*Atellan fables.

**fairy tale** (F. conte de fées; G. Märchen; S. cuento de hadas): a short narrative dealing with supernatural be-

ings and fantastic events. (**fantasy fiction; narrative poetry; tale.)

**fairy story**=*fairy tale.

**falcon theory**: *Falkentheorie.

**Falkentheorie** [G. falcon theory]: according to the German poet Paul Heyse (1830 - 1914), a good *novella must revolve around a *leitmotif, exactly as in the novella by Boccaccio (the ninth novella of the fifth day of the *Decamerone*, 1353) in which a falcon is an indispensable part of the *theme. (**Münchner Dichterkreis.)

**fallacy**: *poetic fallacy.

**falling action** (F. chute de l'action; G. fallende Handlung; S. acción decreciente): the part of the *action which follows the *climax and leads to the *catastrophe. (**catabasis; catastasis; epitasis; Freytag's pyramid; peripetia; protasis.)

**falling foot**=*falling meter.

**falling meter; falling foot** (F. pied à rythme descendant; G. fallendes Metrum; S. ritmo descendente): a metrical foot that begins with a stressed syllable such as a trochee (‿◡) or dactyl (‿◡◡). (**rhythm.)

**falling rhythm**=descending *rhythm.

**fantasy fiction** (F. récit fantastique; G. phantastische Erzählung; S. narración fantástica): a fictional work that deals with strange settings, implausible incidents, and supernatural beings. (**cock-and-bull story; exemplum; fabliau; fairy tale; folk tale; magical realism; myth; narrative poetry; science fiction; tall tale; Utopian fiction; yarn.)

**farce** [L. stuffing]; (F. farce, G. Farce, Posse, Schwank, Burleske, Streich; S. farsa): *low comedy.

**fatras:** a French verse form that consists of a *distich and a strophe of eleven lines rhyming ab aabaabbabab; its theme, which is included in the distich, is usually a humorous one. Depending on the grade of coherence and lucidity, one distinguishes between fatras possible and fatras impossible.

**Félibrige** [a name used in a Prov. folk song]: a French poetic circle founded in 1854 in Fontségugne near Avignon to revive *Provençal language and literature; among its members one finds F. Mistral and J. Roumanille.

**feminine caesura** (F. coupe féminine; G. weibliche Zäsur; S. cesura femenina): a slight pause after an unstressed or short syllable. (**break, caesura.)

**feminine ending** (F. terminaison féminine; G. weiblicher Versausgang; S. terminación femenina.): occurs when the line ends with an unstressed, usually hypermetric, syllable. (**feminine rhyme.)

**feminine rhyme** (F. rime féminine; G. weiblicher Reim, klingender Reim; S. rima femenina): occurs when the rhyming parts consist of a stressed syllable followed by an unstressed one. (**double rhyme; feminine ending; rhyme.)

**Fescennine verses** [from Fescennia, ancient town in Etruria, Italy]; (F. vers fescennins; G. Feszenninen; S. versos fesceninos): a crude and abusive song in dialogue form without a fixed metrical pattern; it was sung at harvest festivals, weddings, and births. (**amoebean verse; flyting.)

**Festschrift** [G. writings for a celebration]: a collection of *essays by different scholars to honor a colleague or a famous writer on a special occasion.

**feuilleton** [F. small sheet]; (F. feuilleton; G. Feuilleton; S. folletín): a literary work written for publication in the feature section of a newspaper; usually entertaining and unpretentious. (**penny-a-liner.)

**fiction** [L. invention, fabrication]; (F. fiction, oeuvre de fiction; G. erzählerische Dichtung, epische Dichtung; S. ficción): a blanket term that encompasses all narrative forms and particularly those in prose. (**narrative poetry; narrative techniques.)

**figura etymologica:** *paronomasia(1).

**figurative** (F. figuré; G. figürlich, übertragen, bildlich; S. figurativo): the implicit and suggestive meaning of words as opposed to their *literal meaning. (**connotation; denotation.)

**figurative language** (F. langage figuré; G. bildliche Sprache; S. lenguaje figurado): ornamental language. (**figurative; rhetorical figures.)

**figures of speech** (F. figures de rhétorique; G. Redefiguren; S. figuras retóricas)=*rhetorical figures.

**fin de siècle** [F. end of the century]: *decadence.

**first person narrative** (F. récit à la première personne; G. Ich-Form; S. narración en primera persona): the narration of a story by one of the characters. (**indirect interior monologue; interior monologue; narrative techniques; stream of consciousness; third person narrative; voice.)

**flashback; retrospect** (F. retour en arrière, flashback; G. Rückblende; S. retrospección, flashback): a literary device reached by interrupting the chronological sequence of events and recalling incidents from the past or presenting earlier *episodes. (**narrative techniques.)

**flat character** (F. caractère sans imprévu; G. Typ; S. personaje bidimensional, flat character): a fixed or predictable character, hence, an undramatic one; opposite of *round character. (**archetype; character; characterization; stock character.)

**Fleshly School of Poetry, the:** a term used by the English critic Robert Buchanan in 1871 in his attack on D. G. Rossetti, Swinburne, and Morris whom he denounced for being "fleshly."

**fliting**=*flyting.

**flyting** [OHG. quarrel]; (F. tenson; G. Streitgedicht; S. polémica satírica en verso): an abusive dispute in verse between two poets. (**amoebean verse; débat; dialogue; enthymeme; Fescennine verses; polemic; syllogism; tenzone.)

**foil** [L. leaf]; (F. repoussoir; G. Gegenspieler, Gegner; S. antagonista): a person who serves as a contrast to the leading *character in dramas and narratives. (**antagonist; protagonist.)

**folio** [L. leaf]; (F. in-folio; G. Folio; S. folio): a large size book containing sheets of paper that are folded once. (**quarto.)

**folk ballad; popular ballad; traditional ballad** (F. ballade populaire; G. Volksballade; S. romance folklórico, romance tradicional, romance popular): a *ballad characterized by the anonymity of its author and by its unelevated style, and simple—if not faulty—language. (**art ballad; ballad stanza; Chevy-Chase stanza; folk poetry; minstrel; narrative poetry.)

**folk drama**=*folk play.

**folk epic; primitive epic; primary epic** (F. épopée primitive; G. Volksepos; S. épica primitiva): a stately narrative poem usually written by an unknown poet, for recitation to the nobility. Folk epics are usually divided into *heroic epics and *national epics. (**art epic; folk poetry; narrative poetry.)

**folk poetry** (F. poésie populaire; G. Volksdichtung; S. poesía tradicional): the different kinds of poetry that are of unknown authorship and which are usually handed down by oral tradition; it encompasses folk epic, folk ballad, folk song, folk tale, charm, riddle, and folk play. (**incremental repetition; oral poetry.)

**folk play; folk drama** (F. pièce populaire; G. Volksschauspiel, Volksstück; S. comedias tradicionales, comedias populares): includes *carnival comedies, popular plays of a simple and unpretentious nature, and plays of unknown authorship. (**drama; folk poetry.)

**folk song; popular song** (F. chanson populaire; G. Volkslied; S. canción popular): a popular song of unknown origin marked for its simple structure, plain language, and unsophisticated melody; usually transmitted orally. (**folk poetry; lyric poetry; song.)

**folk tale** (F. récit, légende populaire; G. Volkssage, Volkserzählung; S. cuento popular): a popular short narrative that deals with mythical, historical, or fantastic figures and events; usually of unknown authorship and handed down by oral tradition. (**chapbook; cock-and-bull story; fabliau; fairy tale; fantasy fiction; narrative poetry; tale; tall tale; tradition; yarn.)

**folly literature** (F. sotie, bouffonnerie, satire burlesque; G. Narrendichtung; S. bufonada): a form of satirical literature that is hidden behind the mask of buffoonery or madness. (**diatribe; dit; doggerel; lampoon; pasquinade; satire; silloi; skit; sotie.)

**foot** [OHG. step, foot as a measure]; **metrical foot** (F. mesure, pied; G. Versfuß; S. pie): the smallest rhythmical unit which usually consists of one stressed (or one long) syllable and one or two unstressed (or short) syllables (**accentual verse; amphibrach; amphimacer; anapaest; antibacchius; antispast; dactyl; falling meter; iamb; Ionic; molossus; paeon; proceleusmatic; pyrrhic; quantitative verse; rising meter; scansion; spondee; tribrach; triple meter(2); trochee.)

**foreshadowing:** *anticipation.

**foreword** [trans. of G. Vorwort=before word]; (F. avant-propos; G. Vorwort; S. prefacio)=*prologue.

**form** [L. shape]; (F. forme; G. Form; S. forma): (1)=*genre; (2)=*structure.

**formalism** (F. formalisme; G. Formalismus; S. formalismo): (1) strict adherence to extrinsic rules; little attention is paid to content; (2) a Russian literary movement (1915 - 1930) which overemphasized the extrinsic aspects of literary works; although it had a great influence on literary criticism, it was attacked in 1927 by followers of government-sponsored *socialist realism. Rep. V. Slovskij, B. Eichenbaum, R. Jacobson. (**acmeism; constructivism; futurism.)

**formula** [L. rule, formula]; (F. formule; G. Formel; S. fórmula): a formal statement, a fixed figure of speech, or a conventionalized expression used in popular literary genres (such as folk epics, folk songs, fairy tales, riddles, and legends), especially during the Middle Ages. (**cliché; dead metaphor; hackneyed expression.)

**fourteener** (F. vers iambique de sept pieds; G. Vierzehnsilber; S.—): a line of seven iambic feet (=fourteen syllables): ◡—◡—◡—◡—◡—◡—◡—◡— .

**fragment** [L. fraction]; (F. fragment; G. Fragment; S. fragmento): a literary work that consists of disconnected and not fully developed parts; also a work that is left incomplete. (**collage; montage.)

**frame story** (F. récit à tiroir; G. Rahmenerzählung; S.—): a story that encloses other shorter stories or *episodes; these episodes are known as inset stories. (**enveloping structure; episodic structure; play within a play.)

**free rhythm**=*free verse.

**free verse** (F. vers libre; G. freier Rhythmus; S. verso suelto): a verse form that does not adhere to a fixed metrical pattern; it differs from *prose in that the stress accents recur at fairly regular time intervals. (**imagism; polyphonic prose; prose poem; vers libre; verset.)

**Freytag's pyramid** (F. pyramide de Freytag; G. Gustav Freytags Pyramide; S. pirámide de Freytag): according to the German poet Gustav Freytag *(Die Technik des Dramas*, 1863), the dramatic action rises constantly till it reaches the *climax, after which it starts to fall down rapidly toward the *catastrophe; this gives a play a pyramid-like structure. (**catabasis; catastasis; epitasis; dramatic techniques; peripetia; protasis.)

**frottola** [It. crowd]: a joyous Italian popular song with satirical and didactic elements; also known as barzelletta.

**full rhyme:** *perfect rhyme.

**futurism** (F. futurisme; G. Futurismus; S. futurismo): a radical Italian literary movement within *expressionism (the first manifesto was published in 1909); it attacked traditional forms and concepts in an attempt to free poetry from sentimentality and formalism. In 1924 it blended with *cubism, *Dadaism, and *surrealism. Rep. F. T. Marinetti, Papini, Govoni. (**Hermeticism; vorticism.)

# G

**galliamb; galliambus; galliambic** [Gk. named after the songs of the Galli, the priests of Cybele]; (F. galliambe; G. Galliamb, Galliambus; S. galiambo): a line in *quantitative poetry which usually consists of four minor *Ionics: ᴜᴜ_ _ᴜᴜ_ _ᴜᴜ_ _ᴜᴜ_ _.

**Gallicism** [F. Gallic]; (F. gallicisme; G. Gallizismus; S. galicismo): the adoption of a French expression by another language. (**macaronic poetry.)

**genre** [L. origin, species]; (F. genre; G. Gattung, Genre; S. género): a poetic form or a literary type (e.g. epic, ballad, short story, etc.). (**drama; lyric poetry; narrative poetry.)

**genre picture** (F. peinture de genre; G. Genrebild; S. cuadro costumbrista): a short realistic prose description of a typical situation from everyday life. (**idyll; sketch; vignette.)

**Georgian poets; Georgianism:** a group of poets during the reign of George V of England (reigned 1910 - 1936) noted for their conventional forms, romantic themes, and sentimental moods. Rep. R. Brooke, J. Drinkwater, W. H. Davies. (**Caroline period; Cavalier poets; Edwardian; Elizabethan age; Jacobean; neo-romanticism; Restoration; Victorian.)

**georgic** [after Vergil's poem *Georgics*]; (F. géorgique; G. Georgika; S. geórgica): a poem which describes the farmer's world without idealizing it. (**bucolic poetry; eclogue; pastoral poetry.)

**gest; geste** [L. deeds]; (F. geste; G. Gesta; S. gesta)=*chanson de geste.

**ghazel; ghazal; gazel** [Arab. love song]; (F. ghazel; G. Ghasel, Gasel, Ghazel, Ghasal; S. zejel): a rhymed Arabic poem of varying length—usually between six and thirty lines—which deals with *erotic or mystical love. (**courtly love; mysticism; qasida.)

**glosa**=*gloss(3).

**gloss** [Gk. tongue, language]; (F. glose; G. Glosse; S. glosa): (1) an unusual or obscure word; (2) the explanation or translation of words or a text;
- (3) a Spanish lyric poem of four ten-line stanzas; each stanza is a variation or an explanation of the main theme which is presented in a four-line stanza at the beginning of the poem.

**Glyconic** [named after the Greek poet Glycon]; (F. glyconique; G. Glykoneus; S. gliconio): a Greek verse that usually consists of eight syllables:
⏑⏑ —⏑⏑ — ⏑⏑.

**gnomic poetry; gnome** [Gk. judgment, maxim]; (F. poésie gnomique; G. Gnome, Spruch; S. poesía gnómica): a short aphoristic statement, usually in verse. (**aphorism; apophthegm; epigram; maxim; sentence.)

**Goliardic verse** [L. glutton]; (F. poésie goliardique; G. Goliarden, Goliardendichtung, Vagantendichtung; S. poesía goliardesca): medieval satiric and profane poetry sung by wandering poets in praise of earthly pleasures. (**carpe diem; minstrel; ubi sunt motif.)

**Gongorism** [named after the Spanish poet Luis de Góngora y Argote, 1561 - 1627]; (F. gongorisme; G. Gongorismus; S. gongorismo): it usually refers pejoratively to works written in imitation of the style of Góngora. This style is pretentious, inflated, and highly rhetorical. (**baroque; culteranism; cultism; estilo culto; logorrhoea; Neo-Gongorism; orotund; preciosity; euphuism; verbosity.)

**Göttinger Hain; Göttinger Dichterbund; Hainbund** [after Klopstock's ode "Der Hügel und der Hain"]: an association of young, patriotic German poets, founded in Göttingen in 1772. The members of this group protested against the rigid rationalism of the *Enlightenment and attempted to free German poetry from foreign influence; organ: *Der Göttinger Musenalmanach;* rep. Voβ, Hölty. (**irrationalism; Preromanticism; Sturm and Drang.)

**Gothic novel** (F. roman gothique; G. Schauerroman; S. novela gótica): the horror novel of the eighteenth and nineteenth centuries; noted for its cruel characters, macabre incidents, and medieval settings; it could be regarded as a forerunner of *detective and mystery stories. (**event-novel; penny dreadful; thriller.)

**grand style:** *high style.

**Graveyard School:** melancholic English poetry of the eighteenth century that dealt with death and often had the grave as its *leitmotif (e.g. Robert Blair's *The Grave*, 1743). (**metaphysical poets.)

**grotesque** [It. cave]; (F. grotesque; G. grotesk; S. grotesco): a style noted for its comic absurdity, ridiculous ugliness, or ludicrous *incongruity. (**antimasque; irony; theater of the absurd.)

# H

**hackneyed** [OF. a horse suitable for ordinary riding] **expression; hackneyed quotation** (F. cliché, poncif; G. abgenutzter Ausdruck, Klischee; S. expresión gastada): a once effective phrase, theme, or motif that has lost its freshness and power to impress due to its frequent use. (**cliché; dead metaphor; formula.)

**hagiography** [Gk. holy writing]; (F. hagiographie; G. Hagiographie; S. hagiografía): the idealized *biography of a saint.

**haiku; hokku; haikai; Hai-kai; hokko** [Jap. first half line]: a Japanese lyric poem of three lines which have five, seven, and five syllables respectively.

**Hainbund**=*Göttinger Hain.

**hamartia** [Gk. error]; **tragic flaw** (F. erreur tragique; G. Hamartie, Hamartia; S. error trágico): the hero's oversight, misunderstanding, or error which causes a *tragic situation. (**anagnorisis; catharsis; dramatic irony; Hybris; nemesis.)

**Hanswurst:** *harlequinade.

**harangue** [ML. public speech]; (F. harangue; G. hetzerische Ansprache; S. arenga): an emotional speech or a rabble-rousing text. (**enthymeme; epideictic speech; homiletics; invective; syllogism; tirade.)

**Harlequin:** *harlequinade.

**harlequinade** (F. arlequinade; G. Harlekinade, Hanswurstspiel; S. arlequinada): a play that revolves around a comical figure (in England: Harlequin, Punch; in Germany: Hanswurst, Kasperle; in France: Arlequin, Scaramouche; in Italy: Bajazzo, Pantalone, Arlecchino, Columbina) and the preposterous situations he gets into. (**low comedy.)

**headless line** (F. vers acéphale; G. Akephal; S. verso acéfalo): a verse beginning with an incomplete metrical foot. (**acephalous; catalectic.)

**head rhyme:** *alliteration(1).

**hemiepes** [Gk. half verse]; (F. hemiepes; G. Hemipes; S. hemiepes): a dactylic trimeter whose last foot is incomplete: ＿∪∪＿∪∪∟.

**hemistich** [Gk. half line]; (F. hémistiche; G. Hemistichon, Hemistichus, Kurzvers, Kurzzeile; S. hemistiquio): half a metrical line; it usually ends with, or starts after, a diaeresis. (**diaeresis(2); Nibelungenstrophe.)

**hemistichomythia** [Gk. dialogue in half lines]; (F. hémistichomythie; G. Hemistichomythie; S. hemistecomitia): *stichomythia.

**hendecasyllable** [Gk. of eleven syllables]; (F. hendécasyllabe; G. Hendekasyllabus; S. endecasílabo):

a metrical line of eleven syllables. (**Phalaecean; rispetto; Sapphic; Sicilian octave; strambotto; versi sciolti.)

**hendiadys** [Gk. one through two]; (F. hendiadys; G. Hendiadyoin; S. hendíadis): a rhetorical figure: using two words joined by "and" to express one idea or describe one thing. (**asyndeton; epanalepsis; pleonasm; polysyndeton; tautology.)

**hephthemimeral** [Gk. seventh half]; (F. hepthémimère; G. Hephthemimeres; S. heptemímeris): a *caesura after the fourth stressed (or long) syllable (=after the seventh half foot). (**hexameter; penthemimeral; trithemimeral.)

**heptameter** [Gk. seven meters]; (F. heptamètre; G. Heptameter; S. heptámetro): a line of seven metrical feet; sometimes known as septenary. (**hexameter; pentameter.)

**heptastich** [Gk. seven verses]; (F. septain; G. Heptastichon; S. séptima): a *stanza of seven lines. (**hexastich; pentastich.)

**heptasyllable** [Gk. of seven syllables]; (F. heptasyllabe; G. Heptasyllabus; S. heptasílabo): a metrical line of seven syllables.

**heretical novel**=*experimental novel.

**Hermeticism** [named after the Greek mythological figure Hermes]; (F. hermétisme; G. Hermetismus; S. hermetismo): an Italian literary school (It. ermetismo) at the beginning of the twentieth century which, inspired by *symbolism and *decadence, dealt with sound patterns, extremely subjective images, and magical symbols. Rep. E. Montale, G. Ungaretti, S. Quasimodo. (**futurism.)

**hero** [Gk. a divine or immortal person]; (F. héros; G. Held; S. héroe): *protagonist.

**heroic couplet** (F. vers héroïque; G. heroisches Reimpaar; S. dístico heroico): a rhyming *couplet in iambic pentameter ($\cup\_\cup\_\cup\_\cup\_\cup\_$). (**heroic meter.)

**heroic epic** (F. chanson de geste; G. Heldenepos; S. épica heroica): a stately narrative poem which deals with the heroic deeds of a person who often has superhuman or divine traits. (**art epic; chivalric romance; courtly epic; epic; folk epic; heroic meter; heroic stanza; heroic verse; metrical romance; mock epic.)

**heroic line:** *heroic verse.

**heroic meter** (F. vers épique, vers héroïque; G. heroischer Vers; S. verso épico): the meter used in heroic poetry such as hexameters in Greek and Latin poetry, blank verse or heroic couplets in English and German, the Alexandrine in French, and the endecasillabo in Italian. (**heroic stanza; heroic verse.)

**heroic play** (F. théâtre héroïque; G. Heldendrama; S. drama heroico): a play in rhymed couplets which deals with heroic, noble, or aristocratic characters and is noted for its rhetorical style and operatic elements; popular in the sixteenth and seventeenth centuries. (**baroque; heroic poetry.)

**heroic poetry** (F. poésie héroïque; G. Heldendichtung; S. poesía heroica): poetry that deals with the adventurous deeds of a historical or legendary hero; it is usually written in *heroic meter. (**heroic epic; heroic verse.)

**heroic quatrain:** *heroic stanza.

**heroic stanza** (F. quatrain héroïque, quatrain de pentamètres iambiques; G. Quatrain, heroische Strophe; S. estrofa heroica): a *stanza of four iambic pentameters ($\cup\_\cup\_\cup\_\cup\_$ $\cup\_$). (**heroic verse.)

**heroic verse; heroic line** (F. vers héroïque; G. heroischer Vers; S. verso heroico): the verse used in heroic poetry; in English it is the iambic pentameter ($\cup\_\cup\_\cup\_\cup\_\cup\_$). (**heroic meter; heroic stanza.)

**heterodox** [Gk. of another opinion] **novel** (F. roman hétérodoxe; G. heterodoxer Roman; S. novela heterodoxa): a term used in connection with the *experimental novel, the so-called nouveau roman, which differs in all aspects from the traditional novel. (**antinovel; chosisme; novel; tropisme.)

**hexameter** [Gk. six meter]; (F. hexamètre; G. Hexameter; S. hexámetro): a classical verse of six metrical feet: five dactyls and one trochee or spondee ($\_\cup\cup\_\cup\cup$ $\_\cup\cup\_\cup\cup\_\cup\cup\_\_\cup$), the first four dactyls could be replaced by trochees or spondees; the *caesura is either penthemimeral, hephthemimeral, or trithemimeral. (**distich; Pythian verse; silloi; spondaic verse.)

**hexastich** [Gk. six verses]; (F. sixain; G. Hexastichon; S. hexastiquio): a *stanza of six verses. (**heptastich; pentastich.)

**hiatus** [L. to gape]; (F. hiatus; G. Hiat, Hiatus; S. hiato): a pause or a gap between two vowels; it is sometimes regarded as dissonance and therefore eliminated by means of *aphaeresis, *crasis, *elision, or *synaloephe. (**diaeresis(1); synaeresis.)

**hidden alliteration:** *alliteration(2).

**high comedy** (F. haute comédie; G. Komödie; S. alta comedia): *comedy.

**high style; grand style** (F. style noble; G. erhabener Stil; S. estilo alto): an ornate, mannered, sometimes pompous and inflated style. (**bombast; culteranism; cultism; euphuism; Gongorism; logorrhoea; low style; Marinism; middle style; mock epic; orotund; preciosity; verbosity.)

**historic epic** (F. épopée historique; G. historisches Epos; S. épica histórica): a stately narrative that describes a past era or glorifies a particular historical event. (**epic; narrative poetry.)

**historical novel** (F. roman historique; G. historischer Roman; S. novela histórica): a long prose narrative that deals with historical characters, events, or settings. (**novel; time-novel.)

**historical present** (F. présent narratif, présent historique; G. historisches Präsens; S. presente histórico): the use of the present tense to give past events a more immediate effect. (**narrative techniques.)

**historical play; history play** (F. pièce historique; G. historisches Drama, Geschichtsdrama; S. comedia histórica): a play that deals with historical characters, conflicts, or episodes; it differs from the *chronicle play in that it portrays the historical epoch, comments on the events, and analyzes the characters and their motivations. (**drama.)

**hokku:** *haiku.

**homiletics** [Gk. art of conversation]; (F. homilétique; G. Homiletik, Predigtlehre; S. oratoria sagrada): the art of effective preaching. (**epideictic speech; harangue; homily; rhetoric.)

**homily** [Gk. meeting]; (F. homélie; G. Homilie; S. homilía): a religious discourse or a moralizing lecture. (**homiletics.)

**homoeomeral** [Gk. of equal parts]; (F. homoeomère; G. isometrisch; S. isométrico): of identical meters or having the same number of lines.

**homoeoteleuton; homoeuteleuton** [Gk. of the same ending]; (S. homéotéleute; G. Homöioteleuton, Homöoteleuton; S. homeoteleuton): a rhetorical figure: placing words of similar endings near each other; it could be regarded as an early form of *end rhyme; opposite of *homoiarcton. (**homoioptoton; paronomasia.)

**homographs** [Gk. the same writing]; (F. homogrammes, homographes; G. Homographen; S. homógrafos): words identical in spelling but different in pronunciation. (**homonyms; homophones.)

**homoiarcton** [Gk. of the same beginning]; (F. homoiarchton; G. Homoiarkton; S.—): a rhetorical figure: words whose first syllables are similar are placed near each other or at the beginning of successive sentences; opposite of *homoeoteleuton. (**homoioptoton.)

**homoioptoton** [Gk. similar case-endings]; (F. homéoptote; G. Homoioptoton; S. homoioptoton): a rhetorical figure: placing words of similar case-endings near each other. (**homoeoteleuton; paronomasia.)

**homoioteleuton**=*homoeoteleuton.

**homonyms** [Gk. the same name]; (F. homonymes; G. Homonyme; S. homónimos): words identical in spelling and pronunciation but different in meaning. (**homographs; homophones; paronomasia; pun.)

**homophones** [Gk. of the same sound]; (F. homophones, homophone équivoque; G. Homophone; S. homófonos): words different in meaning or spelling but identical in pronunciation. (**homographs; homonyms; paronomasia; pun; rime riche.)

**Horatian ode** [named after the Latin poet Horace, 65 - 8 B.C.]; (F. ode horatienne; G. horazische Ode; S. oda horaciana): a stanzaic poem of contemplative and philosophic nature. (**ode.)

**hovering accent:** *distributed stress.

**hubris:** *hybris.

**Hudibrastic verse** [named after Samuel Butler's satirical poem *Hudibras*, 1663]: a satirical poem in *octosyllabic couplets.

**huitain** [F. from huit=eight]; (F. huitain; G. Huitain; S. octava): a poem or a *stanza of eight lines; also known as octastich.

**Humanism** (F. humanisme; G. Humanismus; S. humanismo): a scholarly movement in Europe in the fifteenth and sixteenth centuries (*Renaissance) which was devoted to classical ideas in matters of philosophy, literature, religion, and education. Rep. Erasmus, Johann Reuchlin, Sir Thomas More. (**classicism; neohumanism; Reformation; Scholasticism.)

**humanitarian novel** (F. roman humanitaire; G. sozialkritischer Roman; S. novela social, novela humanitaria): a novel that deals with social issues and moral questions. (**novel; time-novel.)

**humor** [L. moisture, fluid of the body]; (F. humour; G. Humor; S. humor): a cheerful attitude toward life; it is the ability to discover and appreciate amiable traits in other human beings and to smile understandingly at other people's as well as one's own weaknesses and eccentricities. (**comic; irony; satire; wit.)

**humoresque** (F. récit humoristique; G. Humoreske; S. humorada): a witty and humorous short narrative. (**narrative poetry.)

**hybris; hubris** [Gk. excess, beyond measure]; (F. hybris, orgueil fatal; G. Hybris, Überheblichkeit; S. orgullo fatal): the hero's arrogance and superciliousness which make him misjudge the situation; this causes his downfall. (**anagnorisis; catharsis; dramatic irony; dramatic techniques; hamartia; nemesis; tragic.)

**hymn** [Gk. song of praise]; (F. hymne; G. Hymne; S. himno): a solemn lyrical poem without any fixed metrical pattern which praises gods or holy creations; if it praises or honors human beings it is called an *ode. (**common meter; paean; psalm.)

**hymnal stanza:** *common meter.

**hypallage** [Gk. interchange]; **transferred epithet** (F. hypallage; G. Hypallage; S. hipálage): a rhetorical figure: the normal syntactical structure of a sentence is changed and some terms are transferred from their logical place. (**amphibology; anastrophe; hyperbaton; inversion.)

**hyperbaton** [Gk. to go beyond]; (F. hyperbate; G. Hyperbaton, Hyperbasis, Sperrung; S. hipérbaton): deviation from the normal syntactical order for rhetorical or rhythmical reasons. (**amphibology; anastrophe; hypallage; inversion.)

**hyperbole** [Gk. to throw beyond, excess]; (F. hyperbole; G. Hyperbel; S. hipérbole): exaggeration for rhetorical reasons. (**amplification; irony; litotes; meiosis.)

**hypercatalectic**=*hypermetric.

**hypermetric** [Gk. overmetrical]; (F. hypermètre; G. Hyperkatalektisch; S. hipérmetro): exceeding the metrical pattern or having an extra syllable. (**acatalectic; paragoge.)

**hypotaxis** [Gk. subordination]; (F. hypotaxe; G. Hypotaxe; S. hipotaxis): the subdivision of a statement into principal and subordinate clauses; opposite of *parataxis.

**hysteron proteron** [Gk. the latter earlier]: a rhetorical figure: reversing the natural or logical order of events. (**anachronism; in medias res; prochronism.)

# I

**iamb; iambus** [Gk. throw]; (F. iambe; G. Jambus; S. yambo): a metrical foot; one unstressed (or short) syllable is followed by a stressed (or long) one: ∪— . (**diiamb; dochmius; foot; rising meter; trochee.)

**iambic** (F. iambique; G. jambisch; S. yámbico): having to do with *iambs.

**iambic dimeter:** a classical meter that consists of two iambic dipodies: ◡_◡_ ◡_◡_ .

**ictus** [L. beat]; (F. ictus; G. Iktus; S. ictus): metrical *stress or rhythmical beat.

**idealism** (F. idéalisme; G. Idealismus; S. idealismo): a philosophical and literary theory that stresses the importance of subjectiveness, imagination, and the spiritual aspects of reality. (**irrationalism; Junges Deutschland; realism; romanticization; Romanticism; Sturm und Drang.)

**identical rhyme** (F. rimes identiques; G. identischer Reim; S. rima idéntica): repetition of the same word to produce a *rhyme. (**homographs; homonyms; homophones.)

**idiom** [Gk. peculiar]; (F. idiome; G. Idiom, Redewendung; S. modismo): a special expression established within a language or a literature in spite of its peculiarity. (**jargon; phraseology; provincialism; regionalism; vernacularism.)

**idyll** [Gk. a small picture]; (F. idylle; G. Idylle; S. idilio): a short idealized description of rustic life or pastoral scenes; usually written in verse. (**bucolic poetry; genre picture; vignette.)

**image** [L. picture, imitation]; (F. image; G. Bild; S. imagen): the representation and illustration of unreal things by means of real objects, e.g. the reproduction of feelings and sensations by means of words; also used as a blanket term for *simile, *metaphor, *symbol, *chiffre, and *emblem. (**catachresis; synaesthesia.)

**imagery** (F. imagerie, langage imagé, style imagé; G. Bildlichkeit; S. imágenes): the mental images and imaginary pictures evoked by words; it is an essential part of poetry. (**image.)

**imagism; imagists; imagist poets** (F. imagisme; G. Imagismus; S. imagismo): a literary movement in England and the USA before and during the First World War; inspired by *symbolism, the representatives of this movement (T. E. Hulme, Ezra Pound, Hilda Doolittle, Amy Lowell) experimented with new forms, concrete images, free rhythm, modern subject matter, and common speech. (**vorticism.)

**imitation; mimesis** [Gk. imitation]; (F. imitation, mimèse; G. Imitation, Mimesis, Nachahmung; S. imitación, mimesis): (1) imitation of life as a literary and artistic principle; opposite of *romanticization; (2) a literary work which is designed and executed in the manner of another author. (**epigonism; Münchner Dichterkreis; Parnassians; parody; pastiche; travesty.)

**imperfect rhyme** (F. rime défectueuse, rime apophonique; G. unreiner Reim; S. rima imperfecta): occurs when the rhyming syllables have no identical consonant-sounds or no identical vowels; also known as approximate rhyme, embryonic rhyme, consonance, near rhyme, oblique rhyme, and para-rhyme. (**assonance; rhyme.)

**impressionism** [named after Monet's painting *Impression: Soleil Levant*, 1874]; (F. impressionnisme; G. Impressionismus; S. impresionismo): an artistic movement in Europe between 1890 and 1910; inspired by the paintings of Monet, Pissaro, and Renoir, poets like Rimbaud, Verlaine, and Mallarmé attempted to capture and reproduce their immediate subjective impressions of objects regardless of logic, form, or objective reality. (\*\*expressionism; Jung-Wien.)

**impressionistic criticism** (F. critique impressioniste; G. impressionistische Kritik; S. crítica impresionista): literary criticism that is based on the reader's impression of a work and the critic's reaction to it rather than on a detailed examination of its intrinsic and extrinsic characteristics. (\*\*affective fallacy; analysis; critique; intentional fallacy; new criticism; objectivism.)

**incantation** [L. enchanting]; (F. incantation; G. Beschwörung, Zauberspruch, Zauberformel; S. encantación): the use of obscure words mainly for their sound rather than for their meaning, as in a magic spell or a \*charm. (\*\*cacophony; dissonance; euphony; jingle; onomatopoeia.)

**incongruity** [L. unsuitability]; (F. incongruité; G. Mißverhältnis, Widersinnigkeit; S. incongruencia): the lack of consistency, logic, or harmony; an important element in humorous, ironic, comic, and grotesque writings. (\*\*comic; grotesque; humor; irony; oxymoron; theater of the absurd.)

**incremental** [L. increase] **repetition** (F. refrain; G. Refrain; S. repetición): a rhetorical device used in folk poetry; certain lines are repeated with some variations at the most crucial moments. (\*\*anaclasis(2); burden; refrain; repetend; repetition.)

**index** [L. indicate]; (F. index; G. Index; S. índice): (1) an alphabetical list of names, titles, or subjects; (2) abbreviation for *Index Librorum Prohibitorum*, the list of books forbidden by the Catholic Church. (\*\*canon(2); bowdlerize.)

**Index Librorum Prohibitorum:** \*index(2).

**indirect interior monologue; substitutionary narration** (F. style indirect libre; G. erlebte Rede; S. estilo indirecto libre): the representation of a character's thoughts and feelings from his own point of view; although in a \*third person narrative, only the indicative verb form is used. (\*\*first person narrative; interior monologue; narrative techniques; stream of consciousness.)

**inform; inner form; internal form**=\*intrinsic structure.

**initial incident** (F. événement initial, épitase; G. Ausgangsereignis; S. epítasis, acontecimiento inicial): the incident with which the dramatic entanglement begins; also known as initiating action or \*epitasis. (\*\*dramatic techniques.)

**initial rhyme:** \*alliteration(2).

**initiating action:** \*initial incident.

**in medias res** [L. into the midst of it]: a narrative and dramatic device; the story begins in the middle of the \*plot in order to arouse the reader's or the viewer's interest and to capture his attention. (\*\*dramatic techniques; hysteron proteron; narrative techniques.)

**inner form**=\*intrinsic structure.

**innuendo** [L. to hint]; (F. insinuation; G. Andeutung, Anspielung; S. insinuación): hidden or equivocal *allusion. (**anticipation; narrative techniques.)

inset story: *frame story.

insinuation= *innuendo.

intentional fallacy (F. critique des intentions; G.—; S. crítica intencionada): interpreting and judging a literary work according to the intention of its author; this attitude is regarded by many critics as fallacious. (**affective fallacy; analysis; critique; impressionistic criticism; objectivism.)

interior monologue; direct interior monologue (F. monologue intérieur; G. innerer Monolog; S. monólogo interior): the representation of a character's thoughts and feelings by attempting to reproduce the monologue that takes place within himself. (**indirect interior monologue; narrative techniques; stream of consciousness technique.)

interlinear [L. between lines]; (F. traduction interlinéaire; G. Interlinearversion, Interversion; S. traducción interlineal): a book that consists of a text and its translation printed on alternate lines. (**interpolation; polyglot; triglot.)

interlude [L. within+play]; (F. intermède; G. Interludium, Zwischenspiel; S. entremés): (1) a short, independent, and humorous play presented as part of a festival or in the intervals of a banquet; (2) a short play with music and songs presented between the acts of another play; also known as intermezzo. (**drama; prelude.)

intermezzo [It. intermedium]; (F. intermède, interlude; G. Intermezzo; S. intermedio): *interlude(2).

internal form= *intrinsic structure.

internal rhyme (F. rime intérieure; G. Binnenreim, Schlagreim, Mittelreim; S. rima interna): rhyme between two words within one or two metrical lines. (**Leonine rhyme; Leonine verse; rhyme.)

interpolation [L. alteration, falsification]; (F. interpolation; G. Interpolation; S. interpolación): the insertion of a spurious text into a book for the purpose of explanation or falsification. (**interlinear.)

interpretation [L. explanation, translation]; (F. interprétation; G. Interpretation; S. interpretación): explanation and elucidation of the intrinsic and extrinsic characteristics of a literary work. (**analysis; anagoge; apparatus criticus; exegesis; explication; interpolation; paraphrase.)

intrigue [It. confusion, intricacy]; (F. intrigue, comédie d'intrigue; G. Intrige, Intrigenstück; S. intriga): intricate plot; a play noted for its complex action and intricate plot. (**comedy of intrigue; drama.)

intrinsic structure (F. structure intrinsèque; G. innere Form; S. estructura intrínsica): the inner form of a literary work, i.e. all the characteristics related to theme, subject matter, motifs, and intellectual content; as opposed to *extrinsic structure. (**architectonics; atmosphere; content; meaning; message; structure; texture; tone.)

invective [L. abusive]; (F. invective; G. Invektive, Schmäschrift, Schmärede; S. invectiva): a critical text or a violent speech noted for its abusive language. (**epideictic speech; harangue; rhetoric.)

**inversion** [L. reversal]; (F. inversion; G. Inversion; S. inversión): reversal of the normal order of words for metrical or rhetorical reasons. (\*\*amphibology; anastrophe; hypallage; hyperbaton.)

**invocation** [L. to call, to invoke]; (F. invocation; G. Invokation, Anrufung; S. invocación): an appeal for help or support addressed to a deity or a muse at the beginning of a literary work. (\*\*apostrophe; epigraph; exordium; oration; prologue.)

**Ionic** [Gk. named after the Ionic dialect]; (F. ionique; G. Ionikus; S. jónico): a metrical foot in \*quantitative verse that consists of two long and two short syllables; if it starts with the two long syllables it is known as major, or greater Ionic (‗ ‗ ◡◡); if it begins with the short ones, it is called a minor or a lesser Ionic (◡◡‗ ‗). (\*\*foot; galliamb)

**Irish Literary Renaissance:** \*Celtic Renaissance.

**irony** [Gk. to simulate ignorance]; (F. ironie; G. Ironie; S. ironía): an ostensibly earnest but mockingly overstated or understated remark which touches upon and ridicules the most striking characteristics of a person, thing, or situation. (\*\*Byronic; caricature; comic; dramatic irony; grotesque; humor; irony of fate; litotes; meiosis; romantic irony; sarcasm, satire; Socratic irony; verbal irony; wit.)

**irony of fate; cosmic irony** (F. ironie du sort; G. Ironie des Schicksals; S. ironía del destino): the suffering of a well-meaning person for reasons beyond his control. (\*\*dramatic irony; hamartia; hybris; irony.)

**irrationalism** (F. irrationalisme; G. Irrationalismus; S. irracionalismo): a philosophical point of view which emphasizes feeling, faith, and intuition as opposed to the rigid rationalism of the \*Enlightenment; it had a great influence on some of the literary movements of the eighteenth century such as \*Pietism, \*Preromanticism, \*Sturm und Drang, and \*Göttinger Hain.

**irrelevant digression:** \*digression.

**Italian sonnet:** \*sonnet.

# J

**Jacobean** [L. Jacobus=James]; relating to James I of England and his reign (1603 - 1625). (\*\*Caroline period; Cavalier poets; Edwardian; Elizabethan age; Georgian poets; Restoration; Victorian.)

**jargon** [F. unintelligible talk]; (F. jargon; G. Jargon; S. jerga): the special vocabulary or characteristic idioms used by a particular group of people. (\*\*idiom; provincialism; regionalism; vernacularism.)

**jestbook** [L. gesta=deeds]; (F. ana; G. Scherzbuch, Witzbuch; S. libro de chistes): a collection of humorous tales, ludicrous stories, or frivolous jokes. (\*\*chapbook.)

**jeu parti:** \*partimen.

**jingle** [of imitative origin]; (F. tintement de vers; G. Reimgeklingel; S. rima pueril): a verse rich in sound effects but poor in meaning. (**cacophony; euphony; incantation; onomatopoeia.)

**joc partit:** *partimen.

**journal** [L. daily]=*diary.

**Jugendstil** [G. early style]; **art nouveau** (F. art nouveau; G. Jugendstil; S. arte nuevo): a highly decorative style in art and literature associated with the beginning of the twentieth century; a few neoromantic Austrian writers (A. Schnitzler, H. v. Hofmannsthal, R. M. Rilke) are sometimes regarded as exponents of this style. (**Jung-Wien; neoromanticism.)

**Junges Deutschland** [G. Young Germany]; (F. jeune-Allemagne; G. Junges Deutschland; S. la joven Alemania): a group of German writers (circa 1830 - 1850) known for their strong opposition to all kinds of *idealism and for their complete devotion to social, moral, and political changes. Rep. L. Wienbarg, H. Laube, K. Gutzkow. (**Biedermeier poets.)

**Jung-Wien** [G. Young Vienna]; (F. jeune-Vienne; G. Jung-Wien; S. la joven Viena): a group of Austrian authors and critics writing at the beginning of the twentieth century; they were known for their opposition to *naturalism and for their nearness to *impressionism, *symbolism, *neoromanticism, and *decadence. Rep. H. Bahr, A. Schnitzler, H. v. Hofmannsthal. (**Jugendstil.)

# K

**kabuki** [Jap. of singing and dancing]: a popular Japanese play noted for its rich décor and elaborate scenery.

**Kasperle:** *harlequinade.

**katharsis**=*catharsis.

**kenning** [Old Norse=to know]: a standard compound *metaphor used in Old Germanic poetry.

**key novel** (F. roman à clef; G. Schlüsselroman; S. novela en clave): a novel in which real persons and historical events are referred to, but in a more or less veiled manner. (**allusion; novel.)

**Khayyam quatrain:** *Ruba'i

**kind**=*genre.

**Knittelvers** [G. rhymed verse]: a German verse of rhymed couplets with four stressed syllables and either eight (sometimes nine) unstressed syllables (as by Hans Sachs), or any number of unstressed syllables (Goethe's *Urfaust*). (**tumbling verse.)

**Künstlerroman:** *novel of the artist.

# L

lai; lay [Breton: song]; (F. lai; G. Lai; S. lai): a short non-stanzaic medieval poem of love or adventure. (**courtly love.)

laisse: *chanson de geste.

Lake Poets; Lake School; Lakers: a name given to the three English romantic poets Wordsworth, Coleridge, and Southey who lived in the Lake District and were noted for their sentimental and elegiac attitude towards nature. (**Romanticism.)

lament [L. wailing]; (F. thrénodie; G. Klage; S. lamento): a mournful lyric poem in which the poet laments the loss of something or someone dear to him. (**commus; complaint; dirge; elegy; epicedium; monody; planh.)

lampoon [F. let us drink excessively]; (F. pasquinade, satire, libelle; G. Schmäschrift, Invektive; S. pasquín): a personal, malicious, and vulgar *satire in prose or verse. (**diatribe; folly literature; pasquinade; persiflage; philippic; silloi; skit; vulgarism.)

Langzeile: *Nibelungenstrophe.

lapsus linguae [L. lapse or error in language]: *malapropism.

l'art pour l'art: *aestheticism.

lauda [L. praise]: a popular Italian religious song.

lay: *lai.

legend [L. to be read]; (F. légende; G. Legende; S. leyenda): a short story or tale that deals with the life of a saint; it can also depict the fantastic deeds of a historical or mythical figure. (**hagiography; narrative poetry; tradition.)

Leich [Gothic: game, dance]: a medieval German lyric poem in irregular stanzas.

leitmotif; leitmotiv [G. leading motif]; (F. leitmotiv; G. Leitmotiv; S. leitmotiv): a certain idea, mood, or feeling evoked by the reappearance of a person, thing, word, or situation; its reoccurrence throughout a literary work forms an indispensable part of the work's theme. (**blind motif; central motif; Falkentheorie; motif; objective correlative.)

leitsymbol [G. leading symbol]=*central motif.

Leonine rhyme [*Leonine verse]; (F. rime interne, rime léonine; G. Leoninischer Reim; S. rima leonina): the *internal rhyme used in *Leonine verse. (**rhyme.)

Leonine verse [probably named after the twelfth-century poet Leoninus]; (F. vers léonin; G. Leoninischer Vers; S. verso leonino): a verse, usually a hexameter or a *distich, in which the last word rhymes with the word preceding the *caesura.

lesser Ionic: *Ionic.

letrilla [S. short letter]: a Spanish stanzaic poem with a refrain (*estribillo).

letterism [L. letter]; (F. lettrisme; G. Lettrismus, Buchstabismus; S. letraismo): a literary and artistic movement in France in the forties inspired by Isidore Isou (*First Letterist Manifesto*, 1946) and Maurice Lemaître which deals with the use of letters and meaningless syllables in literary and artistic creations as for instance in folk songs and the poetry of *Dadaism. (**concretism.)

**libretto** [It. small book]; (F. livret; G. Libretto, Operntext; S. libreto): the text of an opera, operetta, or a musical drama. (**scenario.)

**light fiction**= *trivial literature.

**light rhyme** (F. rime légère; G.—; S. rima átona): the rhyming of unstressed syllables. (**feminine ending; feminine rhyme.)

**light verse** (F. poésie légère, poésie de circonstance; G. Gelegenheitsdichtung; S. poesía ocasional): all kinds of elegant and witty poems which are written for no informative, instructive, or poetic reasons, but merely to amuse and entertain such as *vers de société or *occasional verse. (**autotelic; clerihew; limerick; macaronic poetry; mock epic; scolion.)

**limerick** [named after the Irish town of Limerick]; (F. limerick; G. Limerick; S. copla humorística de cinco versos): a humorous, sometimes grotesque poem consisting of five lines rhyming aabba. (**occasional verse; light verse.)

**line** (F. ligne; G. Zeile, Vers; S. verso)= *verse.

**line endings** (F. fin du vers, clausule; G. Versausgang; S. final del verso): depending upon the nature of the last syllable of a verse, one distinguishes between *feminine ending and *masculine ending.

**linguistics** [L. the study of languages]; (F. linguistique; G. Linguistik, Sprachwissenschaft; S. lingüística): the science of languages and the study of their different aspects such as grammar (morphology, syntax), *semantics, and phonology.

**lipogram** [Gk. omitting a letter]; (F. lipogramme; G. Leipogramm, Lipogramm; S. lipograma): a text in which one specific letter is never used.

**lira** [the name was taken from the first line ("Si de mi baja lira") of the canción "A la flor de Gnido" by Garcilaso de las Vega (1503 - 1536)]: a Spanish poem of five lines rhyming ababb.

**litany** [Gk. supplication]; (F. litanie; G. Litanei; S. letanía): a prayer recited alternately by clergy and congregation.

**literal meaning** (F. sens littéral; G. wörtlich; S. sentido literal): the exact and explicit meaning of words regardless of their metaphorical or suggestive function. (**connotation; denotation; figurative.)

**literary ballad:** *art ballad.

**literary epic:** *art epic.

**literature** [L. writing]; (F. littérature; G. Literatur; S. literatura): (1) the literary works of a nation or a historical epoch; (2) written works that deal with a particular subject; (3) works written in verse or prose and which are noted for their literary merits and human relevance. (**belletristic literature; didactic literature; esoteric; exoteric; poesie, poetry; trivial literature.)

**litotes** [Gk. simple, plain]; (F. litote; G. Litotes; S. lítote): understatement for rhetorical reasons: negating the opposite of what is meant. (**amplification; hyperbole; irony; meiosis.)

**liturgical** [Gk. public service] **drama; liturgical play** (F. drame liturgique; G. geistliches Drama; S. drama litúrgico): the dramatic treatment of dogmatic-ecclesiastical subject matter, biblical figures, or Christian *Weltanschauung (such as *passion, *mystery, *miracle, *morality plays). (**canticle; carol(1); Christian epic; Corpus Christi play; drama; virgin play.)

**living newspaper** (F. pièce didactique et expérimentale; G. Lehrstück, Agitprop-Stücke; S. obra didáctica experimental): an informative and instructive play of experimental character which deals with current events and problems of immediate interest. It was developed in the USA in the thirties and was used in England during the Second World War for propaganda and education. (**agit-prop; epic drama.)

**local color** (F. couleur locale; G. Lokalkolorit; S. color local): a literary work in which the characteristics of a certain locality or the features of a particular milieu play an important part. (**setting.)

**logaoedic** [Gk. speech and song]; (F. logaédique; G. logaödische Verse; S. ritmo logaédico): a rhythmical unit that consists of dactyls and trochees or anapaests and iambs mixed together.

**logical stress** (F. accent d'insistance; G. rhetorische Betonung; S. acento expresivo): the stressing of a syllable for no metrical reason but merely to emphasize the meaning of a certain word; also known as rhetorical stress. (**distributed stress; recessive accent.)

**logogriph** [Gk. word riddle]; (F. logogriphe; G. Logogriph; S. logogrifo): a word puzzle based on omitting, adding, or transposing one or more

letters so that a new word is formed. (**anagram; cryptogram; logomachy; metaplasm; metathesis; prothesis; spoonerism.)

**logomachy** [Gk. word fight]; F. logomachie; G. Logomachie, Wortstreit; S. logomaquia): a dispute over words or a game involving letters and words. (**anagram; cryptogram; logogriph.)

**logorrhoea** [Gk. word flow]; (F. logorrhée; G. Logorrhöe; S. verborragia): extreme volubleness or excessive use of words. (**bombast; euphuism; high style; Marinism; orotund; preciosity; purple passage; verbosity.)

**long line:** *Nibelungenstrophe.

**long meter; long measure** (F. quatrain de tétramètres iambiques; G.—; S. cuarteto iámbico): a stanza of four iambic tetrameters ($\cup\_\cup\_\cup\_\cup\_$) rhyming abcb or abab.

**long-short story** (F. longue nouvelle; G. Romannovelle; S. novela corta): a dubious term used sometimes in connection with prose narratives which are longer than a *short story and shorter than a *novel. (**narrative poetry; novelette.)

**long syllable** (F. syllabe longue; G. Länge; S. sílaba larga): *short syllable.

**longueur** [F. length]: a tedious part of a literary work.

**love poetry** (F. poésie d'amour; G. Liebesdichtung; S. poesía amorosa): *erotic poetry; courtly love; ghazel; Petrarchism.

**low comedy** (F. comédie bouffonne; G. Lustspiel; S. baja comedia): as opposed to *comedy, or high comedy, low comedy (farce, slap-stick, droll, mime) depends on jokes, preposterous situations, and physical actions rather than on the *comic. (**Atellan fables; drama; harlequin-ade; mime; repartee; satyr play; sotie.)

**low style; plain style** (F. style simple; G. leichter Stil; S. estilo sencillo): plain and precise style used for communication and for the trans-mission of information. (**high style; middle style; platitude; primitivism; reportage; vulgarism.)

**lyric poetry; lyric** [Gk. singing to the lyre]; (F. poésie lyrique; G. Lyrik, lyrische Dichtung; S. poesia lírica): lyric, *dramatic, and *narrative are the three main categories of poetry. Lyric poetry, which is not necessarily in verse, deals with moods, impres-sions, and feelings rather than with events, ideas, or characters; lyric poetry is often written in the fol-lowing forms: *ode, *hymn, *sonnet, and *song. (**ballad; folk song; melic poetry; poem; poetry; prose poem.)

# M

**macaronic** [It. macaroni] **poetry; maca-ronic verse** (F. poésie macaronique; G. makkaronische Dichtung; S. poesía macarrónica): humorous verse containing a mixture of lan-guages. (**descort; light verse.)

**machinery** [Gk. mechanical device, plan]; (F. le merveilleux; G. Ma-schinerie; S. máquina, tramoya): a supernatural figure (god, angel, demon) who appears in an epic to guide or rescue the hero. (**deus ex machina.)

**macron** [Gk. long]; (F. marque de longueur; G. Längestrich; S. mac-ron): a sign used in *quantitative verse to indicate a long syllable. (**metron; mora; number.)

**madrigal** [It. shepherd's poem]; (F. madrigal; G. Madrigal; S. madrigal): a short, monostrophic lyric poem with no metrical pattern or defi-nite rhyme scheme.

**magical realism** (F. réalisme magique; G. magischer Realismus; S. realismo mágico): a term coined by the German art critic Franz Roh in 1925 in connection with postexpressionist painters. In literature it refers to the representation of real persons and everyday objects in a strange and fantastic atmosphere. (**expression-ism; fantasy fiction; Neue Sachlich-keit; realism; socialist realism; verism.)

**major Ionic:** *Ionic.

**makame; maqama** [Ar. stay, residence]: a long Arabic prose narrative that consists of adventurous episodes, humorous tales, and lyric passages; it might have served as a model for the *picaresque novel. Rep. Hariri, 1054 - 1122.

**mālahǎttr:** a four-line stanza used in the Old Icelandic poem *Edda*; the lines, which are linked by initial and inter-nal alliterations, consist of four accented and six unaccented syl-lables with a caesura in the middle. (**medial caesura.)

**malapropism** [after Mrs. Malaprop, in Sheridan's *The Rivals*, 1775]; **lapsus**

linguae [L. lapse or error in language]: the ridiculous misapplication of words.

male rhyme=*masculine rhyme.

mannerism [L. of the hand, way of handling]; (F. maniérisme; G. Manierismus; S. manierismo): ornate, affected, and highly rhetorical style; popular in Europe in the sixteenth and seventeenth centuries. (**baroque; euphuism; Gongorism; Marinism; preciosity.)

man-novel (F. roman de caractères; G. Menschen-Roman; S. novela de personajes): a novel that has one or more figures at the center of the action; it deals mainly with the private lives of the characters as well as with their different activities in the world around them. The novel of development (Entwicklungsroman), apprenticeship novel (Bildungsroman), novel of educational formation (Erziehungsroman), novel of the artist (Künstlerroman), psychological novel, picaresque novel, love romance, saga, and other similar novels can be regarded as man-novels. (**narrative poetry; novel.)

maqama: *makame.

Marinism [after the Italian poet Giambattista Marino, 1569 - 1625]; (F. marinisme; G. Marinismus; S. marinismo): a flamboyant, flowery, and rambling style. (**baroque; culteranism; cultism; euphuism; Gongorism; logorrhoea; mannerism; orotund; preciosity; verbosity.)

masculine caesura (F. coupe masculine; G. männliche Zäsur; S. cesura masculina): a *caesura after a stressed syllable.

masculine ending (F. terminaison masculine; G. männlicher Versausgang; S. acento agudo, terminación masculina): a verse ending with a stressed syllable. (**feminine ending; verso tronco.)

masculine rhyme; male rhyme; single rhyme (F. rime masculine; G. männlicher Reim, stumpfer Reim; S. rima aguda, rima masculina): occurs when the rhyming words end with a stressed syllable. (**feminine rhyme; rhyme.)

mask: *masque.

masque; mask [origin unknown]; (F. masque; G. Masque, Maskenspiel; S. mascarada, comedia mitológica): a highly spectacular play that deals with allegorical, mythological, and fantastic themes combining dancing and music; usually performed by masked noblemen; popular as court entertainment in Europe in the sixteenth and seventeenth centuries. (**antimasque; drama; mummery.)

maxim [L. greatest]; (F. maxime; G. Maxime; S. máxima): a short, pointed statement in verse or in prose which expresses a general truth or summarizes a rule of conduct. (**aphorism; apophthegm; closed couplet; epigram; gnomic poetry; sentence.)

meaning [OHG. to intend, to have in mind]; (F. sens, signification; G. Gehalt; S. sentido): the sum of ideas expressed in a literary work or the intellectual substance of a text. (**argument; atmosphere; content; intrinsic structure; message; subject matter; theme; tone.)

measure=*meter.

medial caesura (F. césure médiane; G. Binnenpause; S. cesura): a *caesura in the middle of a long line dividing it into two equal parts known as short lines. (**Alexandrine; diaeresis; mālahāttr.)

**medieval** [L. middle ages] **period; middle ages** (F. époque médiévale, moyen âge; G. Mittelalter; S. época medieval): a period of European history between ancient and modern times, i.e. between circa 500 A.D. and 1500 A.D.

**meiosis** [Gk. belittling]; (F. litote; G. Meiosis; S. meiosis): a rhetorical figure; the importance of a thing is emphasized by lessening its significance. (**hyperbole; irony; litotes.)

**Meistergesang; Meistersang** [G. master+song]: songs composed in Germany in the fourteenth, fifteenth, and sixteenth centuries. The poets were usually burghers (Meistersinger) and they composed according to a strict set of rules (Tabulator). The compositions were appraised by a poetic judge known as a Merker.

**Meistersinger** [G. master singer]: *Meistersang.

**melic poetry** [Gk. melos=song]; (F. poésie mélique; G. Melik, melische Dichtung; S. poesía mélica): *lyric poetry or any poetry written for singing. (**song.)

**melodrama** [Gk. song+action]; (F. mélodrame; G. Melodrama; S. melodrama): (1) a play that includes songs and music; (2) a suspenseful, sensational, and bathetic play. (**comedy of tears; drama; drame.)

**memoirs** [F. memory]; (F. mémoires; G. Memoiren; S. memorias): an *autobiography, or a part of an autobiography in which the author gives a detailed account of certain historical events as witnessed by him. (**diary; open form.)

**Merker:** *Meistergesang.

**mesode** [Gk. a song in between]; (F. mésode; G. Mesodos; S. mesode): a part that lies between strophe and antistrophe in Greek drama. (**proode.)

**mesostich** [Gk. middle of verse]; (F. mésostiche; G. Mesostichon; S. mesosticha): occurs when the letters in the middle of successive verses form a word or a phrase. (**abecedarian; acrostic; acroteleutic; cryptogram; telestich.)

**message** [L. to send]; **moral** [L. custom]; (F. thèse, message, morale; G. Lehre, Moral; S. tesis, mensaje, moral): the author's intellectual intention or the work's moral significance. (**argument; atmosphere; content; meaning; subject matter; theme; tone.)

**metalepsis** [Gk. substitution]; (F. métalepse; G. Metalepsis; S. metalepsis): a rhetorical figure; words that denote things or describe their effects are used instead of their proper names; a form of *metonymy. (**antonomasia; periphrasis.)

**metaphor** [Gk. transfer]; (F. métaphore; G. Metapher; S. metáfora): a rhetorical figure; a word, or words, that denote a certain object are used to describe another object from a different area; usually the two objects share one or more *tertium comparationis. (I. A. Richards calls the object described "tenor," the other part of the metaphor is the "vehicle.") (**chiffre; conceit; dead metaphor; image; kenning; metaphysical conceits; mixed metaphor; Petrarchan conceits; trope.)

metaphysical conceits (F. concetti méta-physiques; G. metaphysische Kon-zetti; S. conceptos metafísicos): in-genious metaphors drawn from areas not usually regarded as poetic; widely used in metaphysical poetry and in the poetry of the late nine-teenth and early twentieth centuries. (**conceits; Graveyard School; metaphysical poets.)

metaphysical poets (F. poètes méta-physiques; G. metaphysische Dich-ter; S. poetas metafísicos): a group of English poets in the seventeenth century (J. Donne, R. Crashaw, G. Herbert, A. Marvell . . .) noted for their ingenious metaphors, inventive imagery, paradoxical statements, and intellectual themes. (**Grave-yard School; metaphysical conceits.)

metaplasm [Gk. recasting]; (F. méta-plasme; G. Metaplasmus; S. meta-plasmo): transposition of a letter within a word or a word within a sentence. (**logograph; metathesis; prothesis; spoonerism.)

metathesis [Gk. transposition]; (F. méta-thèse; G. Metathese; S. metátesis): the transposition of sounds or letters in a word. (**logograph; metaplasm; spoonerism.)

meter [Gk. measure ]; (F. mètre; G. Metrum; S. metro): the rhythmical pattern of a verse; it is determined by the type and number of feet. (**foot; prosody; rhythm; scansion.)

metonymy [Gk. change of name]; (F. métonymie; G. Metonymie; S. metonimia): the use of a character-istic as a substitute for the object described and vice versa. (**antono-masia; metalepsis; periphrasis; synecdoche; trope.)

metrical foot=*foot.

metrical romance (F. épopée galante; G. höfisches Epos, heroisch-galantes Epos; S. novela en verso): an ad-venturous story in verse. (**Arthuri-an romance; chivalric romance; courtly epic; heroic epic; narrative poetry.)

metrics [Gk. art of measures]; (F. métri-que; G. Metrik; S. métrica): the study of metrical structure. (**pros-ody; scansion.)

metron [Gk. measure]; (F. mètre; G. Metron; S. metron, metro): the smallest unit of measurement in classical prosody; it consists of one or more feet. (**macron; mora; number.)

middle ages: *medieval period.

middle rhyme=*internal rhyme.

middle style (F. style naturel; G. mittlerer Stil; S. estilo medio): a poetic, elevated but lucid and un-affected style. (**high style; low style.)

Miltonic sonnet (F. sonnet miltonien; G. Milton Sonett; S. soneto mil-toniano): a sonnet form introduced by John Milton (1608 - 1674) which varies from the English (Shakespear-ian) and Italian (Petrarchan) sonnets because of the *enjambment of the eighth line with the ninth and the different rhyme scheme (abba abba cdc dcd). (**sonnet; Spenserian sonnet.)

mime [Gk. to represent or imitate]; (F. mime; G. Mimus; S. mimo): a play which depends mainly on gestures and imitations. (**low comedy.)

mimesis [Gk. imitation]; (F. mimèse; G. Mimesis; S. mimesis): *imitation.

**minnesong; Minnesang** [G. love song]: German lyric poetry of the middle ages noted for its artistic forms and conventional themes: chivalrous love, disciplined devotion to woman, idealization of womanhood, the parting of lovers at dawn (Tagelied). (**courtly love; dolce still nuovo; minnesinger.)

**minnesinger; Minnesänger** [*minnesong]: German lyric poets of the middle ages who composed highly artistic love songs (*minnesong); rep. Walther von der Vogelweide. (**troubadour; trouvère.)

**minor Ionic:** *Ionic.

**minstrel** [L. official attendant]; (F. ménestrel; G. Bänkelsänger; S. trovador, juglar): a professional singer, performer, and comedian of the middle ages who sang folk ballads, recited narrative poems and familiar stories, played the harp, and acted as an acrobat or buffoon. (**bard; Goliardic verse; rhapsodist; scop; skald.)

**miracle play** (F. miracle; G. Mirakelspiel; S. milagro): a medieval *liturgical play that deals with the supernatural powers of a saint or martyr. (**drama; virgin play.)

**mise-en-scène** [F. putting on the stage]; (F. mise-en-scène; G. Inszenierung; S. representación): the staging and performing of a play. (**dramaturgy.)

**mixed metaphor** (F. métaphore incohérente, métaphore disparate; G. gemischte Metapher; S. metáfora disparatada): a rhetorical figure based on a combination of two or more *metaphors which do not share a *tertium comparationis.

**mock epic; mock heroic** (F. épopée badine, poème héroï-comique; G. parodistisches Epos, komisches Epos; S. épica burlesca): a literary work that ridicules *heroic epics by using a flowery and lofty style to describe a trivial and frivolous action. (**light verse; parody; pastiche; travesty.)

**modulation** [L. to measure]; (F. modulation; G. Modulation; S. medida anárquica): the poet's departure from the original metrical pattern of his poem, usually for rhetorical reasons. (**barbarism; equivalence; poetic licence; solecism; substitution.)

**molossus** [Gk. of Molossis, a district in Greece]; (F. molosse; G. Molossus; S. moloso): a classical metrical foot of three long syllables ($-\ -\ -$). (**quantitative verse.)

**monodrama** [Gk. single+action]; (F. pièce à un personnage; G. Monodrama; S. monodrama): a play or a *dramatic monologue performed or narrated by one person. (**drama.)

**monody** [Gk. singing alone]; F. monodie; G. Klagelied, Monodie; S. monodia): an elegiac poem expressing the grief of one person. (**complaint; dirge; elegy; lament.)

**monologue** [Gk. speaking alone]; (F. monologue; G. Monolog; S. monólogo): a literary work or a part of a literary work that is written as a *soliloquy or speech. (**dramatic monologue; monodrama.)

**monometer** [Gk. single measure]; (F. monomètre; G. Monometer; S. monometro): a verse of one metrical foot or one *dipody.

**monopody** [Gk. single foot]; (F. monopodie; G. Monopodie; S. mono-podia, monométrico)=*monometer.

**monorhyme** [Gk. single rhythm]; (F. monorime; G. gehäufter Reim; S. monorrima): occurs when all lines of a strophe or a poem have the same end *rhyme. (**qasida.)

**monostich** [Gk. single verse]; (F. monostique; G. Monostichon; S. poema de una línea): a poem of one single line. (**distich; heptastich; hexastich; octastich; pentastich; tetrastich; tristich.)

**monosyllabic** [Gk. of one syllable]; (F. monosyllabique; G. einsilbig; S. monosilábico): consisting of one syllable. (**disyllabic; polysyllabic.)

**montage** [F. to mount]; (F. montage; G. Montage; S. montaje): the juxtaposition of heterogeneous images, themes, motifs, or styles to produce a single literary work. (**analects; cento; collage; fragment.)

**mood** [L. custom]; (F. ambiance; G. Stimmung; S. ambiente): *atmosphere.

**mora** [L. delay]; (F. more; G. More, Mora; S. mora): the minimal time unit in *quantitative verse equivalent to the duration of a *short syllable (a long syllable equals two morae). (**macron; metron; number.)

**moral** [L. custom, manner]; (F. morale; G. Moral; S. moral): *message.

**morality play** (F. moralité; G. Moralität; S. moralidad): a popular play of the fifteenth and sixteenth centuries noted for its allegorical characters, personified abstractions, and moral-didactic bent. (**allegory; drama; personification.)

**mosaic** [L. of the muses, artistic] **rhyme** (F. rimes empérières, rimes couronnées, vers holorimes; G. Schüttelreim; S. rima imperial): occurs when the rhyming element includes more than one word. (**broken rhyme; end rhyme; polysyllabic rhyme; rhyme.)

**motif** [L. to move]; (F. motif; G. Motiv; S. motivo): a certain idea or a typical situation which appears in a literary work and is of some relevance to its theme. (**blind motif; burden(2); central motif; leitmotif; objective correlative; stock situation; ubi sunt motif.)

**motivation** [L. move]; (F. motivation; G. Motivation; S. motivación): the act of supplying a character with the motives which determine and justify his actions. (**characterization.)

**multiple rhyme:** *polysyllabic rhyme.

**mummery** [F. masquerade]; (F. mascarade; G. Maskenspiel; S. mascarada, momería): a theatrical performance or a *pantomime show given by actors wearing masks. (**dumb show; masque.)

**Münchner Dichterkreis** [G. Munich's Poetic Circle]: a group of German poets who resided in Munich at the court of King Maximilian II of Bavaria (1811 - 1864); noted for their opposition to *realism and for their epigonous imitation of the literary works of Goethe's times. Rep. P. Heyse, E. Geibel. (**epigonism; Parnassians.)

**musical:** *musical drama.

**musical comedy:** *musical drama.

**musical drama; musical comedy; musical** (F. comédie musicale; G. Musikdrama; S. comedia musical): a light play or a comedy which includes musical numbers and songs. (**ballad opera; cantata; drama; opera; operetta; revue.)

**mystery novel; mystery story:** a blanket term that encompasses the *detective story, the *Gothic novel, the *thriller, the *whodunit, the *penny dreadful, and other similar stories.

**mystery** [Gk. to initiate into religious rites] **play** (F. mystère; G. Mysterienspiel; S. misterio): a medieval *liturgical play based on the Bible. (**drama; pageant.)

**mysticism** [Gk. to initiate into mysteries]; (F. mysticisme; G. Mystik; S. misticismo): a religious-ascetic theory based on the belief that a union between God and the human soul is possible by means of ecstasy, visions, and contemplations; it had some influence on a number of writers in the seventeenth and eighteenth centuries as well as on *Romanticism. (**Pietism; Preromanticism.)

**myth** [Gk. tale, fable, mystery]; (F. mythe; G. Mythos; S. mito): a story that explains natural and supernatural phenomena as well as the religious rites and beliefs of a nation or a group of people. (**fantasy fiction; mythology.)

**mythology** [Gk. study of myth]; (F. mythologie; G. Mythologie; S. mitología): a body of *myths; the entirety of traditional stories and legendary tales of a nation or a group of people. (**epyllion.)

# N

**narrative poetry; epic poetry** (F. poésie épique; G. epische Dichtung, Epik; S. poesía épica): narrative, dramatic, and lyric are the three main categories of poetry. Narrative poetry encompasses all literary genres which tell a story either in verse or in prose. Narrative genres can be divided according to the following criteria: the nature of the plot, the characters presented, the setting, the intellectual content, style, and *narrative techniques. However, the simplest way is to classify them according to extrinsic qualities. Lengthy genres: (a) in verse: epic; (b) in prose: novel or saga. Short genres: (a) in verse: romance, idyll, ballad (which also has dramatic and lyrical elements), and verse tale (which is used as a blanket term for other short genres like fable, legend, folk tale, and fairy story when told in verse); (b) in prose: short story, folk tale, novella, anecdote, fable, parable, legend, or fairy story. (**art epic; Arthurian romance; cautionary tale; chivalric romance; cock-and-bull story; courtly epic; exemplum; fabliau; fairy tale; fantasy fiction; fiction; folk epic; historic epic; humoresque; long-short story; metrical romance; myth; novelette; pastourelle; rhapsody; tale; tall tale; tradition; yarn.)

**narrative techniques:** **action; allusion; anticipation; chosisme; digression; enveloping structure; episodic structure; epistolary novel; fable(2); fable time; first person narrative; flashback; historical present; indirect interior monologue; in medias res; innuendo; interior monologue; machinery; narrative time; omniscient narrator; point of view; slice-of-life; story(1); stream of consciousness technique; third person narrative; tropisme; voice.

**narrative time; reading time** (F. temps de lecture; G. Erzählzeit; S. tiempo narrativo): the length of time needed to perform a play or narrate a story; usually given in hours or in pages. (**action; fable time; narrative techniques; plot; story.)

**national epic** (F. épopée nationale; G. Nationalepos; S. epopeya nacional): a stately narrative poem which reflects the beliefs of a nation, dignifies its history, or glorifies its heroes. (**art epic; folk epic; narrative poetry.)

**naturalism** (F. naturalisme; G. Naturalismus; S. naturalismo): a European literary movement in the late nineteenth century which decreed that works of literature should project an accurate and objective picture of reality without any selection or alteration. The naturalist's close adherence to nature was not as detached and dispassionate as he claimed it to be; he overrated the role of heredity and environment and magnified the ugly, unpoetic, and uncouth aspects of his subjects. Rep. E. Zola, Ibsen, G. Hauptmann. (**expressionism; Jung-Wien; neo-humanism; neoromanticism; slice-of-life; verism.)

**near rhyme**= *imperfect rhyme.

**nemesis** [Gk. retribution]; (F. némésis; G. Nemesis; S. némesis): the down-

fall of evil as an inevitable result of *poetic justice or the punishment of the hero for his *hybris. (**anagnorisis; catharsis; dramatic irony; hamartia; tragic.)

**neoclassicism** (F. néo-classicisme; G. Klassizismus; S. neoclasicismo)= *classicism(2).

**Neo-Gongorism** [*Gongorism]; (F. néo-gongorisme; G. Neogongorismus; S. neogongorismo): the revival of *Gongorism in Spain in the twentieth century; rep. Gerardo Diego, Rafael Alberti.

**neo-humanism; new humanism:** a conservative literary movement in the USA in the 1920's opposed to romantic, realistic, and naturalistic schools; its representatives (I. Babbitt, P. E. More) stressed the ethical and humanistic rather than the aesthetic aspects of poetry. (**classicism; epigonism; Humanism.)

**neologism** [Gk. new word]; (F. néologisme; G. Neologismus; S. neologismo): the coinage of new—sometimes senseless or useless—words or expressions. (**nonce word; nonsense verse.)

**neoromanticism** (F. néo-romantisme; G. Neuromantik; S. neorromanticismo): the revival of *Romanticism at the end of the nineteenth and beginning of the twentieth centuries in opposition to *naturalism. (**epigonism; Jugendstil; Jung-Wien.)

**Neue Sachlichkeit** [G. new objectivity]: a term used in art criticism in the twentieth century; in literature it refers to the realistic, objective, and dispassionate literary style used in Germany in the twenties; often opposed to *expressionism. Rep. E.

Kästner, A. Döblin, C. Zuckmayer. (\*\*magical realism; realism; socialist realism; verism.)

**new criticism** (F. nouvelle critique; G. textimmanente Interpretation; S. crítica interna): a school in criticism in the twentieth century which relies intensively upon the analysis of the intrinsic and extrinsic elements of the text rather than on biographical, historical, or sociological aspects. (\*\*analysis; apparatus criticus; critique; impressionistic criticism; intentional fallacy; interpretation; objectivism; primary source; secondary sources.)

**new objectivity:** \*Neue Sachlichkeit.

**Nibelungenstrophe** [G. Nibelungen stanza]: the four-line stanza used in the Middle High German national epic *Nibelungenlied*, circa 1200 (the Song of the Nibelungs) which has the rhyme scheme aabb. Each line, known as "Langzeile" (long line), consists of two \*hemistichs, and each hemistich has four stressed syllables, with the exception of the second, fourth, and sixth which have three stressed syllables.

**Nō; Nō-plays** [Jap. skill, proficiency]; (F. Nô; G. Nō-Spiel; S. no-gaku): a short traditional Japanese play in verse or prose with dance and music that deals with mythological, religious, or legendary subject matter.

**nom de guerre** [F. war name]= \*pseudonym.

**nom de plume** [F. pen name]=\*pseudonym.

**nonce** [ME. for the one occasion] **word** (F. mot de circonstance; G. Gelegenheitsbildung; S. neologismo circunstancial): a word coined by a writer for a particular context. (\*\*neologism; nonsense verse.)

**nonobjective**=\*abstract.

**nonsense verse** (F. jeu de rime, vers amphigouriques; G. sinnlose Verse; S. verso incoherente, juego): a group of words arranged according to a certain metrical or rhythmical pattern but with no sense or meaning. (\*\*neologism; nonce word.)

**nouveau roman** [F. new novel]: French \*experimental novel.

**nouveau nouveau roman** [F. new new novel]: an extremely \*experimental novel.

**novel** [L. new]; (F. roman; G. Roman; S. novela): a plausible narrative in prose of extended length. Novels can be divided according to their extrinsic (e.g. \*epistolary novel) or intrinsic (e.g. \*psychological novel) characteristics. Novels can be arranged into three main groups according to their subject matter: \*man-novels, \*time-novels, and \*event-novels. (\*\*antinovel; experimental novel; heterodox novel; key novel; long-short story; narrative poetry; narrative techniques; roman-fleuve; sentimental novel.)

**novelette** [dim. of \*novel]; (F. nouvelle, petit roman à bon marché; G. kurzer Roman, Romannovelle; S. novela corta): a dubious term sometimes used in connection with short \*novellas, long-short stories, or brief \*novels.

**novella; novelle** [It. new]; (F. nouvelle; G. Novelle; S. cuento): a plausible narrative in prose of limited length noted for its taut structure and unity of action. (\*\*Falkentheorie; leitmotif; narrative poetry; novelette.)

novel of development; Entwicklungs-roman (F. roman d'évolution psy-chologique; G. Entwicklungsroman; S. novela de formación): a novel that depicts the different stages of a person's development from his early years until his maturity or old age. *Apprenticeship novel, *novel of educational formation, and *novel of the artist could be regarded as sub-ordinate types of the novel of development. (**man-novel; novel.)

novel of educational formation; Erziehungsroman (F. roman de forma-tion éducative, roman pédagogique; G. Erziehungsroman; S. novela de formación): a novel that depicts and analyzes the educational factors and conditions which play a major role in the development of an individual. (**man-novel; novel; novel of de-velopment.)

novel of ideas (F. roman philosophique, roman à thèse; G. Ideenroman; S. novela de ideas, novela intelectual): a novel that is mainly devoted to the discussion of abstract ideas (political, philosophical, sociological, etc.) rather than to the narration of

amusing incidents. (**novel; time-novel.)

novel of manners (F. roman de moeurs; G. Sittenroman, Gesellschaftsroman; S. novela de costumbres): a novel that deals with the social and moral norms of a particular society. (**novel; time-novel.)

novel of the artist; Künstlerroman (F. roman d'un artiste; G. Künstler-roman; S. novela del artista): a novel that depicts the positive and negative experiences of an artist or a poet; various artistic schools and theories are discussed. (**novel; novel of development.)

novel of the soil (F. roman paysan, roman rustique, roman régionaliste; G. Bauernroman, Heimatroman; S. novela de la tierra): a novel that deals with man's struggle to keep or to cultivate his land. (**man-novel; novel.)

number (F. nombre; G. Numerus; S. número): in classical prosody: the number of morae (*mora) in a verse. (**macron; metron; quantitative verse.)

nursery rhyme: *children's song.

# O

objective correlative (F. symbole à valeur psychologique; G. objektives Korrelat; S. objetos simbólicos): a term introduced by T. S. Eliot in 1919 that refers to certain objects or specific events which embody and symbolize particular feelings and emotions, thus helping to evoke them in the reader. (**central motif; leitmotif; motif; symbol; symbol-ism.)

objectivism (F. objectivisme; G. Objek-tivismus; S. objetivismo): a mode of writing and a theory of criticism that emphasizes the extrinsic aspects rather than the intrinsic characteris-tics of a literary work. (**critique; impressionistic criticism; intentional fallacy; new criticism; objectivity.)
objectivity (F. objectivité; G. Objektivi-tät; S. objetividad): a literary work can be described as objective or sub-

jective according to the author's attitude toward the external world that surrounds him and his degree of reliance upon the internal world within himself. He is objective if he leans towards the former (i. e. the external world) and subjective if he tends towards the latter (i. e. his internal world). (**abstract; antinovel; concrete; meaning; point of view; tone.)

**oblique rhyme:** *imperfect rhyme.

**occasional verse** (F. poésie de circonstance; G. Gelegenheitsdichtung; S. poesía ocasional): a poem written for a special occasion (birthday, wedding, death, anniversary, inauguration, etc.). (**light verse; vers de société.)

**octameter; octometer** [Gk. eight measures]; (F. octamètre; G. Oktameter; S. octámetro): a line of eight metrical feet. (**verse.)

**octapody** [Gk. eight measures]; (F. octopode; G. Oktapodie; S. octómetro, octapodia)=*octameter.

**octastich; octastichon** [Gk. of eight lines]; (F. huitain; G. Oktastichon, Oktett; S. octava): a poem or *stanza of eight lines; also known as huitain.

**octave; octet** [L. eighth]; (F. octave; G. Oktave, Stanze; S. octava): a group of eight lines. (**ottava rima; Sicilian octave.)

**octet; octette** [L. eight]; (F. huitain; G. Oktett; S. octava)=*octastich.

**octonarius** [L. consisting of eight]; (F. octonaire; G. Oktonar; S. octonario): a classical verse of eight metrical feet or four dipodies.

**octonary** [L. consisting of eight]= *octastich.

**octosyllabic** [Gk. of eight syllables] **couplet** (F. distique d'octosyllabes; G. oktosyllabisches Reimpaar; S. dístico octosilábico): a *stanza of two iambic or two trochaic tetrameters. (**Hudibrastic; quintilla; redondilla.)

**octosyllabic** [Gk. of eight syllables] **verse** (F. octosyllabique; G. oktosyllabische Zeile; S. verso octosilábico): a line of eight syllables (=four iambs or four trochees). (**copla; verse.)

**ode** [Gk. song]; (F. ode; G. Ode; S. oda): a stanzaic lyric poem noted for its highly artistic form and exalted tone. (**dithyramb; Horatian ode; hymn; mesode; paean; panegyric; parabasis; Pindaric ode; proode.)

**Omar Khayyam quatrain:** *Ruba'i.

**omniscient narrator** (F. narrateur omniscient; G. auktorialer Erzähler, allwissender Erzähler; S. narrador omnisciente): a fictitious character created by the author to narrate the story, explain the characters' motivations, and comment on the events. (**narrative techniques.)

**one-act play** (F. pièce en un acte; G. Einakter; S. obra en un acto): a concise and dramatically compact play which consists of only one act. Well-known writers of one-act plays are Strindberg, Shaw, Wilde, Lorca, and Beckett. (**drama.)

**onomatopoeia** [Gk. to make names]; (F. onomatopée; G. Onomatopöie, Onomatopoesie, Klangmalerei, Lautmalerei; S. onomatopeya): the formation of a word or group of words which imitate a natural sound, or the use of words whose sound suggests or reinforces their meaning. (**cacophony; euphony; incantation; jingle.)

**open couplet** (F. strophe à enjambement; G.—; S. dístico con encabalgamiento): a *couplet that does not consist of a complete sentence and therefore depends on *enjambment.

**open form** (F. forme lâche; G. offene Form; S. forma abierta): literary forms that have a loose extrinsic structure such as the diary, the dialogue, the essay, or the letter.

**opera** [L. work]; (F. opéra; G. Oper; S. ópera): one can distinguish between (1) *musical drama: in which the spoken word has some importance; (2) *operetta: in which there is a balance between speech, song, and music and (3) opera: in which song and music predominate. (**ballad opera; cantata; drama; libretto; oratorio; revue.)

**operetta** [It. small opera]; (F. opérette; G. Operette; S. opereta): a light musical drama which includes dialogues, songs, and occasionally dancing scenes. (**ballad opera; cantata; drama; libretto; opera; revue.)

**oral poetry** (F. poésie orale; G. mündlich überlieferte Dichtung; S. poesía oral): oral poetry encompasses different kinds of *folk poetry such as folk epic, folk ballad, folk song, folk tale, charm, riddle, etc. which were handed down by oral tradition; it is usually of unknown authorship.

**oration** [L. speech, discourse]; (F. allocution, discours; G. Ansprache; S. oración): a formal speech or an elaborate discourse delivered on a special occasion. (**epideictic speech; harangue; homiletics; invocation; paean; panegyric; peroration.)

**oratorio** [It. from the Oratorio di San Filippo Neri in Rome where similar compositions were performed]; (F. oratorio; G. Oratorium; S. oratorio): a musical composition usually of a religious nature which is performed without scenery; it consists of arias, recitatives, and choruses with organ or orchestral accompaniment. (**opera.)

**organic form; organic unity** (F. unité organique; G. organische Form, organische Einheit; S. forma orgánica): two terms used in connection with literary works which demonstrate a complete harmony between their intrinsic and extrinsic elements. (**Apollonian; balance; classic(3); decorum; structure.)

**organic unity:** *organic form.

**orotund** [L. with round mouth] **style** (F. style emphatique, style ampoulé; G. bombastischer Stil; S. rotundo): a pompous, flamboyant, and pretentious style. (**baroque; bombast; euphuism; Gongorism; high style; logorrhoea; Marinism; preciosity; purple passage; verbosity.)

**Ossianic poems** (F. poésie ossianique; G. Ossianische Dichtung; S. poesía osiánica): the two epic poems *Fingal* and *Temoro* published in 1762 and 1763 by James Macpherson (1736 - 1796), purporting to be English translations from a third-century Gaelic bard by the name of Ossian. The poems—noted for their rhythmic prose, romantic atmosphere, and melancholic mood—had a great impact on *Romanticism. (**Preromanticism.)

**ottava rima** [It. eight rhyme]; (F. ottava rima; G. Ottaverime; S. octava rima): a *stanza of eight iambic pentameters (◡—◡—◡—◡—◡—), rhyming abababcc.

**oxymoron** [Gk. sharp+foolish]; (F. oxymoron; G. Oxymoron; S. oxímoron): a combination of contradictory terms or incongruous images. (**antithesis; antonym; catachresis; grotesque; incongruity; paradox.)

# P

**paean; pean** [dedicated to Paian, an epithet of Apollo]; (F. paean, Péan; G. Päan, Paian, Paean; S. peán): a *hymn or choral song of praise or thanksgiving. (**ode; oration; paeon; panegyric.)

**paeon** [for its use in *paeans]; (F. péon; G. Päon, Paeonicus; S. peón): a metrical foot that consists of one long (or stressed) and three short (or unstressed) syllables. According to the position of the long (or stressed) syllable, it is known as first (‿◡◡◡), second (◡‿◡◡), third (◡◡‿◡), or fourth paeon (◡◡◡‿). (**epitrite; paean.)

**pageant** [L. page, stage]; (F. mansion, décors juxtaposés; G. Wagenbühne, Bühnenwagen; S. carro): a movable stage upon which medieval *mystery plays were performed.

**palilogy; palillogy; palilogia** [Gk. to restate]; (F. palilogie; G. Palillogie, Palilogia; S. palilogia): a rhetorical figure: repeating a word or group of words for emphasis. (**anadiplosis; anaphora; epanalepsis; epiphora; ploce; polyptoton.)

**palimbacchius** [Gk. back+bacchius]; (F. palimbacchée; G. Palimbacchius; S. antibaquio)=*antibacchius.

**palindrome** [Gk. running backward]; (F. palindrome; G. Palindrom; S. palíndromo): a word, sentence, verse, or text which has the same meaning when read either forwards or backwards. (**anastrophe; cryptogram.)

**palinode** [Gk. revocation]; (F. palinodie; G. Palinodie, Palinode, dichterischer Widerruf; S. palinodia): a poem in which the poet retracts an earlier statement made by him. (**correctio.)

**palinodic** [Gk. *palinode]; (F. palinodique; G. palinodisch; S. estrofa palinódica): a group of four lines or four strophes which correspond—intrinsically or extrinsically—to the pattern abba. (**enclosing rhyme.)

**panegyric** [Gk. solemn assembly]; (F. panégyrique; G. Panegyrikos, Panegyrikus; S. panegírico): a speech or a song glorifying a deed, celebrating an occasion, praising an institution, honoring a hero (encomium), or commemorating a victory (epinicion). (**epideictic speech; epithalamium; eulogy; harangue; ode; oration; paean; rhetoric.)

**Pantaloon; Pantalone:** *harlequinade.

**pantomime** [Gk. imitate, act]; (F. pantomime; G. Pantomime; S. pantomima): an independent dramatic act which is communicated by means of mimicry and gestures. (**dumb show; drama; masque; mummery.)

**pantoum** [from Malayan: pantun, a verse form in Malay]; (F. pantoum; G. Pantun, Pantum; S. pantoum): a poem that consists of quatrains rhyming abab bcbc cdcd . . . xaxa (i.e. the second and fourth lines of each quatrain are repeated as the first and third lines of the next; the second and fourth lines of the last quatrain being the third and first lines of the poem respectively).

**pantun**: *pantoum.

**parabasis** [Gk. step aside]; (F. parabase; G. Parabase; S. parábasis): an *ode addressed to the audience and delivered by the chorus in the middle of Old Greek comedies. (**aside; epilogue; exodus; parodos; stasimon.)

**parable** [Gk. comparison]; (F. parabole; G. Parabel; S. parábola): a short narrative that illustrates a moral principle. (**allegory; cautionary tale; emblem; exemplum; symbol.)

**paradox** [Gk. contrary to opinion]; (F. paradoxe; G. Paradox, Paradoxon; S. paradoja): a rhetorical figure; a seemingly self-contradictory statement which under certain circumstances can be shown to be true. (**antithesis; antonym; oxymoron.)

**paragoge** [Gk. to lead over]; (F. paragoge; G. Paragoge; S. paragoge): the addition of one or more letters to the end of a word for rhetorical or metrical reasons. (**catalectic; hypermetric.)

**paragraph** [Gk. a new section of writing]: *verse paragraph.

**paraliterature** [Gk.+L. beside writing]; (F. paralittérature, littérature marginale; G. trivialliteratur, Konsumliteratur; S. paraliteratura): a term sometimes used instead of popular fiction or *trivial literature.

**parallelism** [Gk. beside each other]; (F. parallélisme; G. Parallelismus; S.

paralelismo): a rhetorical figure based on the use of groups of words which correspond to each other. (**enallage; antithesis; chiasmus; correlative verse; parataxis.)

**paraphrase** [Gk. adding to a speech]; (F. paraphrase; G. Paraphrase; S. paráfrasis): rendering the meaning of a text in another form. (**analysis; explication; interpretation; periphrasis.)

**para-rhyme**=*imperfect rhyme.

**parataxis** [Gk. placing side by side]; (F. parataxe; G. Parataxe; S. parataxis): a rhetorical figure: placing a group of principal clauses one after another without the customary connectives; usually done to indicate emotional excitement. (**asyndeton; hypotaxis; parallelism.)

**Parnassians** [of Parnassus, a Greek mountain regarded as the residence of Apollo and the Muses]; (F. Parnassiens; G. Parnassiens; S. parnasianos): a group of French poets in the second half of the nineteenth century who rejected the excessive sentimentalism of the romantic era and used traditional verse forms. Rep. Th. Gautier, Leconte de Lisle. (**epigonism; Münchner Dichterkreis.)

**parodos; parodus** [Gk. entrance]; (F. parodos; G. Parodos, Einzugslied; S. parodos): the choral part of a Greek drama which is sung as the chorus enters for the first time; opposite of exodus. (**parabasis; stasimon.)

**parody** [Gk. mock song]; (F. parodie; G. Parodie; S. parodia): a literary work that imitates the style of an-

paroemiac

other work in order to ridicule its subject matter. (**burlesque(1); extravaganza; imitation; mock epic; pastiche; persiflage; travesty.)

**paroemiac** [Gk. proverb]; (F. parémiaque; G. Parömiakos; S. paremia): an anapaestic dimeter catalectic used in proverbs; one of the oldest Greek verse forms.

**paronomasia** [Gk. to call with a changed name]; (F. paronomase; G. Paronomasie; S. paronomasia): a rhetorical figure: juxtaposing words that have (1) a common ancestral form but different meanings (also known as figura etymologica); or (2) similar sounds but different meanings (also called annominatio). (**conundrum; homoeoteleuton; homographs; homoioptoton; homonyms; homophones; polyptoton; pun; rime riche; word play.)

**pars pro toto** [L. part for the whole]: *synecdoche.

**partimen** [Prov. division]; **joc partit; jeu parti** (F. jeu parti; G. Partimen; S. contrapunto poético): a *tenzone in which the first poet suggests the topic of the dispute and gives his opponent the chance to choose one of the two points of view. (**amoebean verse; débat.)

**pasquil:** *pasquinade.

**pasquinade; pasquil** [It. lampoon]; (F. pasquin; G. Pasquill, Pasquinade; S. pasquín): an anonymous *lampoon usually posted in a public place.

**passion** [L. suffering] **play** (F. mystère de la Passion; G. Passionsspiel; S. auto sacramental): a *liturgical play based on the sufferings of Jesus. (**Corpus Christi play; drama.)

**pastiche** [It. paste]; (F. pastiche; G. Pastiche; S. pastiche): a literary work that ridicules another work by imitating and accumulating its stylistic features. (**parody; travesty.)

**pastoral** [L. shepherd] **poetry** (F. pastorale, églogue; G. Schäferdichtung, Pastorale; S. poesía pastoril): poetry that deals with the simple and untroubled life of shepherds; usually written in an idealized way and in a conventional manner. (**Arcadia; bucolic poetry; eclogue; georgic; idyll; pastourelle; villanelle.)

**pastourelle; pastorelle** [L. shepherd]; (F. pastourelle; G. Pastorelle, Pastourella; S. pastorela): a medieval narrative poem that deals with love between a knight and a shepherdess. (**bucolic; courtly epic; narrative poetry; pastoral.)

**pathos** [Gk. suffered]; (F. pathos; G. Pathos; S. pathos): a sad element that evokes pity, sorrow, or compassion in the reader or the beholder. Pathetic elements differ from *tragic ones in that they are not based on free will or choice, but merely on luck or fate. (**bathos; dramatic techniques.)

**pattern poetry:** *carmen figuratum.

**pause:** *break.

**pen name:** *pseudonym.

**penny-a-liner** (F. écrivaillon, lignard; G. Zeilenschreiber, Schreiberling, Zeilenschinder; S. gacetillero): a writer paid at a low rate; usually a journalist or a feuilletonist. (**feuilleton; potboiler.)

**penny dreadful; dreadful; dime novel; shilling shocker; shocker** (F. feuilleton à gros effets, roman à deux sous, roman à sensation, roman pour concierges; G. Groschenroman, Schauerroman, Hintertreppenroman, Schundroman, Kolportageroman; S. folletín): an inexpensive *event-novel noted for sensationalism and violence. (**detective story; Gothic novel; thriller.)

**pentameter** [Gk. five measures]; (F. pentamètre; G. Pentameter; S. pentámetro): a line of five metrical feet. (**distich.)

**pentapody** [Gk. five feet]; (F. pentapodie; G. Pentapodie; S. pentámetro): a group of five metrical feet. (**dipody; monopody; tetrapody; tripody.)

**pentarsic** [Gk. of five rises or stresses]; (F. vers à cinq arsis; G. Pentarsik; S. verso de cinco arsis): having five arses (*arsis).

**pentastich** [Gk. five lines]; (F. quintil; G. Pentastichon; S. quintilla): a group of five lines. (**stanza.)

**penthemimer** [Gk. of five halves]; (F. penthémimère; G. Penthemimeres; S. verso pentamímero): a metrical unit that consists of two and one half feet. (**penthemimeral caesura.)

**penthemimeral** [Gk. fifth half] **caesura** (F. césure penthémimère; G. Penthemimeres; S. pentemímeris): a *caesura after the third stressed (or long) syllable (the fifth half-foot). (**hepthemimeral; hexameter; penthemimer; trithemimeral.)

**penult** [L. before the last]; (F. pénultième; G. Pänultima; S. penúltimo): the second syllable counting from the end of the word. (**antepenult.)

**perfect rhyme; full rhyme; true rhyme** (F. rime riche; G. reiner Reim; S. rima perfecta): the correspondence of the stressed vowel and all following consonants. (**end rhyme; rhyme.)

**period** [Gk. circuit, cycle]; (F. période; G. Periode, Satzgefüge; S. período): (1) a rhythmical unit that consists of two or more cola (*colon); (2) a sentence that has several clauses.

**peripeteia; peripety** [Gk. sudden change]; **reversal** (F. péripétie; G. Peripetie; S. peripecia): a sudden and unexpected dramatic turning point. (**catabasis; catastasis; catastrophe; climax(2); dramatic techniques; epitasis; Freytag's pyramid; protasis; volta.)

**peripety:** *peripeteia.

**periphrasis** [Gk. rephrase]; (F. périphrase; G. Periphrase; S. perífrasis): a rhetorical figure: the use of a longer phrasing instead of a shorter one. (**antonomasia; circumlocution; euphemism; metalepsis; metonymy.)

**peroration** [L. end of speech]; (F. péroraison; G. Peroration; S. per oración: the concluding part or summary of a speech. (**epilogue; oration.)

**persiflage** [L. to whistle]; (F. persiflage; G. Persiflage; S.—): a witty and frivolous derision. (**burlesque (1); lampoon; parody; philippic.)

**persona** [L. mask]; (F. personnage; G. Figur, Charakter; S. personaje): a *character in a literary work. (**antagonist; characterization; protagonist; voice.)

**personae:** plural of *persona.

**personification** [L. making a mask]; (F. personnification; G. Personifikation; S. personificación): a rhetorical figure: the representation of non-human things and creatures as persons. (\*\*allegory; anthropomorphism, apostrophe; empathy; metaphor; poetic fallacy; prosopopoeia.)

**Petrarchan conceits** (F. concetti pétrarquistes; G. Petrarkische Konzetti; S. conceptos petrarquistas): certain far-fetched \*metaphors first used by Petrarch (1304 - 1374) and then employed by successive generations. (\*\*conceit; Petrarchism.)

**Petrarchan sonnet** [of Petrarch, 1304 - 1374]: \*sonnet.

**Petrarchism; Petrarchianism** [of or related to the Italian poet Petrarch, 1304 - 1374]; (F. pétrarquisme; G. Petrarkismus; S. petrarquismo): a poetic style inspired by Petrarch's lyric poetry (antitheses; farfetched metaphors, detailed description of physical beauty). (\*\*Petrarchan conceits.)

**Phalaecean** [named after the Greek poet Phalaecus]; (F. phalécien; G. phaläkischer Vers; S. verso faleuco): a classical verse of eleven syllables: ⏑⏑ — ⏑⏑ — ⏑ — ⏑ — ⏑. (\*\*hendecasyllable.)

**Pherecratean; Pherecratic** [named after the Greek poet Pherecrates, circa 450 B.C.]; (F. phérécratéen; G. Pherekrateus; S. verso ferecracio): a classical verse of seven syllables: — ⏑⏑ — ⏑ — ⏑. (\*\*reizianum.)

**philippic** (F. philippique; G. Philippika; S. filípica): a harsh, abusive, and highly rhetorical speech denouncing someone; named after Philip II, king of Macedon, who was attacked by the Greek orator Demosthenes (384 - 322 B.C.).

(\*\*diatribe; lampoon; persiflage; vulgarism.)

**phraseology** [Gk. study of phrases]; (F. phraséologie; G. Phraseologie; S. fraseología): the study of \*idioms, choice of words, and structure of sentences. (\*\*cant; syntax.)

**picaresque; picaresque novel** [S. pícaro= rogue]; (F. roman picaresque; G. Picareske, picarischer Roman, Schelmenroman; S. picaresco, novela picaresca): a prose fiction of Spanish origin; it describes the life and adventures of a delinquent or rogue, and usually has an \*episodic structure. (\*\*makame; man-novel.)

**Pietism** (F. piétisme; G. Pietismus; S. pietismo): a religious movement in Germany within Protestantism (founded by Jacob Spener in 1670) which emphasized the importance of personal religious experience. A few German writers (Klopstock, Herder, Goethe) were influenced by this movement. (\*\*irrationalism; mysticism; Preromanticism.)

**Pindaric ode** [named after the Greek poet Pindar, circa 518 - 446 B.C.]; (F. ode pindarique; G. pindarische Ode; S. oda pindárica): an \*ode of several stanzas, each of which has three parts: strophe, antistrophe, and epode.

**Pindaric stanza:** \*Pindaric ode.

**plagiarism** [L. kidnap]; (F. plagiat; G. Plagiat; S. plagio): the use of words or ideas of another writer without crediting the source. (\*\*quotation.)

**plain style:** \*low style.

**plaint** [L. to beat the breast]; (F. plainte, lamentation; G. Klage; S. lamento)=\*lament.

**planh** [L. lament]: a Provençal *lament.

**platitude** [F. flat]; (F. platitude; G. Platitüde, Plattheit, Gemeinplatz; S.—): a dull idea, insipid thought, or trite style. (**low style; primitivism.)

**play within a play** (F. pièce dans la pièce; G. Spiel im Spiel; S. comedia dentro de una comedia): a short independent play included in a longer play; it usually has some relevance to the main plot. (**drama; dramatic techniques; enveloping structure; frame story.)

**Pléiade** [derived from the seven stars of the Pleiades]: a literary movement in France in the second half of the sixteenth century. Holding ancient Greek and Roman works as models, the seven members of this group (Ronsard, J. Dorat, J. du Bellay, J. A. Baïf, R. Belleau, P. de Tyard, E. Jodelle) tried to renovate certain aspects of French literature. (**classicism(2).)

**pleonasm** [Gk. superfluity]; (F. pléonasme; G. Pleonasmus; S. pleonasmo): a rhetorical figure: using more synonymous words than are actually needed to express one idea or describe one thing. (**asyndeton; epanalepsis; hendiadys; polysyndeton; tautology.)

**ploce** [Gk. complication]; (F. ploque, répétition; G. Ploke, Wiederholung; S. repetición, eco): a rhetorical figure in which a certain word is repeated to stress its significance. (**anadiplosis; echo; epanalepsis; palilogy; polyptoton; symploce.)

**plot** [F. complot=conspiracy]; (F. intrigue, action, trame; G. Handlung, Fabel, Konflikt; S. trama): the sequence of events in a narrative or dramatic work as they have been arranged by the author. (**action; argument; commedia dell'arte; dramatic techniques; fable(2); in medias res; retardation; scenario; story; subplot.)

**poem** [Gk. creation, invention, work]; (F. poème; G. Gedicht; S. poema): any lyrical, dramatic, or narrative composition in verse. (**lyric poetry; poetry; prose poem.)

**poem in prose**=*prose poem.

**poesie; poesy** [Gk. creation]; (F. poésie; G. Poesie; S. poesía): art of poetic composition. (**literature; poetic diction; poetry.)

**poeta doctus:** *epyllion.

**poetic contraction**=*elision.

**poetic diction** (F. diction; G. Diktion, Wortwahl; S. dicción poética): the choice of words which by their *denotation and *connotation are poetically effective. (**poesie.)

**poetic fallacy** (F. personnification, prosopopée; G. Personifikation, Prosopopöe; S. prosopopeya): the attribution of human feelings to inanimate objects; the phrase was coined in 1856 by John Ruskin. (**anthropomorphism; apostrophe; empathy; personification; prosopopoeia.)

**poetic justice** (F. justice poétique; G. poetische Gerechtigkeit; S. némesis): a justice found in poetry but seldom in real life, according to which the virtuous are rewarded and the vicious are punished. (**deus ex machina; hamartia; hybris; nemesis.)

**poetic licence** (F. licence poétique; G. dichterische Freiheit, poetische

Lizenz, poetische Freiheit; S. licencia poética): the poet's ability to change language, forms, and facts for purely artistic reasons. (**barbarism; modulation; solecism.)

**poetics** [Gk. the art of poetry]; (F. la poétique; G. Poetik; S. poética): *rhetoric.

**poet laureate** [L. crowned poet]; (F. poète lauréat; G. Poeta laureatus; S. poeta laureado): a court poet or a poet honored as the most eminent of his country.

**poetry** [Gk. creation, composition]; (F. poésie; G. Dichtung; S. poesía): the art of using words to reproduce a certain human experience and to give it a general and lasting validity. The three main categories of poetry are *narrative, *dramatic, and *lyric. (**literature; oral poetry; poesie; trivial literature; universality; ut pictura poesis.)

**point of view** (F. point de vue; G. Perspektive, Standpunkt; S. punto de vista): the narrator's standpoint; he may observe the incidents or participate in them; he may merely record the actions of the characters, or explain their motivations. (**narrative techniques; objectivity.)

**polemic** [Gk. war]; (F. polémique; G. Polemik; S. polémica): a controversial discussion or vigorous scholarly dispute. (**débat; enthymeme; flyting; silloi; syllogism; tract.)

**political novel** (F. roman politique; G. politischer Roman; S. novela política): a novel that discusses political issues and deals with ideological questions. (**novel; time-novel.)

**polyglot** [Gk. many-tongued]; (F. édition polyglotte; G. Polyglotte; S. polígloto): a book that contains a text in different languages. (**interlinear; triglot.)

**polyphonic** [Gk. having many tones or melodies] **prose** (F. prose polyphonique; G. polyphonische Prosa; S. prosa polifónica): a term coined by Amy Lowell in 1918 in connection with her own *free verse. In general it could mean as much as a poem in prose. (**prose poem; verset; vers libre.)

**polyptoton** [Gk. many cases]; (F. polyptote; G. Polyptoton; S. poliptoton): a rhetorical figure: the repetition of the differing forms of a single word in close proximity to one another. (**anadiplosis; echo; epanalepsis; palilogy; paronomasia; ploce; symploce; tautology.)

**polysyllabic** [Gk. having many syllables]; (F. polysyllabique; G. vielsilbig; S. polisílabo, polisilábico): consisting of several syllables. (**disyllabic; monosyllabic.)

**polysyllabic rhyme; multiple rhyme** (F. rimes polysyllabiques, rimes empérières, rimes couronneés; G. erweiterter Reim, reicher Reim; S. rima polisilábica): the rhyming of three (triple rhyme) or more syllables. (**end rhyme; rhyme.)

**polysyndeton** [Gk. binding together]; (F. polysyndéton; G. Polysyndeton; S. polisíndeton): a rhetorical figure: stringing related words together without omitting the conjunctions; opposite of asyndeton. (**hendiadys; pleonasm; tautology.)

**popular ballad:** *folk ballad.

**popular song:** *folk song.

**pornography** [Gk. writing of whores]; (F. pornographie; G. Pornographie; S. pornografía): *erotic poetry.

**portmanteau** [F. carry+mantle] **word:** *blend.

**potboiler** (F. littérature alimentaire; G. Brotarbeit; S. literatura comercial): an inferior literary work written only for money; also one who writes this kind of book. (**penny-a-liner.)

**poulter's measure** [poulterers used to add one or two extra eggs to each dozen sold]; (F.—; G. Geflügel-händler-Maß; S. dístico irregular): a *couplet that consists of one twelve-syllabic and one fourteen-syllabic line.

**preamble** [L. to walk in front]; (F. préambule; G. Präambel, Vorspiel, Vorwort; S. preámbulo): the introductory part of a book. (**prologue.)

**preciosity** [L. value]; (F. préciosité; G. Preziösität; S. preciosismo): an affected, inflated, and mannered style; popular in France in the seventeenth century. (**baroque; conceptism; culteranism; cultism; euphuism; Gongorism; logorrhoea; mannerism; Marinism; orotund; purple passage; verbosity.)

**preface** [L. to speak beforehand]; (F. préface; G. Vorwort, Einleitung; S. prefacio)=*prologue.

**prelude** [L. to play beforehand]; (F. prélude; G. Präludium, Vorspiel, Vorwort; S. preludio): a *prologue or dramatic scene preceding the main drama. (**exordium; interlude.)

**Pre-Raphaelite Brotherhood** (F. préraphaélites; G. Präraffaeliten; S. prerrafaelistas): a group of writers and painters formed in England in 1848 who were devoted to the artistic principles of Italy before Raphael, 1483 - 1520; it was noted for its *realism and attention to detail. Rep. D. G. Rossetti, Chr. Rossetti, William Morris.

**Preromanticism** (F. préromantisme; G. Vorromantik; S. prerromanticismo): a blanket term that encompasses several literary and artistic movements of the eighteenth century which were opposed to the rigid rationalism of the *Enlightenment such as *Pietism, *Sturm und Drang, *rococo, *Göttinger Hain, and the sentimental literature of Fielding, Sterne, and Ossian. (**irrationalism; mysticism; Ossianic poems; Romanticism.)

**primary epic:** *folk epic.

**primary source** (F. source de première main; G. Primärliteratur; S. fuente primaria): the text of a literary work. (**analysis; apparatus criticus; bibliography; new criticism; secondary sources.)

**primitive epic:** *folk epic.

**primitivism** [L. original, first]; (F. primitivisme; G. Primitivismus; S. primitivismo): a literary style marked by spontaneity, naïveté, and formal simplicity. (**diatribe; folk ballad; folk song; low style; platitude.)

**problem play** (F. pièce à thèse; G. Problemstück; S. obra de tesis social): a play that deals with a social problem; also known as a thesis play. (**drama.)

**procatalepsis** [Gk. anticipate]; (F. hypobole, procatalepse; G. Prokatalepsis; S.—): a rhetorical figure: anticipating a question and answering it. (**anticipation; refutation; rhetorical question.)

**proceleusmatic** [Gk. forestall]; (F. procéleusmatique; G. Prokeleusmatikos; S. proceleusmático): a classical metrical foot that consists of four short syllables: ◡ ◡ ◡ ◡. (**dispondee; pyrrhic.)

**prochronism** [Gk. before the time]; (F. prochronisme; G. Prochronismus; S. procronismo): an *anachronism based on assigning the events to a date earlier than the actual one. (**hysteron proteron.)

**proclitic** [Gk. to lean forwards]; (F. proclitique; G. Proklise, Proklisis; S. proclítico): the pronunciation of a word which has no independent accent as part of the following word. (**enclitic; distributed stress; recessive accent.)

**proem; proemium** [Gk. prelude]; (F. proème; G. Proömium; S. proemio) =*exordium.

**prolepsis** [Gk. anticipation]; (F. prolepse; G. Prolepse; S. prolepsis): (1)=*procatalepsis; (2)=*anticipation.

**prologue** [Gk. openning speech]; (F. prologue; G. Prolog, Vorrede, Vorwort, Vorspiel; S. prologo): the introductory part of a book or play; as opposed to *epilogue. (**exordium; invocation; preamble; prelude.)

**proode** [Gk. before the song]; (F. proode; G. Proodos; S.—): a *strophe preceding an *ode. (**mesode.)

**prose** [L. direct]; (F. prose; G. Prosa; S. prosa): an unrhymed language that does not adhere to any metrical pattern. (**free verse; polyphonic prose; prose poem; verset; vers libre.)

**prose poem** (F. poème en prose; G. Prosagedicht; S. poema en prosa): a text, usually of a lyrical nature, that is written in a poetic and rhythmic style but does not adhere to a metrical pattern. (**free verse; lyric poetry; poetic diction; polyphonic prose; prose; verset; vers libre.)

**prosodiac; prosodion** (F. prosodiaque; G. Prosodiakos; S. prosodion): a Greek verse that usually consists of three *anapaests; it was sung during religious processions (prosodia).

**prosodion:** *prosodiac.

**prosody** [Gk. a song sung to instrumental accompaniment]; (F. prosodie; G. Prosodie, Metrik, Verslehre; S. prosodia): the study of versification, i.e. the theory of metrical structures, rhythmical patterns, *rhyme schemes, and verse forms. (**metrics; rhythm; scansion.)

**prosopopoeia** [Gk. to make a person]; (F. prosopopée; G. Prosopopöe, Prosopopöie; S. prosopopeya): (1) *personification; (2) representing an absent, dead, or imaginary person as present. (**anthropomorphism; poetic fallacy.)

**protagonist** [Gk. competitor, fighter]; (F. protagoniste; G. Protagonist, Held, Hauptfigur; S. protagonista): the leading character in dramas and narratives, also called hero. The second most important character or actor is known as the deuteragonist, and the third as the tritagonist. (**antagonist; antihero; character; confidant; foil.)

**protasis** [Gk. put forward]; (F. protase, exposition; G. Protasis, Exposition; S. prótasis): the part of a drama in which the main characters are introduced and the background exposed; also known as exposition. (\*\*catabasis; catastasis; catastrophe; dramatic techniques; epitasis; Freytag's pyramid; peripetia.)

**prothalamion** [Gk. bridal song]; (F. prothalame; G. Prothalamion, Epithalamium; S. epitalamio)=\*epithalamium.

**prothesis** [Gk. placing before]; (F. prothèse, prosthèse; G. Prothese; S. prótesis): the addition of one or more letters at the beginning of a word; a form of \*metaplasm. (\*\*logogriph; metathesis; spoonerism.)

**Provençal literature** (F. littérature provençale: G. provenzalische Literatur; S. literatura de Provenza): the medieval literature of Provence, a region in southeastern France. (\*\*cobla; cobla esparsa; courtly love; courtly song; descort; ensenhamen; Félibrige; planh; retroensa; sirvente; tenzone; tornada; troubadour.)

**proverb** [L. before the word]; (F. proverbe; G. Sprichwort; S. proverbio): a popular saying that expresses a general truth. (\*\*adage; apophthegm; aphorism; bon mot; epigram; maxim; paroemiac; refrán; sentence.)

**provincialism** (F. provincialisme; G. Provinzialismus; S. provincialismo): words, phrases, manners, or attitudes characteristic of a certain region. (\*\*idiom; jargon; regionalism; vernacularism.)

**psalm** [Gk. a poem sung to the harp]; (F. psaume; G. Psalm; S. salmo): a poem praising a deity; also one of the 150 \*hymns included in the Bible (Book of Psalms).

**pseudonym** [Gk. false name]; **pen name; nom de guerre; nom de plume** (F. pseudonyme; G. Pseudonym, Deckname; S. seudónimo): a name assumed by an author. (\*\*anonymous.)

**psychological novel** (F. roman psychologique; G. psychologischer Roman; S. novela psicológica): a novel that deals mainly with the thoughts and emotions of its characters. (\*\*interior monologue; man-novel; narrative techniques; stream of consciousness technique.)

**pun** [It. puntiglio: quibble]; (F. calembour, jeu de mots; G. Wortspiel, Wortwitz; S. equívoco): a rhetorical figure: the use of words with similar sounds but different meanings. (\*\*conundrum; homographs; homoioptoton; homonyms; homophones; paronomasia; quip; repartee.)

**purism** [L. purity]; (F. purisme; G. Purismus; S. purismo): a rigid literary doctrine that insists on rejecting foreign words, common idioms, and unrefined expressions.

**purple passage; purple patch** (F. morceau de bravoure; G. Glanzstelle; S. pasaje preciocista, pasaje exagerado): a pretentious and highly ornate passage within a plain and common literary work. (\*\*orotund; preciosity; tirade.)

**pyrrhic** [Gk. related to war dance]; (F. pyrrhique; G. Pyrrhichius; S. pirriquio): a metrical foot that consists of two short (or unstressed) syllables: ∪ ∪. (\*\*proceleusmatic.)

**Pythiambic** [Gk. *Pythian+iambic]; (F. pythiambique; G. pythiambisches Maß; S. pitiyambo): a *distich that consists of a *Pythian verse and an iambic trimeter acatalectic.

**Pythian verse** [Gk. of Pytho=Delphi]; (F. vers pythique; G. pythischer Vers; S. hexámetro dactílico): a dactylic *hexameter: ‿‿‿‿‿‿‿‿ ‿‿‿‿‿‿‿.

# Q

**qasida; kasida** [Ar. poem]; (F. qasida; G. Kasside; S. casida): a monorhymed Arabic poem of unlimited length. (**ghazel.)

**quantitative verse** (F. vers quantitatif, vers métrique; G. quantitierende Dichtung; S. verso cuantitativo): the classical Greek and Latin verse which is metrically based on the length of time it takes to pronounce the syllables (*short syllables and long syllables). (**accentual verse; atonic; macron; metron; mora; number; thesis; tonic.)

**quarto** [L. the fourth]; (F. quarto; G. Quartformat; S. libro en cuarto): a book containing sheets of paper that are folded into four leaves. (**folio.)

**quatorzain** [F. of fourteen]; (F. quatorzain; G. Vierzehnzeiler; S. soneto irregular): a poem of fourteen lines which does not adhere to the rules of the *sonnet.

**quatrain** [L. four]; (F. quatrain; G. Quatrain, Quartett, Vierzeiler; S. cuarteto): a stanza of four lines. (**elegiac stanza; pantoum; rondeau redoublé; Ruba'i; short meter.)

**quintilla:** a rhymed Spanish stanza of five *octosyllabic lines.

**quip** [origin unknown]; (F. mot piquant, sarcasme; G. Wortspiel, Wortwitz; S. concepto, agudeza): a humorous *pun or witty remark. (**repartee.)

**quotation** [L. numeration]; **citation** [L. summon]; (F. citation; G. Zitat; S. cita): a passage read or written from another work and acknowledged as such. (**collage; hackneyed expression; plagiarism.)

# R

**radio play** (F. pièce radiophonique; G. Hörspiel; S. radio teatro): a purely acoustic play written or adapted for the radio and noted for its uncomplicated plot and limited number of characters. (**television play.)

**rationalism** [L. ratio=reason]; (F. rationalisme; G. Rationalismus; S. racionalismo): a philosophical doctrine that relies on reason and experience rather than on sense perception, emotions, or intuition. (**Enlightenment; irrationalism.)

**reading time:** *narrative time.

**realism** [L. actual]; (F. réalisme; G. Realismus; S. realismo): a nineteenth-century European literary movement that differed from the preceding *idealism and the ensuing *naturalism in that it rejected the subjectivity and sentimentalism of the first and avoided the banality and bluntness of the second. Representatives of this movement (Balzac, Dickens, Dostoevski, Th. Fontane . . .) depicted the everyday world and dealt with familiar experiences, without magnifying the ugly and uncouth, nor dispensing with feelings and moods. (**magical realism; Münchner Dichterkreis; neo-humanism; Neue Sachlichkeit; Pre-Raphaelite Brotherhood; slice-of-life; socialist realism; surrealism; verism.)

**rebus** [L. by things]; (F. rébus; G. Rebus, Bilderrätsel; S. alegoría): the representation of words by means of *symbols. (**allegory; emblem.)

**recension** [L. revision, review]; (F. recension, texte révisé; G. Rezension; S. recensión): the critical revision of a text; also the definitive text established by such a revision. (**analysis; apparatus criticus; definitive edition.)

**recessive** [L. withdraw] **accent** (F. accent remontant, accent régressif; G. Enklise; S. acento enclítico): the accent of a disyllabic word is sometimes shifted from the second syllable—where it normally belongs—to the first syllable. (**distributed stress; enclitic; logical stress; proclitic; syllaba anceps.)

**recognition:** *anagnorisis.

**redondilla** [S. dim. of redonda= round]: a Spanish stanza of four *octosyllabic lines rhyming abba. (**embracing rhyme; enclosing rhyme.)

**Reformation** [L. form again]; (F. réforme; G. Reformation; S. Reforma): a religious movement led by Martin Luther (1483 - 1546) in the first half of the sixteenth century; it aimed at reforming the Roman Catholic Church, and led to the establishment of the Protestant Church. Luther's translation of the Bible (1522 - 1534) and his writings had a great influence on German language and literature. (**Humanism; Pietism; Renaissance.)

**refrain** [L. to break off]; (F. refrain; G. Refrain, Kehrreim; S. estribillo): a metrical or rhythmical unit that consists of a few words, a line, or a group of lines which are repeated regularly within a poem, especially at the end of the *stanzas. (**burden(1); estribillo; incremental repetition; letrilla; repetend; ritornello; rondeau; rondel; serenade.)

**refrán:** a popular Spanish *proverb in verse form.

**refutation** [L. repel]; (F. réfutation; G. Refutation; S. refutación): in rhetoric: part of a speech which refutes the opponent's argument. (**anticipation; procatalepsis; rhetorical question.)

**regionalism** [L. district]; (F. régionalisme; G. Regionalismus, Heimatkunst; S. regionalismo): emphasizing the influence of a particular locale on the action, characters, style, and intellectual content of a literary work. (**idiom; jargon; provincialism; vernacularism.)

**reizianum** [named after the German scholar J. W. Reiz, 1733 - 1790]; (F. reizianum; G. Reizianum; S. reizianismo): an *acephalous *Pherecratean: ◡＿◡◡＿◡＿.

**relevant digression:** *digression.

**Renaissance** [F. rebirth]; (F. Renaissance; G. Renaissance; S. Renacimiento): the revival of humanistic and classical (Greek and Latin) studies in Europe during the fourteenth, fifteenth, and sixteenth centuries; it emphasized the importance of the intellect, of individualism, and of worldliness. (**classicism; Humanism; Reformation.)

**repartee** [F. to retort]; (F. repartie; G. Schlagfertigkeit; S. agudeza): a witty reply or a sharp retort; an important element in the *commedia dell'arte and in other forms of *low comedy. (**pun; quip.)

**repetend** [L. repeated]; (F. refrain; G. Refrain; S. refrán): a word or a group of words repeated irregularly within a poem. (**anadiplosis; burden; incremental repetition; refrain.)

**repetition** [L. to attack again]; (F. répétition; G. Wiederholung; S. repetición): an important and unifying element which depends on repeating a rhythmical unit, sound, or metrical pattern. (**anaclasis(2); anadiplosis; burden; incremental repetition; refrain.)

**reportage** [L. bring back]; (F. reportage; G. Reportage; S. reportaje): the unimaginative reporting of factual events in a straightforward and unembellished style. (**low style.)

**requiem** [L. rest]; (F. requiem; G. Requiem; S. réquiem): a *dirge or a mass for the dead. (**elegy; lament.)

**resolution** [L. untying]; (F. dénouement; G. Lösung; S. desenlace): *catastrophe.

**resolved stress:** *distributed stress.

**responsive verse:** *antiphon.

**rest** [OHG. peace]; (F. pause; G. Pause, Zäsur; S. pausa): a *break, *caesura, or rhythmical pause that compensates for the absence of an unstressed syllable. (**compensation.)

**Restoration** (F. restauration; G. Restauration; S. Restauración): the restoration of Charles II to the English throne in 1660. As a period in English literature, it extends to the end of the seventeenth century. (**Caroline period; Cavalier poets; Edwardian; Elizabethan age; Georgian poets; Jacobean; Victorian.)

**retardation** [L. to delay]; (F. ralentissement; G. Retardation, retardierendes Moment; S. retardación): an abnormal slowness in the development of the plot. (**blind motif; dramatic techniques.)

**retroensa; retroencha; retrouenge; retroänge; rotrouenge; rotrouänge:** a *Provençal lyrical poem of five stanzas with a *refrain at the end of each one.

**retrospect:** *flashback.

**reverdie; reverdi** [F. to become green again]: an old French lyric poem which celebrates the return of spring.

**reversal:** *peripeteia.

**review** [F. to look over]; (F. critique; G. Rundschau, Kritik, Rezension; S. reseña): a critical article on a book or a performance; also a periodical containing such articles. (**analysis; essay.)

**revue** [*review]; (F. revue; G. Revue, Kabarett; S. revista): a theatrical performance that consists of songs, dances, spectacles, and satirical *sketches. (**burlesque(3); drama; musical drama; opera; operetta; skit; vaudeville.)

rhapsodist [*rhapsody]; (F. rhapsode; G. Rhapsode; S. rapsoda): a wandering *minstrel. (**bard; Goliardic verse.)

rhapsody [Gk. songs stitched together]; (F. rhapsodie; G. Rhapsodie; S. rapsodia): (1) a narrative poem planned for recitation; (2) a highly emotional literary work noted for its loose and disconnected structure. (**epic; narrative poetry.)

rhetoric [Gk. art of speech]; (F. rhétorique; G. Rhetorik; S. retórica): whereas poetics is the theory of literary representation and poetic formation, rhetoric is the theory of expressive and effective speech. (**eloquence; enthymeme; epideictic speech; harangue; homiletics; oration; paean; panegyric; rhetorical figures; tirade.)

rhetorical figures (F. figures de rhétorique; G. rhetorische Figuren; S. figuras retóricas): ornaments of speech such as anaphora, antithesis, metaphor, etc. (**rhetoric.)

rhetorical question (F. interrogation oratoire; G. rhetorische Frage; S. pregunta retórica): a statement or an exclamation made in the form of a question merely for rhetorical effect. (**anticipation; procatalepsis; refutation.)

rhetorical stress: *logical stress.

Rhétoriqueurs [F. orators]: a group of French poets of the fifteenth century noted for their extensive use of rhetorical figures and highly artistic forms. Rep. J. Lemaire, A. Chartier.

rhopalic verse; ropalic [Gk. thicker toward the end]; (F. vers rhopaliques; G. Rhopalikos, Keulenvers; S. verso ropálico): a verse in which each word is one syllable longer than the word preceding it.

rhyme; rime [Gk. rhythm]; (F. rime; G. Reim; S. rima): correspondence of word sounds, especially of the last stressed vowels and the following consonants of two or more words; it is also known as rhyme proper. (**alternate rhyme; alliteration; analyzed rhyme; approximate rhyme; assonance; broken rhyme; cauda; chain rhyme; consonance; cross rhyme; double rhyme; embracing rhyme; embryonic rhyme; enclosing rhyme; end rhyme; eye rhyme; feminine rhyme; identical rhyme; imperfect rhyme; internal rhyme; Leonine rhyme; masculine rhyme; mono rhyme; mosaic rhyme; near rhyme; para-rhyme; perfect rhyme; polysyllabic rhyme; rhyme royal; rhyme scheme; rime riche; tail rhyme; vowel rhyme.)

rhyme proper: *rhyme.

rhyme royal; Chaucerian stanza (F. strophe chaucerienne; G. Chaucer-Strophe; S. estrofa chauceriana): a seven-line stanza in iambic pentameters (υ—υ—υ—υ—υ—), rhyming ababbcc. (**septet.)

rhyme scheme (F. disposition des rimes; G. Reimschema; S. combinación métrica, versificación): the arrangement of the rhyming words within a stanza or a poem. (**rhyme.)

rhythm [Gk. to flow]; (F. rythme; G. Rhythmus; S. ritmo): the melodic curve of a line, verse, paragraph, or stanza. Rhythm is affected by the meaning and length of the words, the accentuation of the syllables, and the syntactical pauses. The ascending part of the melodic curve is known as ascending rhythm; the descending part, as descending rhythm. (**break; caesura; colon; counterpoint rhythm; diaeresis; duple rhythm; duration; free verse; logaoedic; period(1); rest; rising meter; rocking rhythm; running rhythm; scansion; slack; sprung rhythm; syllaba anceps.)

**rhythmical pause:** *rest.

**riddle** [OE. opinion]; (F. devinette; G. Rätsel; S. acertijo, adivinanza): a mystifying question or a puzzling formula in verse or prose. Like charms, gnomes, proverbs, myths, legends, and traditions, the riddle is one of the earliest forms of literature. (**charade; conundrum; pun.)

**rime:** *rhyme.

**rime riche** [F. rich rhyme]; (F. rime riche; G. rime riche, reicher Reim; S. rima homónima): occurs when the rhyming words are identical in sound but different in meaning. (**homophones; paronomasia(2); rhyme.)

**rising action**=*epitasis. (**Freytag's Pyramid.)

**rising foot:** *rising meter.

**rising meter; rising foot; rising rhythm** (F. rythme ascendant; G. steigend; S. ritmo ascendente): a metrical foot that ends with a stressed syllable such as an *iamb (∪—) or an *anapaest (∪∪—); opposite of falling meter. (**rhythm.)

**rising rhythm:** *rising meter.

**rispetto** [It. respect]: a lyric poem often written in "respectful" praise of the beloved, and consisting of eight hendecasyllables rhyming abadccdd or abababcc. (**courtly love; dolce stil nuovo; minnesong.)

**ritornello; ritornelle; ritornel** [It. return];

(F. ritournelle; G. Ritornell; S. ritornelo): an Italian stanza of three lines rhyming aba; often used as a *refrain.

**rocking rhythm** (F. rythme balance, rythme de berceuse; G. Schaukel-Rhythmus; S. ritmo anfíbraco, ritmo de vaivén): a rhythm based upon *amphibrachs. (**running rhythm; sprung rhythm.)

**rococo** [F. rocaille=rockwork, shellwork]; (F. rococo; G. Rokoko; S. rococó): an artistic style of the eighteenth century marked by excessively ornate forms and playful themes. Rep. Hagedorn, Wieland, Prévost, Voltaire. (**anacreontic poetry; vers de société.)

**roman à clef** [F. novel with a key]= *key novel.

**romance** [OF. tale]; (F. romance; G. Romanze; S. romance): (1)=*chivalric romance; (2)=*metrical romance.

**romance:** a Spanish *ballad. (**romancero.)

**romancero:** a collection of Spanish ballads (romances).

**roman-fleuve** [F. river novel]; **saga novel** (F. roman fleuve; G. Saga, Familienroman, Generationenroman; S. saga): a long, usually multivolume novel that deals with the life of a large family or a community. (**narrative poetry; novel.)

**romantic irony** (F. diasyrme, ironie romanesque; G. romantische Ironie; S. ironía poética): a remark made by an author within his work which destroys the illusion he has just created and reveals the discrepancy between ideals and realities. (**Byronic; epic drama; irony; Romanticism.)

**Romanticism** [from OF. *romant:* romance]; (F. romantisme; G. Romantik; S. romanticismo): a European literary and philosophical movement of the late eighteenth and early nineteenth centuries, sometimes contrasted with *neoclassicism. Authors of this movement (Novalis, Brentano, Eichendorff, Victor Hugo, Lamartine, Byron, Shelley, Keats, Wordsworth . . .) were noted for their subjectivity, melancholy, and metaphysical tendencies. They emphasized emotions, spontaneity, and the power of imagination. Recurring themes were worship of nature, unfulfilled longing for the unknown, exaltation of the primitive, and the search for a mystical union with God. (**Byronic; Dionysian; Georgian poets; idealism; irrationalism; Lake poets; mysticism; neohumanism; neoromanticism; Ossianic poems; Parnassians; Pre-romanticism; romantic irony; Satanic school; sensibility; spasmodic school.)

**romanticization** [*Romanticism]; (F. romancer; G. Romantisierung; S. romantización): presenting people and incidents in a romantic way, i.e. stressing the emotional, adventurous, and idealized aspects of life. (**idealism; Romanticism.)

**rondeau** [F. round]; (F. rondeau; G. Rondeau; S. rondó): a stanzaic poem usually of thirteen (sometimes twelve, fourteen, or fifteen) lines with two rhymes and a *refrain. (**rondeau redoublé; roundel.)

**rondeau redoublé:** a stricter form of the *rondeau that consists of six quatrains with two alternating rhymes. The lines of the first quatrain are used consecutively as the last lines of the following four quatrains. The opening words of the poem are used as a *refrain after the last quatrain. The rhyme scheme is ABÁB̂ babA abaB babÁ abaB̂ baba+ refrain (the capital letters indicate the repeated lines.)

**rondel** [F. round]: a poem of thirteen or fourteen lines divided into three stanzas with two rhymes. The first two lines are used as a *refrain in the second and third stanzas.

**rondelet** [F. little *rondel]; (F. petit rondel; G. Rondelet; S.—): a short poem of five lines with two rhymes; the first line, or part of it, is used as a *refrain (R) after the second and the fifth lines. Rhyme scheme: abRabbR.

**round character** (F. personnage complexe, personnage énigmatique; G. voller Charakter; S. personaje completo): a many-sided, unpredictable, and thus highly dramatic character; as opposed to *flat character. (**archetype; character; characterization; stock character.)

**roundel** (F. rondeau à la façon de Swinburne; G. Roundel; S. rondó al estilo de Swinburne): a form of the French *rondeau as developed by Swinburne (1837 - 1909). Rhyme scheme: abaB bab abaB, where B is a *refrain taken from the opening of the poem and rhyming with the second line.

**roundelay** [*rondel + *lay]: a short lyrical poem with *refrain.

**Ruba'i; Ruba'iyat; Omar Khayyam quatrain:** a quatrain rhyming aaxa used by the Persian poet Omar Khayyam (1045 - 1122).

running rhythm; common rhythm (F. rythme coulant, rythme cadencé; G. alternierender Rhythmus; S. ritmo cadencioso): a rhythm based on the alternation of stressed and unstressed syllables. (\*\*rhythm; rocking rhythm; sprung rhythm.)

run-on line: \*enjambment.

# S

saga [Old Norse: story]; (F. saga; G. Saga; S. saga): (1) Norwegian and Icelandic prose narratives of the middle ages which deal with historical, heroic, and legendary events; (2) saga novel (\*roman-fleuve). (\*\*narrative poetry; novel.)

Sapphic [named after the Greek poetess Sappho, circa 600 B.C.]; (F. vers saphique; G. Sapphische Zeile; S. sáfico): a line of eleven syllables: one dactyl placed between two trochaic dipodies; also a stanza of three such lines and an \*Adonic. (\*\*Alcaic strophe; Asclepiadic strophe; choriamb; hendecasyllable.)

Sapphic stanza [\*Sapphic]; (F. strophe saphique; G. Sapphische Strophe; S. estrofa sáfica): \*Sapphic.

sarcasm [Gk. to gnash the teeth, to tear flesh, to laugh bitterly]; (F. sarcasme; G. Sarkasmus; S. sarcasmo): bitter, contemptuous, and offensive \*irony. (\*\*cynicism; satire.)

Satanic school: a term coined by Robert Southey (1774 - 1843) in connection with the romantic poets Byron, Shelley, and Keats condemning them because of their exotic, cruel, and sensual themes. The term could be applied to other romantic poets like Hugo, Musset, Kleist, and particularly to E. T. A. Hoffmann. (\*\*Byronic; Cockney School of Poetry; Romanticism.)

satire [L. full dish, hotchpotch]; (F. satire; G. Satire; S. sátira): a literary work which wittingly repudiates, and ironically ridicules folly, vice, and wickedness. However, if it is offensive or contemptuous, then it is no longer satirical but cynical. (\*\*capitolo; caricature; cynicism; diatribe; dit; folly literature; humor; irony; lampoon; silloi; skit; wit.)

satyr play; satyric drama [named after the Greek mythological figure Satyros]; (F. drame satyrique, satyre; G. Satyrspiel; S. sátira): a farcical play performed after a \*trilogy of tragedies in ancient Greece. (\*\*drama; low comedy.)

scald: \*skald.

scansion [L. ascend]; (F. scansion; G. Skansion; S. escansión): the division of a rhythmical unit into metrical feet; the stressed and unstressed syllables are identified and represented by means of symbols ($\cup$ = unstressed or short syllable; $\_$ = stressed or long syllable). (\*\*prosody; rhythm.)

scazon [Gk. limping]: \*choliamb.

scenario [\*scene]; (F. scénario; G. Drehbuch; S. guión): a film script or \*plot outline. (\*\*libretto.)

scene [Gk. stage]; (F. scène; G. Szene, Bild, Auftritt; S. escena, jornada): \*act.

scenery=\*background.

**Scholasticism** [Gk. leisure, school]; (F. scolastique; G. Scholastik; S. escolasticismo): a philosophical and dogmatic-theological movement of the middle ages which preceded both *Humanism and the *Enlightenment. Rep. Abélard, Albertus Magnus, Aquinas . . .

**science fiction** (F. roman d'anticipation, roman de science-fiction; G. Zukunftsroman; S. ciencia ficción): a novel or story that deals with the rapid progress of science and technology and projects a fantastic picture of future times. (**fantasy fiction; novel; time-novel; Utopian fiction.)

**scolion** [Gk. bent, winding]; (F. scolie, chanson de table; G. Skolion; S. escolio): a lyric or satirical poem sung at banquets and symposia; usually improvised by the guests. (**light verse; occasional verse; vers de société.)

**scop** [Old Saxon=poet]; (F. scop; G. Skop, Skob; S. bardo): an Old English *minstrel, bard, or ballad singer. (**rhapsodist.)

**scriptural play**=*mystery play.

**sdrucciola**=*verso sdrucciolo.

**secondary epic:** *art epic.

**secondary sources** (F. sources secondaires; G. Sekundärliteratur; S. fuentes secundarias): all the works that deal with the different intrinsic and extrinsic aspects of a text. (**analysis; apparatus criticus; bibliography; interpretation; new criticism; primary source.)

**semantics** [Gk. significance]; (F. sémantique; G. Semantik; S. semántica): the study of the meanings of words as well as the development, expansion, and adaptation of those meanings. (**linguistics.)

**senarius** [L. of six parts]; (F. sénaire; G. Senar; S. senario): a verse that consists of three iambic dipodies or six iambic feet: $\smile\_\smile\_\smile\_\smile\_\smile\_\smile\_$.

**sensibility** [L. to feel]; (F. sensibilité; G. Empfindsamkeit, Sensibilität; S. sensibilidad): emotions and feelings are emphasized rather than reason and will (as for example in the sentimental novel—S. Richardson, O. Goldsmith—of eighteenth-century England). (**Empfindsamkeit; Preromanticism; Romanticism; sentimentality.)

**sentence; sententia** [L. opinion]; (F. sentence; G. Sentenz; S. sentencia): a short saying or brief statement that expresses a general truth. (**aphorism; apophthegm; epigram; gnomic poetry; maxim.)

**sententia:** *sentence.

**sentimentality** [L. to feel]; (F. sentimentalité, sensiblerie; G. Sentimentalismus, Sentimentalität, Empfindsamkeit; S. sentimentalidad): excessive *sensibility and indulgence in pathetic feeling and tender emotion. (**Empfindsamkeit; futurism; Preromanticism; Romanticism.)

**sentimental novel** (F. roman sentimental; G. empfindsamer Roman; S. novela sentimental): *sensibility.

**septenarius** [L. of seven parts]; (F. septénaire; G. Septenar; S. septenario): a line of seven feet and one additional syllable, or of three complete and one incomplete dipody.

**septenary** [L. of seven parts]; (F. septénaire; G. Septenar; S. septenario): *heptameter.

septet

septet; septette [L. seven]; (F. septain; G. Septett; S. septeto): a poem or stanza of seven lines. (**rhyme royal.)

serenade [It. evening song]; (F. sérénade; G. Serenade; S. serenata): a love *song in which the word evening (Prov.=sera) is not only a *refrain but also a central motif of the poem. (**aubade.)

serpentine verse (F. rime serpentine; G. Serpentinenvers; S. versos serpentinos): a line that begins and ends with the same word. (**echo.)

sestet [L. six]; sextet (F. sixain, sizain; G. Sextett; S. sextina): a stanza or poem of six lines.

sestina [It. the sixth]; (F. sextine; G. Sestine, Sextine; S. sextina): an unrhymed poem that consists of six stanzas of six lines each and a three-line envoi. The end words of the first stanza are repeated in the other stanzas but always in a different order. (**courtly song.)

setting (F. arrière-plan, décor; G. Schauplatz, Hintergrund, Bühnenbild; S. escenario): the *background, the scenery, or environment of a story or play. (**local color; unities.)

sextet: *sestet.

Shakespearean sonnet: *sonnet.

shanty [F. to sing]; shantey; sea shanty; chantey; chanty (F. chanson de marin, chanson de bord, refrain de mer; G. Shanty, Matrosenlied, Seemannslied; S. canción marinera): a rhythmical *song sung by sailors during their work.

shaped poetry: *carmen figuratum.

shilling shocker: *penny dreadful.

shocker: *penny dreadful.

short measure:*short meter.

short meter; short measure; s. m.: a *quatrain of three iambic trimeters (the first, the second, and the fourth lines) and one iambic tetrameter; the rhyme scheme is either abab or abcb.

short story (F. nouvelle; G. Kurzgeschichte; S. cuento): a plausible short narrative usually marked by a stupefying ending. (**long-short story; narrative poetry; story(3).)

short syllable (F. syllabe brève; G. Kürze; S. sílaba breve): whereas *accentual verse is measured according to stressed and unstressed syllables, *quantitative verse is based on short and long syllables, i.e. on the length of time it takes to pronounce the syllables. A short syllable equals one *mora; a long syllable equals two morae. (**macron; metron; number; scansion.)

Shrovetide play=*carnival comedy.

Sicilian octave; Siciliana [L. of Sicily]; (F. sicilienne; G. Siziliane; S. octava siciliana): a stanza of eight *hendecasyllables rhyming abababab.

Sicilian school (F. école sicilienne; G. Sizilianische Schule; S. escuela siciliana): a group of poets at the court in Palermo of the Hohenstaufen kings Friedrich II (1194 - 1250) and his son, Manfred. The school lasted over fifty years; new poetic forms were developed and Italian was established as a literary language.

Silesian schools (F. écoles silésiennes; G. Schlesische Dichterschulen; S. escuelas silesianas): two groups of German poets of the seventeenth century. The first Silesian school is of great importance to German *baroque literature; members are Martin Opitz, Gryphius, Logau, Dach, Fleming. Members of the second Silesian school are Hofmannswaldau, Lohenstein, and Zigler.

**sillographer** (F. sillographe; G. Sillograph; S. silógrafo): writer of *silloi.

**silloi** [Gk. satirical poems]; (F. sille; G. Sillen; S. poemas siloicos): satirical and polemic poems in hexameters. (**lampoon; sillographer.)

**silva:** a Spanish poem that consists of *hendecasyllables and *heptasyllables.

**simile** [L. similar]; **comparison** (F. similé; G. Vergleich; S. símil): a comparison between two things which are derived from two different areas but share a *tertium comparationis. A simile is usually introduced by a particle such as "like" or "as." (**chiffre; conceit; image; metaphor.)

**sincerity** [L. purity]; (F. sincérité; G. Aufrichtigkeit; S. sinceridad): a term used in connection with the poet's attitude toward his subject; it suggests that he is genuine, unfeigned, and serious in expressing his feelings, ideas, and convictions. (**atmosphere; meaning; message; tone.)

**single rhyme:** *masculine rhyme.

**sirvente; sirventès; serventois; sirventois** [Prov. servant]: a short satirical poem of the Provençal *troubadours. (**courtly song.)

**skald; scald** [Old Norse: poet]; (F. scalde; G. Skalde; S. bardo): a Norse *minstrel or an ancient Scandinavian *bard.

**sketch** [Gk. extempore]; (F. sketch, saynète, esquisse dramatique; G. Sketch, Skizze; S. boceto): a short independent dramatic scene; also a brief descriptive composition or the tentative draft of a literary work. (**character(2); essay; genre picture; skit; vignette.)

**skit** [origin unknown]; (F. pièce satirique, charge, satire; G. Stichelei; S. boceto burlesco, parodia): a satirical or parodical *sketch. (**diatribe; folly literature; lampoon.)

**slack** [L. loose]; (F. thésis, faible; G. Senkung; S. átonas): the unstressed syllables in a metrical foot or the slow part of a rhythmic unit. (**rhythm.)

**slant rhyme:** *imperfect rhyme.

**slapstick** [slap+stick: a stick with flapping ends used in low comedy to simulate a severe blow]; (F. farce, arlequinades; G. Farce, Schwank, Posse; S. farsa): *low comedy.

**slice-of-life; tranche de vie** (F. tranche de vie; G. Sekundenstil; S. trozo de vida): the accurate and unselective reproduction of all the mental and physical reactions of the characters regardless of their relevance; a literary device of *naturalism. (**chosisme; narrative techniques; stream of consciousness technique.)

**sloka** [Sanskrit: hymn]: the verse form of the Sanskrit epics of India (e.g. Mahâbhârata) that consists of two lines (distich) of sixteen syllables each.

**s. m.**=*short meter, short measure.

**socialist realism** (F. réalisme socialiste; G. sozialistischer Realismus; S. realismo socialista): a rigid literary doctrine of communism proclaimed by Maxim Gorky and decreed by the first Soviet Congress of writers in 1934. According to it, writers should depict reality without any individualistic experimentation and in conformity with the optimistic Weltanschauung of communism. Literature should be written in a style understandable to the masses and should deal with the social struggle of positive heroes. (**acmeism; constructivism; formalism(2); magical realism; Neue Sachlichkeit; realism; verism.)

**Socratic irony** [named after the Greek philosopher Socrates, circa 469 - 399 B.C.]; (F. ironie socratique; G. sokratische Ironie; S. ironía socrática): the pretended ignorance and misleading naïveté of a speaker during the course of a discussion, used to weaken and ridicule his partner's point of view. (**irony.)

**solecism** [Gk. incorrect speech]; (F. solécisme; G. Solözismus; S. solecismo): deviation from the accepted rules of grammar and syntax; sometimes regarded as a rhetorical figure (*poetic licence), but usually as an impropriety in speech (*barbarism). (**modulation; substitution.)

**soliloquy** [L. speak alone]; (F. soliloque; G. Soliloquium, Selbstgespräch; S. soliloquio): a discourse or declamation made by a character in a play while standing alone on the stage; it reveals his thoughts and feelings. (**aside; dramatic monologue; dramatic techniques; monodrama; monologue; parabasis.)

**solution**=resolution (*catastrophe).

**song** [OE: to sing]; (F. chanson; G. Lied; S. cancion): a poem, usually stanzaic and rhymed, which could be easily set to music; it is the most popular form of *lyric poetry. (**blues; chanson; courtly song; ditty; folk song; melic poetry; serenade; shanty; spirituals; stave.)

**sonnet** [It. little song]; (F. sonnet; G. Sonett; S. soneto): a poem of Italian origin of fourteen iambic pentameters ($\cup\_\cup\_\cup\_\cup\_\cup\_$) and rhyming abba abba cde cde *or* abba abba cdc dcd (known as the Italian or Petrarchan sonnet). The English or Shakespearean sonnet has the rhyme scheme: abab cdcd efef gg. (**crown of sonnets; curtal sonnet; Miltonic sonnet; quatorzain; sonnet cycle; Spenserian sonnet; tailed sonnet.)

**sonnet cycle; sonnet sequence** (F. cycle de sonnets; G. Sonettenzyklus; S. ciclo de sonetos): a collection of independent *sonnets which deal with the same theme. (**crown of sonnets.)

**Sophoclean irony:** *dramatic irony.

**Sotadean verse** [named after the Greek poet Sotades, circa 250 B.C.]; (F. sotadée; G. Sotadeus; S. verso sotádico): a *brachycatalectic tetrameter of major *ionics: $\_\_\_\cup\cup$ $\_\_\cup\cup\_\_\cup\cup\_\_$

**sotie** [F. foolishness]: a French satirical and farcical play of the fifteenth and sixteenth centuries. (**folly literature; lampoon; low comedy.)

**spasmodic** [Gk. to draw, tug, tear] **school:** a term coined by the English theologian and writer Charles Kingsley in 1853 in connection with a group of popular romantic writers (P. J. Bailey, Alexander Smith) ridiculing them for their emotional outbursts and artistic formlessness. (\*\*Dionysian; dithyramb; Romanticism.)

**spell:** \*charm.

**Spenserian sonnet** [named after the English poet Edmund Spenser, 1552-1599]; (F. sonnet spenserien; G. Spenser-Sonett; S. soneto al estilo de Spenser): a \*sonnet with the rhyme scheme: abab bcbc cdcd ee.

**Spenserian stanza** [named after its inventor Edmund Spenser, 1552 - 1599]; (F. strophe spenserienne; G. Spenser-Strophe; S. estrofa al estilo de Spenser): a \*stanza of eight iambic pentameters and one \*Alexandrine rhyming: ababbcbcc.

**spirituals:** highly rhythmic religious songs of the American negro based among other things on English hymns and French folk songs. (\*\*blues.)

**spondaic verse; spondaic hexameter** (F. vers spondaïque; G. Spondiacus; S. verso espondaico): a \*hexameter whose fifth and sixth feet are \*spondees: ‿‿‿‿‿‿‿‿‿‿‿‿

**spondee** [Gk. of a libation]; (F. spondée; G. Spondeus, Spondäus; S. espondeo): a metrical foot that consists of two long (or two stressed) syllables: ‿‿ ‿.(\*\*dispondee; distributed stress; spondaic verse.)

**spoonerism** [named after the English educator Rev. William A. Spooner, 1844 - 1930]: a comic effect created by the use of \*metathesis—especially of initial sounds—in successive words. (\*\*logogriph; metaplasm; prothesis.)

**sprung rhythm:** a term associated with G. M. Hopkins (1844 - 1889); it refers to rhythm that is based on stressed syllables only, i.e. each foot begins with a stressed syllable followed either by one or more unstressed syllables or by the first stressed syllable of the following foot. (\*\*rhythm; rocking rhythm; running rhythm.)

**stanza** [It. room, living place]; (F. strophe; G. Strophe; S. estrofa): a poem usually consists of a number of uniform or variable rhythmical units called stanzas. A stanza is composed of a certain number of lines arranged according to a fixed metrical pattern. The shortest stanza has two lines (\*couplet), the longest usually has eight lines (\*octave). According to the characteristics of the verse and the rhyme scheme, a stanza can be designated as a heroic \*couplet, \*distich, \*elegiac couplet, \*octosyllabic couplet, \*terza rima, etc. (\*\*Alcaic strophe; astrophic composition; Burns stanza; cinquain; cobla; dizain; elegiac stanza; heptastich; heroic stanza; hexastich; huitain; monostich; octastich; ottava rima; pantoum; pentastich; quatrain; redondilla, rhyme royal; Sapphic; septet; sestet; sestina; Sicilian octave; Spenserian stanza; stave; strophe(3); tercet; tetrastich; triad; triplet; tristich; Venus and Adonis stanza; verse paragraph.)

**stasimon** [Gk. static]: the choral part of ancient Greek tragedy; it follows the \*parodos and alternates with the \*episodes; possibly sung with the chorus standing in its place in the orchestra. (\*\*epirrhema; parabasis.)

**stave** [akin to staff]; (F. couplet; G. Strophe; S. estancia, estrofa): a group of verses or a \*stanza of a \*song.

95

**steady seller:** *best seller.

**stereotype**=*archetype.

**stichomythia; stichomythy** [Gk. dialogue in lines]; (F. stichomythie; G. Stichomythie; S. esticomitia): a dramatic *dialogue spoken in alternating lines to express excitement or anger. If the dialogue is spoken in alternating half lines it is known as hemistichomythia; if spoken in couplets, a distichomythia.

**stock character** (F. type, personnage conventionnel, personnage du répertoire; G. Typ; S. personaje convencional): familiar characters and conventional types. (**archetype; character; commedia dell'arte; flat character; round character.)

**stock epithet:** *epithet.

**stock situation** (F. situation conventionnelle; G. typische Situation; S. situación convencional): a particular situation that recurs in several literary works. (**archetype; motif.)

**Storm and Stress:** *Sturm und Drang.

**stornello** [Prov. contrast]: an Italian folk song of three lines rhyming aba.

**story** [Gk. history, information, narrative]; (F. histoire; G. Geschichte; S. historia, trama): (1) a sequence of incidents arranged exactly as they have occurred; (2) plot outline; (3) a blanket term for short narrative genres such as short story, folk tale, anecdote, fable, fairy story, etc. (**argument; fable(2); narrative poetry; plot.)

**story within a story**=inset story (*frame story).

**strambotto:** an Italian poem of eight *hendecasyllables, which usually rhyme: aabbccdd.

**strategy** [Gk. command of a general]; (F. technique de composition et d'analyse; G. Strategie, Methode; S. enfoque crítico): methods, approaches, and techniques employed by poets and critics in dealing with literary works. (**analysis; apparatus criticus; critique.)

**stream of consciousness technique** (F. technique du flux de conscience; G. Bewuβtseinsstrom-Technik; S. corriente de conciencia): the representation of a character's thoughts and feelings by projecting all the images and ideas that go through his mind no matter how illogical, irrelevant, or inconsistent they might sound (as in E. Dujardin's novel *Les Lauriers sont coupes*, 1887). The term was first used by William James in 1890. (**narrative techniques.)

**stress** [L. to constrain]; (F. accent métrique, ictus; G. Betonung; S. acento tónico): the emphasis given to a syllable or word according to a metrical pattern; a stressed syllable is indicated by the mark: ‿; an unstressed: ◡. (**accentual verse; beat; ictus; logical stress; scansion; slack; tonic.)

**strophe** [Gk. turning]; (F. strophe; G. Strophe; S. estrofa): (1) first part of the choral ode in ancient Greek drama (other parts are *antistrophe and *epode); (2) first part of the triadically constructed *Pindaric stanza; (3) a rhythmic unit of two or more lines within a stanza; (4)= *stanza. (**astrophic composition; mesode; proode; triad; verse paragraph.)

**structure** [L. build]; (F. structure; G. Struktur; S. estructura): the sum of all the intrinsic and extrinsic characteristics of a literary work. A distinction is often made between *intrinsic structure and *extrinsic structure. (**analysis; architectonics; texture.)

**Sturm und Drang** [G. Storm and Stress; the name of a play by Maximilian Klinger, written 1776]; (F. trouble et agitation, tempête et assaut; G. Sturm und Drang; S. Sturm und Drang): a literary movement in Germany in the 1770's and 1780's that was led by young revolutionary writers and directed against the rigid rationalism of the *Enlightenment. Literary works of this movement (Goethe's *Götz*, 1773; Schiller's *Räuber*, 1781) are noted for their realistic language, high emotionalism, rejection of traditional concepts, and subjectivism. The recurring theme is that of the violent revolt of individualistic characters and *Originalgenies* (original geniuses) against injustice. (**Göttinger Hain; irrationalism; Preromanticism.)

**style** [L. an instrument used for writing, manner of writing]; (F. style; G. Stil; S. estilo): the manner in which language is used. (**extrinsic structure; high style; low style; middle style; poetic diction; stylistics.)

**stylistics** [*style]; (F. stylistique; G. Stilistik; S. estilística): the study of the expressive qualities of language. (**style.)

**subaction:** *subplot.

**subjectivity** [L. to throw under, to submit]; (F. subjectivité; G. Subjektivität; S. subjetividad): *objectivity.

**subject matter** (F. sujet; G. Stoff; S. tema, asunto): the factual content of a literary work. (**content; meaning; message; motif; theme; tone.)

**subplot; subaction; counterplot** (F. action secondaire; G. Nebenhandlung; S. intriga secundaria): a secondary plot or subordinate action in a dramatic or narrative work which is related to the main plot. It often parallels the main plot, or relates to the behavior of one of the characters. (**action; plot; unities.)

**substitution** [L. to put in the place of]; (F. substitution; G. Substitution; S. verso cataléctico): a deviation from the metrical pattern; it is caused by substituting one metrical foot for another. (**equivalence; modulation; poetic licence; solecism.)

**substitutionary narration:** *indirect interior monologue.

**surfiction** [L. super-fabrication, above invention]: a term used in connection with extremely experimental fiction and the so-called nouveau nouveau roman. (**antinovel; heterodox novel.)

**surrealism** [F. beyond realism, superrealism]; (F. surréalisme; G. Surrealismus; S. surrealismo): a literary and artistic movement which originated in France after the First World War. It attempted to create the "super-real" by unifying reality and irreality, the conscious and the subconscious regardless of logic, convention, or significance. Rep. André Breton, Paul Eluard. Surrealistic elements can be found in the works of F. Kafka, H. Hesse, J. Joyce, and many others. (**Dadaism; expressionism; futurism; magical realism; realism.)

suspense [L. to hang]; (F. suspense; G. Spannung; S. suspenso): excitement and anxiety caused by uncertainty regarding the outcome of a situation or the resolution of a conflict. *Anticipation, *allusion, *comic, *tragic irony, and similar devices are used to intensify the suspense. (**catastrophe.)

syllaba anceps [L. unstable or doubtful syllable]: a syllable that can be regarded as long or short depending on the metrical pattern and the rhythmic flow of the line. (**distributed stress; recessive accent; rhythm.)

syllable [Gk. to put together]; (F. syllabe; G. Silbe; S. sílaba): an uninterrupted unit of utterance which consists of one or more speech sounds; it is the smallest metrical unit. (**duration; prosody; scansion; syllaba anceps.)

syllepsis [Gk. collection, summary]; (F. syllepse; G. Syllepse; S. silepsis): a grammatical *ellipsis. (**anacoluthon.)

syllogism [Gk. calculation]; (F. syllogisme; G. Syllogismus; S. silogismo): a persuasive, seemingly logical, but often fallacious argument. (**débat; enthymeme; harangue; polemic; tenzone.)

symbol [Gk. sign, token]; (F. symbole; G. Symbol; S. símbolo): a sign that represents an invisible thing or suggests a certain idea. (**allegory; apologue; chiffre; emblem; objective correlative; rebus; symbolism.)

symbolism (F. symbolisme; G. Symbolismus; S. simbolismo): a literary movement which originated in France in the late nineteenth century. It opposed the realistic and naturalistic adherence to the visible and tangible world. The symbolists (Mallarmé, Verlaine, Rimbaud, Rilke, S. George, T. S. Eliot, Yeats, A. Bely, Sologub) aimed at representing ideas, emotions, and "internal realities" by using allusive symbols and words with musical and magical suggestiveness. (**acmeism; futurism; imagism; Hermeticism; Jung-Wien; objective correlative.)

symploce [Gk. plaited together]; (F. symploque; G. Symploke; S.—): a rhetorical figure: a combination of *anaphora and *epiphora. (**anadiplosis, complexio; conduplicatio; palilogy.)

symposium [Gk. drinking together]; (F. symposium; G. Symposion; S. simposio): different opinions expressed at a meeting or collected in a periodical. (**Festschrift; polemic; scolion.)

synaeresis; syneresis [Gk. to contract]; (F. synérèse; G. Synärese; S. sinéresis): occurs when two successive vowels which are ordinarily pronounced separately are pronounced together; usually for metrical reasons. (**aphaeresis; crasis; elision; hiatus; synaloepha.)

synaesthesia; synesthesia [Gk. mixed sensations]; (F. synesthésie; G. Synästhesie; S. sinestesia): the description of sensations or images perceived by one of the senses in terms of another sensory experience.

synaloepha [Gk. fusion]; (F. synalèphe; G. Synalöphe; S. sinalefa): the elimination of a *hiatus by the contraction of the two vowels or the two syllables. (**aphaeresis; crasis; elision; synaeresis.)

**syncope** [Gk. reduction]; (F. syncope; G. Synkope; S. síncope): the intentional omission of a letter or a syllable from the middle of a word. (**apocope; elision; synaloepha.)

**synecdoche** [Gk. understanding along with, seizing at once]; (F. synecdoche, synecdocque; G. Synekdoche; S. sinécdoque): a rhetorical figure: naming a part of an object instead of naming the whole object (pars pro toto); also the other way around. (**antonomasia; metalepsis; metonymy; periphrasis.)

**synonym** [Gk. the same name]; (F. synonyme; G. Synonym; S. sinónimo): a word having the same *denotation—but different *connotation —as another word. (**epanalepsis; pleonasm; tautology.)

**synopsis** [Gk. general view]; (F. synopsis; G. Synopsis; S. sinopsis): *brief.

**syntax** [Gk. arrangement]; (F. syntaxe; G. Syntax; S. sintaxis): the grammatical structure of sentences. (**amphibology; anastrophe; hypallage; hyperbaton; inversion; linguistics; phraseology.)

**syzygy** [Gk. yoked together]; (F. syzygie; G. Syzygie; S. sizigio): the combination of two metrical feet into a *dipody.

# T

**tableau; tableau vivant** [F. living picture]; (F. tableau vivant; G. Tableau; S. cuadro vivo): a spectacular grouping of actors on the stage or of people dressed and posed in imitation of an historical scene or of a famous picture. (**dramatic techniques.)

**Tabulator:** *Meistergesang.

**Tachtigers** [Dutch: of the eighties]: a group of Dutch poets who, in the 1880's, emphasized the importance of spontaneity, individualism, and pure aesthetic values in poetry. Rep. W. Kloos, A. Verwey, L. van Deyssel; organ: *De Nieuwe Gids.* (**aestheticism.)

**Tagelied** [G. dawn song]: *minnesong.

**tailed sonnet** (F. sonnet irrégulier [if consisting of 15 lines: sonnet quinzain; of 16 lines: sonnet seizain; of 18 lines: sonnet à refrains; of 20 lines: sonnet double, or sonnet à codas]; G. Schweifsonett, geschwänztes Sonett; S. soneto irregular): a *sonnet that has more than the usual fourteen lines.

**tail rhyme** (F. rime couée; G. Schweifreim; S.—): the rhyme scheme aabccb. (**rhyme.)

**tale** [OE. story]; (F. récit; G. Erzählung; S. cuento): a prose narrative of limited length and simple structure. (**cautionary tale; exemplum; fabliau; fairy tale; folk tale; narrative poetry; tall tale; tradition.)

**tall tale** (F. histoire extraordinaire; G. Lügendichtung; S. cuento inverosímil): a narrative that deals with highly exaggerated incidents and unbelievable events. (**cock-and-bull story; fairy tale; fantasy fiction; folk tale; narrative poetry; tale; yarn.)

**tautology** [Gk. the same speech]; (F. tautologie; G. Tautologie; S. tautología): a rhetorical figure: using many synonymous words to express one meaning. If the additional words are superfluous and have no poetic merit, it is known as *pleonasm. (**anadiplosis; asyndeton; epanalepsis; hendiadys; polysyndeton.)

**teichoscopy** [Gk. view from the wall]; (F. teichoscopie; G. Teichoskopie, Mauerschau; S. teichoscopía): a dramatic and theatrical device: one of the characters in a play stands on a wall or a watchtower and describes to the other characters—and the audience—something that is ostensibly happening in the distance. (**dramatic techniques.)

**telestich** [Gk. end of verse]; (F. télestiche; G. Telestichon; S. telesticha): occurs when the final letters of the lines or chapters form a word or a phrase. (**acrostic; acroteleutic; cryptogram; mesostich.)

**television play** (F. pièce destinée à la télévision; G. Fernsehspiel; S. teleteatro, comedia televisada): a new dramatic form which relies on the cinema (close-ups, montage, etc.) and on the theater (limited space and limited number of actors). (**radio play.)

**tenor:** *metaphor.

**tenzone** [Prov. quarrel]; (F. tenson; G. Tenzone, Streitgedicht; S. tensón): a stanzaic poem of the Provençal *troubadours in which two poets speak alternate stanzas defending two different points of view. (**amoebean verse; flyting; partimen.)

**tercet** [It. third]; (F. tercet; G. Terzett; S. terceto): a group of three lines of verse. (**stanza; terza rima; triplet.)

**terminal rhyme:** *end rhyme.

**tertium comparationis** [L. the third of the comparison]: a certain characteristic which two basically different things have in common. (**analogy; metaphor; mixed metaphor; simile.)

**terza rima** [It. third rhyme]; (F. terzarima, terzines, rimes-tierces; G. Terzine; S. tercetos encadenados): a poem consisting of *tercets in iambic pentameter ($\cup\_\cup\_\cup\_\cup\_\cup\_$) rhyming aba bcb cdc . . . (**capitolo; stanza.)

**tetralogy** [Gk. four speeches]; (F. tétralogie; G. Tetralogie; S. tetralogía): four independent literary works (dramas, novels) which have a common theme or deal with different aspects of one subject matter. (**dramatic techniques; trilogy.)

**tetrameter** [Gk. four measures]; (F. tétramètre; G. Tetrameter; S. tetrámetro): a line that consists of four metrical feet or of four dipodies. (**verse.)

**tetrapody** [Gk. four feet]; (F. tétrapodie; G. Tetrapodie; S. tetrámetro, tetrapodia): a metrical unit that consists of four feet. (**dimeter; dipody; monopody; tripody.)

**tetrastich** [Gk. four lines]; (F. quatrain; G. Tetrastichon; S. tetrástico): a *stanza or a group of four lines. (**distich; monostich.)

**texture** [L. web]; (F. texture; G. Textur; S. textura): the extrinsic qualities of a limited structural unit. (**architectonics; extrinsic structure; structure.)

**theater of the absurd** (F. théâtre de l'absurde; G. absurdes Drama, absurdes Theater; S. teatro del absurdo): a *grotesque drama that rejects traditional dramatic rules and defies any logical explanation. Rep. Samuel Beckett, Eugène Ionesco. (**drama.)

**theme** [Gk. laid down]; (F. thème; G. Thema; S. tema): the central idea of a literary work or the abstract part of its *subject matter. (**content; meaning; message; motif; tone.)

**thesis** [Gk. down beat, lowering the voice]; (F. thésis; G. Thesis, Senkung; S. tesis): in Gk. prosody: the longer part of a metrical foot; in modern prosody: the unaccented part of a metrical foot. (**arsis; atonic; macron; metron; mora; number; short syllable; tonic.)

**thesis play** (F. pièce à thèse; G. Lehrstück; S. comedia de tesis social): *problem play.

**third person narrative** (F. récit à la troisième personne; G. Er-Form; S. narración en tercera persona): the objective narration of a story by an outsider. (**first person narrative; narrative techniques.)

**three unities:** *unities.

**threnody; threnos** [Gk. lament]; (F. thrénodie; G. Threnodie, Threnos; S. treno)=*dirge.

**thriller** (F. oeuvre à sensation, oeuvre palpitante; G. Reißer; S. novela sensacionalista): an adventurous and highly suspenseful narrative or dramatic work. (**event-novel; penny dreadful; whodunit.)

**time-novel** (F. roman d'une époque; G. Zeit-Roman; S. novela de época): a novel that describes or criticizes the culture and the Zeitgeist of one or more historical epochs such as the historical novel, the period novel, novel of social criticism, sociological novel, political novel, philosophical novel, novel of ideas, humanitarian novel, novel of manners, science fiction, Utopian fiction, and other similar novels. (**narrative poetry; novel.)

**tirade** [F. to pull]; (F. tirade; G. Tirade; S. diatriba): a vehement speech or a pure rhetorical—usually superfluous —passage within a dramatic or narrative work. (**enthymeme; epideictic speech; harangue; purple passage.)

**tmesis** [Gk. cutting]; (F. tmèse; G. Tmesis; S. tmesis): inserting one or more words between the two parts that form a compound word. (**blend.)

**tone** [Gk. tension, cord]; (F. ton; G. Ton; S. tono): the author's frame of mind and his attitude toward the *subject matter, the *theme, the *setting, and the *characters he deals with. (**atmosphere; content; meaning; message; objectivity; sincerity; verisimilitude.)

**tonic** [Gk. with a tone]; (F. tonique; G. tonisch; S. tónico): a stressed syllable. (**atonic; arsis; stress; thesis.)

**topic** [Gk. place]; (F. thème, sujet; G. Topik, Thema; S. tópico)= *theme.

**tornada** [Old Prov. return]: an *envoi or a *refrain.

**tract** [L. discussion]; (F. tract, pamphlet, traité; G. Traktat, Flugschrift, Abhandlung; S. opúsculo): a leaflet, a flyer, or a literary work that is completely devoted to one specific issue, usually a political or religious one. (**essay; polemic.)

tradition [L. handing down, instruction delivered]; (F. tradition; G. Sage; S. tradición): a mythical or historical *folk tale with fantastic elements. (**fairy tale; fantasy fiction; legend; myth; narrative poetry; tale.)

traditional ballad: *folk ballad.

tragedy [Gk. goat's song]; (F. tragédie; G. Tragödie; S. tragedia): the dramatic treatment of a *tragic subject matter. (**bourgeois tragedy; drama.)

tragic (F. tragique; G. tragisch; S. trágico): tragic differs from sad or pathetic (*pathos) in that it refers to a conflict or a struggle between a person obsessed by certain ideals and beliefs (*hamartia, *hybris) and a superior force which leads to his downfall. (**comic; drama; dramatic techniques.)

tragic flow: *hamartia.

tragic irony: *dramatic irony.

tragicomedy [tragic+comedy]; (F. tragicomédie; G. Tragikomödie; S. tragicomedia): (1) a drama that revolves around a tragic conflict but has a happy ending; (2) a tragedy endowed with comic elements (*comic relief). (**drama.)

tranche de vie: *slice-of-life.

transferred epithet: *hypallage.

travelogue; travelog [travel+logue (talk)]; (F. conférence ou livre décrivant un voyage, une expédition; G. Reisebericht, Reisebeschreibung; S. libro de viaje): a lecture on travel or a book that depicts a journey.

travesty [It. to disguise]; (F. parodie, travestissement; G. Travestie; S.

travestía): a literary work that deals with the subject matter of another work whilst ridiculing its style. (**parody; pastiche.)

triad [Gk. a group of three]; (F. triade épodique; G. Triade; S. tríada): a group of three stanzas: *strophe, *antistrophe, and *epode.

tribrach [Gk. three short]; (F. tribraque; G. Tribrachys; S. tribraquio): a metrical foot that consists of three short (in *quantitative verse) or three unstressed (in *accentual verse) syllables: ◡◡◡. (**proceleusmatic; pyrrhic.)

triglot [Gk. three-tongued]; (F. édition triglotte; G. Triglotte; S. trilingüe): a book that contains a text in three different languages. (**interlinear; polyglot.)

trilogy [Gk. three speeches]; (F. trilogie, G. Trilogie; S. trilogía): three independent literary works (dramas or novels) which have a common theme or which deal with different aspects of the same subject. (**satyr play; tetralogy.)

trimeter [Gk. three measures]; (F. trimètre; G. Trimeter; S. trímetro): a line of three metrical feet or of three dipodies. (**verse.)

triolet [F. dim. of It. trio=3]; (F. triolet; G. Triolett; S. triolet): a short epigrammatic poem of eight lines rhyming ABaAabAB (capital letters= repeated lines). (**epigram.)

triple meter (F. tripodie, pied trisyllabique; G. Tripodie; S. trisilábico): (1) a *tripody; (2) a metrical foot of three syllables.

triple rhyme: *polysyllabic rhyme.

triplet [L. triple]; (F. tercet à rimes triplées; G. Dreireim; S. terceto monorrimo): a *tercet usually rhyming aaa.

tripody [Gk. three feet]; (F. tripodie; G. Tripodie; S. tripodia): a single measure that consists of three metrical feet. (**dimeter; dipody; monopody; tetrapody.)

tristich [Gk. three lines]; (F. tercet, tristique; G. Tristichon; S. terceto): a *stanza or a poem of three lines. (**monostich.)

tritagonist: *protagonist.

trithemimeral [Gk. third half]; (F. trihémimère; G. Trithemimeres; S. triemímeris): a *caesura after the second stressed (or long) syllable (the third half foot). (**hephthemimeral; hexameter; penthemimeral.)

trivial literature [L. common writing]; (F. littérature populaire; G. Trivial-literatur; S. seudoliteratura): a kind of literature written for no informative, instructive, or poetic reason, but merely to amuse and entertain the masses of moderately educated readers and help them escape from the hard realities of life into an adventurous and fantastic world. (**belletristic literature; esoteric; exoteric; literature; para-literature; poetry.)

trochee [Gk. running]; (F. trochée; G. Trochäus; S. troqueo): a metrical foot that consists of one stressed (or long) syllable followed by an unstressed (or short) one: _◡. (**foot; ditrochee; iamb; prosody.)

trochaic (F. trochaïque; G. trochäisch; S. trocaico): consisting of *trochees. (**iambic.)

trochaic dimeter: *trochaic; *dimeter.

trope [Gk. turn]; (F. trope; G. Trope, Tropus; S. tropo): a blanket term for rhetorical figures which are based on using words or phrases in a sense that does not properly belong to them, such as *metaphor or *metonymy.

tropisme [Gk. the turning of an organism in response to an external stimulus]: a narrative technique based upon a detailed description of a person's introspective reactions to external stimuli and his subjective impressions of the things surrounding him (Nathalie Sarraute's *Tropismes*, 1939). (**antinovel; chosisme; digression; narrative techniques.)

troubadour [Prov. inventor]: a Provençal lyric poet and *minstrel (twelfth, thirteenth, and fourteenth centuries); contemporary of the *trouvère of northern France and the *minnesinger of Germany. (**courtly love; courtly song; sirvente; tenzone.)

trouvère [F. to find]: narrative and lyric poet of northern France during the twelfth, thirteenth, and fourteenth centuries; contemporary of the *troubadour of southern France and the *minnesinger of Germany. (**chanson de geste.)

true alliteration: *alliteration(1).

true rhyme: *perfect rhyme.

truncation [L. cut off]=*catalexis.

tumbling verse: an English verse of four stressed syllables and any number of unstressed syllables. (**Knittelvers.)

# U

ubi sunt [L. where are] **motif:** a *motif in lyric poetry which refers to the transitory nature of things. (**carpe diem; Goliardic verse.)

Ultraismo; Ultraism [L. beyond]: a Spanish literary movement related to *Creacionismo that started after the First World War and lasted until 1925. Representatives of this movement (the Spaniards G. de Torre and Gerardo Diego; the Latin-Americans C. Vallejo and J. L. Borges) aimed at freeing poetry from rhetorical effects, traditional styles, and conventional images.

understatement: **litotes; meiosis; irony.

unities, the three (F. règle des trois unités; G. die drei Einheiten; S. las tres unidades): a dramatic principle formulated in the sixteenth century and based on Aristotle's *Poetics;* it decrees that a play should observe the three unities of action, time, and place: (1) the action should be free of any irrelevancies such as subplots or independent episodes; (2) the time of the action should not extend beyond one day or twenty-four hours; (3) a play should not have more than one setting or one locale. (**dramatic techniques.)

universality [L. entire, whole]; (F. universalité; G. Universalität; S. universalidad): a quality attributed to literary works which are enduringly valid and relevant to all mankind. (**classic; concrete.)

University Wits: a group of Elizabethan writers with a university training (J. Lyly, Thomas Nashe, George Peele, Robert Greene).

up beat (F. atone; G. atonisch; S. atónico): a term sometimes used instead of *atonic.

Utopian fiction; Utopian novel; Utopian literature [Gk. no place]; (F. création utopiste; G. utopische Literatur; S. literatura utópica): literary works that describe imaginary countries or regions of ideal perfection; named after Sir Thomas More's *Utopia* (1516). (**fantasy fiction; science fiction; time-novel.)

ut pictura poesis [L. like a picture is poetry; Horace: *Ars Poetica,* L361]: a poetic theory which stresses the descriptive function of poetry and compares it with painting.

# V

variable syllable=*distributed stress.

variety show=*burlesque(3); *vaudeville.

vaudeville [F. a song of the valley of Vire]: a musical farce or a variety show. (**burlesque; musical drama; opera; operetta; revue.)

vehicle: *metaphor.

verbosity [L. wordiness]; (F. verbosité, prolixité; G. Wortschwall; S. verbosidad): a tedious style marked by wordiness and prolixity. (**euphuism; logorrhoea; Marinism; orotund; preciosity.)

Venus and Adonis stanza [called after Shakespeare's poem *Venus and Adonis*]: a *stanza of six iambic pentameters (◡‿◡‿◡‿◡‿◡‿) rhyming ababcc.

**verbal irony** (F. ironie d'opposition, antiphrase, anticatastase; G. verbale Ironie; S. ironía verbal): a remark that implies the opposite of what it states. (**irony.)

**Verfremdungseffekt:** *epic drama.

**verisimilitude** [L. appears as true]; (F. vraisemblance; G. Wahrscheinlichkeit; S. verosimilitud): the plausibility of a literary work. (**atmosphere; sincerity; tone.)

**verism** [L. true]; (F. vérisme; G. Verismus; S. verismo): an extreme realistic, rather naturalistic way of depicting reality. (**naturalism; Neue Sachlichkeit; realism; socialist realism.)

**vernacularism** [L. native]; (F. usage vernaculaire, langue vernaculaire; G. mundartlicher Ausdruck, Umgangssprache; S. regionalismo): using the language or the dialect of a particular region rather than the accepted literary language. (**idiom; jargon; provincialism; regionalism; vulgarism.)

**vers de société** [F. society verse]: *light verse noted for its grace, humor, and wit. (**anacreontic poetry; occasional verse; rococo.)

**verse** [L. furrow, row, line, verse]; **line** (F. vers; G. Vers; S. verso): a metrical line of a poem; a rhythmical unit that consists of smaller rhythmical units known as feet. A paragraph of such lines is called a *stanza. Verse is distinguished according to the number (one=monometer; two=dimeter; three=trimeter; four=tetrameter; five=pentameter; six=hexameter; seven=heptameter; eight=octameter) or kind (iambic, trochaic, etc.) of feet it has, or according to both number and kind (trochaic pentameter, iambic hexameter, etc.). (**metrics; octonarius; octosyllabic; prosody; rhyme; rhythm; scansion.)

**verse paragraph** (F. période poétique; G. Vers-Paragraph; S. período poético): a group of metrical lines which form an intrinsical unit. (**stanza; strophe(3).)

**verset** [Prov. dim. of verse]; (F. verset; G.—; S. prosa poética): sonorous and rhythmic prose noted for its long lines and lofty feeling. (**free verse; polyphonic prose; prose poem; vers libre.)

**versification** [L. to make verses]; (F. versification; G. Verskunst, Versbau; S. versificación): *prosody.

**versi sciolti** [It. unbound verse, free verse]: unrhymed *hendecasyllable that was used in medieval Italian epics.

**vers libre** [F. free verse]: a verse form that does not adhere to a fixed metrical pattern; it differs from *free verse in that it uses rhyme. (**polyphonic prose; prose poem; verset.)

**verso sdruccido** [It. sliding verse]: a verse that has a dactylic ending (‿◡◡).

**verso tronco:** in Italian prosody: a verse that ends with an accented syllable. (**masculine ending.)

**Victorian** (F. victorien; G. victorianisch, victorianer; S. victoriano): a term applied to the literature as well as to the moral standards (moralistic, hypocritical, and narrow-minded) of the age of Queen Victoria of England (reigned 1837 - 1901). (**Caroline period; Cavalier poets; Edwardian; Elizabethan; Georgian poets; Jacobean; Restoration.)

**viewpoint**=*point of view.

**vignette** [F. little vine]; (F. pochade, saynète; G. Skizze; S. viñeta): a literary *sketch or a short descriptive *essay. (**idyll; genre picture.)

**villain** [L. pertaining to a farm, peasant]; (F. traître; G. Bösewicht; S. antagonista): the character who opposes the *protagonist, also known as *antagonist or counterplayer. (**character.)

**villancico** [S. of the village]: a Spanish folk song with refrain; also a popular religious song or a Christmas carol.

**villanelle** [It. of the countryside]: a stanzaic *pastoral song with refrain.

**virelay**: *virelai.

**virelai** [F. probably a refrain used in songs]; **virelay; chanson baladée:** a French stanzaic song with two rhymes and a *refrain.

**virgin play** (F. miracle de Notre-Dame; G. Marienspiel; S. comedia mariana, auto sacramental): a *miracle play that deals with the virgin Mother Mary. (**drama; liturgical drama.)

**vision:** *dream allegory.

**voice** [L. to call]; (F. narrateur, commentateur; G. Erzähler; S. voz): the speaker or the narrator who, like other personae, should not be identified with the author. (**narrative techniques.)

**volta** [It. turn]; (F. tournant; G. Volta; S. vuelta): a change in thought or mood; an intrinsical turning point in a poem. (**peripeteia.)

**vorticism** [L. a rotary movement]; (F. vorticisme; G. Vortizismus; S. vorticismo): a short-lived artistic and literary movement in the second decade of the twentieth century (Wyndham Lewis's *Blast*, 1914 - 15) related to *imagism, futurism, cubism, and *abstract poetry. Rep. E. Pound, T. S. Eliot, T. E. Hulme.

**vowel rhyme:** *assonance.

**vulgarism** [L. common, of the mob]; (F. vulgarité; G. Vulgarismus; S. procacidad): the extensive use of profane and coarse expressions in a literary work. (**barbarism; billingsgate; diatribe; lampoon; persiflage; philippic; vernacularism.)

# W

**weak ending** (F. terminaison féminine; G. schwach, weiblich; S. terminación débil, terminación femenina) =*feminine ending.

**wedding poem**=*epithalamium.

**wedge verse**=*rhopalic verse.

**Weltanschauung** [G. world view]: a person's philosophical view or his conception of the world. (**Zeitgeist.)

**Weltschmerz** [G. world pain]: a sentimental and pessimistic outlook caused by a dissatisfaction with the actual state of the world. (**decadence.)

**Western** (F. western; G. Wildwestroman, Wildwestgeschichte; S.

novela del Oeste, western): an adventure story that deals with frontier life in the western parts of the United States during the second half of the nineteenth century. (**event-novel.)

**whodunit** [Engl. who done it]: an exciting and highly suspenseful crime story; also presented as a play or a film. (**event-novel; penny dreadful; thriller.)

**wine song** (F. chanson à boire; G. Weinlied; S. canción anacreóntica): a song that praises wine and glorifies its characteristics and effects.

(**anacreontic poetry; carpe diem; drinking song.)

**wit** [OHG. to know]; (F. repartie, esprit; G. geistreicher Einfall, Esprit, Witz; S. agudeza): ingenuity, creative imagination, and astuteness of perception. Wit is indispensable for creating and appreciating humorous, ironic, and satirical literature. (**bon mot.)

**wordplay** (F. jeu de mots; G. Wortspiel; S. juego de palabras): a speech, a dialogue, or a text which wittingly exploits the peculiarities of words. (**homographs; homonyms; homophones; paronomasia; pun.)

# Y

**yarn** [OHG. a fiber used in manufacturing thread]; (F. conte, histoire; G. Garn; S. cuento popular): an adventurous story or a *tall tale.

(**cock-and-bull story; fantasy fiction; fairy tale; narrative poetry.)
**Young Germany:** *Junges Deutschland.
**Young Vienna:** *Jung-Wien.

# Z

**Zeitgeist** [G. spirit of the time]: the moral tendencies and intellectual trends characteristic of a certain era. (**time-novel; Weltanschauung.)

**zeugma** [Gk. to yoke]; (F. zeugme; G. Zeugma; S. zeugma): the use of one verb to govern two nouns, each in a different way.

# INDEX

## French

A

abstrait: abstract
accent: accent
accent affectif: distributed stress
accent d'insistance: emphasis
    : logical stress
accent emphatique: emphasis
accent mobile: distributed stress
accent régressif: recessive accent
acéphale: acephalous
acmeisme: acmeism
acroteleuton: acroteleutic
acrostiche: acrostic
acrostiche alphabétique: abecedarian
acte: act
action: action
    : plot
action secondaire: subplot
adage: adage
adonique: Adonic verse
adynaton: adynaton
agon: agon
alexandrin: Alexandrine
aliénation: estrangement effect
allégorie: allegory
allitération: alliteration
allocution: oration
allusion: allusion
almanach: almanac
ambiance: mood
ambiguïté: ambiguity
amour courtois: courtly love
amphibologie: amphibology
amphibraque: amphibrach
amphimace: amphimacer
amplification: amplification
ana: ana
    : jestbook
anaclase: anaclasis
anacoluthe: anacoluthon
anacréontique: anacreontic poetry
anacrouse: anacrusis
anadiplose: anadiplosis
anagnorisis: anagnonrisis
anagogie: anagoge
anagramme: anagram
analecta: analects
analectes: analects
analogie: analogy
analyse: analysis

anapeste: anapaest
anaphore: anaphora
anastrophe: anastrophe
anecdote: anecdote
annales: annals
anonyme: anonymous
antagoniste: antagonist
antanaclase: antanaclasis
antépénultième: antepenult
anthologie: anthology
anthropomorphisme: anthropomorphism
antibacchée: antibacchius
anticatastase: verbal irony
anticipation: anticipation
anticlimax: anticlimax
antienne: antiphon
anti-héros: antihero
antimasque: antimasque
antiphrase: verbal irony
antiroman: antinovel
antispaste: antispast
antistrophe: antistrphe
antithèse: antithesis
antonomase: antonomasia
antonyme: antonym
aparté: aside
aphérèse: aphaeresis
aphorisme: aphorism
apocalyptique: apocalyptic
apocope: apocope
apocryphe: apocrypha
apollinien: Apollonian
apologie: apology
apologue: apologue
apophthegme: apophthegm
aposiopèse: aposiopesis
apostrophe: apostrophe
appareil critique: apparatus criticus
Arcadie: Arcadia
archaïsme: archaism
archétype: archetype
architectonique: architectonics
argument: argument
aria: aria
arlequinade: harlequinade
    : slapstick
arrière-plan: setting
arsis: arsis
art nouveau: Jugendstil

**109**

assonance: assonance
asyndète: asyndeton
atellanes: Atellan fables
atmosphére: atmosphere
atone: atonic
   : up beat

attitude: attitude
aubade: aubade
autobiographie: autobiography
avant-garde: avant-garde
avant-propos: foreword

## B

bacchique: bacchius
ballade: ballad
ballade littéraire: art ballad
ballade populaire: folk ballad
bande dessinée: comics
bande illustrée
barbarisme: barbarism
barde: bard
baroque: baroque
belles lettres: belletristic literature
bestiaire: bestiary

best-seller: best seller
bibliographie: bibliography
bienséance: decorum
biographie: biography
bont mot: bon mot
bouffonnerie: folly literature
brachycatalectique: brachycatalectic
brachycatalexe: brachycatalexis
burlesque: burlesque
burletta: burletta
byronien: Byronic

## C

cacophonie: cacophony
cadence: cadence
cadre: background
calembour: pun
canon: canon
cantate: cantata
canticum: canticum
cantique: canticle
canzone: canzone
caractère sans imprévu: flat character
caractérisation: characterization
caricature: caricature
catabase: catabasis
catachrèse: catachresis
catalexe: catalexis
catastase: catastasis
catastase référentielle: comic
catastrophe: catastrophe
catharsis: catharsis
censurer: bowdlerize
centon: cento
césure: break
   : caesura
césure médiane: medial caesura
césure penthémimère: penthemimeral caesura
chanson: chanson
   : song
chanson à boire: drinking song
     : wine song
chanson de bord: shanty
chanson de geste: chanson de geste
     : heroic epic
chanson de marin: shanty
chanson de table: scolion
chanson enfantine: children's song

chanson de toile: chanson de toile
chanson de troubadour: courtly song
chanson de trouvère: courtly song
chansonnette: ditty
chanson populaire: broadside ballad
     : folk song
chant: canto
chant de noël: carol
chant funèbre: dirge
chant mélopée: chant
chapitre: chapter
charade: charade
     : conundrum
charge: skit
chiasma: chiasmus
chiasme: chiasmus
charme: charm
choeur: chorus
choliambe: choliamb
choriambe: choriamb
chrestomathie: chrestomathy
chronique: chronicle
chronogramme: chronogram
chute de l'action: falling action
cinquain: cinquain
circonlocution: circumlocution
citation: quotation
classicisme: classicism
classique: classic
clausule: line endings
clerihew: clerihew
cliché: cliché
     : dead metaphor
     : hackneyed expression
climax: climax

collage: collage
côlon: colon
comédie: comedy
comédie bouffonne: low comedy
comédie carnavalesque: carnival comedy
comédie de caractère: comedy of character
comédie de moeurs: comedy of manners
comédie d'intrigue: comedy of intrigue
: comedy of situation
: intrigue
comédie larmoyante: comedy of tears
comédie musicale: ballad opera
: musical drama
comique: comic
comma: comma
commentateur: voice
compensation: compensation
complainte: complaint
complexion: complexio
composition stichique: astrophic composition
comptine: children's song
conceptisme: conceplism
concetti: conceit
concetti métaphysiques: metaphysical conceits
concetti pétrarquistes: Petrarchan conceits
concret: concrete
concretisme: concretism
conduplication: conduplicatio
confident: confidant
confidente: confidant
conglobation d'impossibilités: adynation
connotation: connotation
consonance: consonance

constructivisme: constructivism
conte: yarn
conte de fées: fairy tale
conte moral: cautionary tale
contenu: content
contraste: antithesis
contrefaçon: contrafacture
contrepoint: counterpoint rhythm
convention: convention
correction: correctio
couleur locale: local color
coupe: break
coupe féminine: feminine caesura
coupe masculine: masculine caesura
couplet: stave
couronne de sonnets: crown of sonnets
crase: crasis
création utopiste: Utopian fiction
crétique: cretic
crise: crisis
critique: critique
: review
critique des intentions: intentional fallacy
critique impressioniste: impressionistic criticism
: affective fallacy
critique par l'effet: affective fallacy
cryptogramme: cryptogram
cubisme: cubism
cultéranisme: culteranism
cultisme: cultism
cycle d'Arthur: Arthurian romance
cycle de sonnets: sonnet cycle
cynisme: cynicism

## D

dactyle: dactyl
dadaïsme: Dadaism
débat: débat
décadence: decadence
décasyllabe: decasyllable
décor: setting
décors: pageant
dénotation: denotation
dénouement: denouement
: resolution
détente comique: comic relief
deutéragoniste: deuteragonist
devinette: riddle
dialogue: dialogue
: duologue
diasyrme: romantic irony
diatribe: diatribe
diction: poetic diction
didactique: didactic literature
diérèse: diaeresis

digression: digression
dïiambe: diiamb
dimètre: dimeter
dionysiaque: Dionysian
dipodie: dipody
discours: oration
discours épidéictique: epideictic speech
dispondée: dispondee
disposition des rimes: rhyme scheme
dissonance: dissonance
dissyllabique: disyllabic
distichomythie: distichomythia
distique: couplet
: distich
distique d'octosyllabes: octosyllabic couplet
distique épigrammatique: closed couplet
dit: dit
dithyrambe: dithyramb
ditrochée: ditrochee
divertissement du carnaval: carnival comedy

dizain: decastich  
: dizain  
dochmiaque: dochmius  
double entente: double entendre  
dramatique: dramatic  
dramaturgie: dramatics  
: dramaturgy  
drame: drama  

: drame  
drame bourgeois: bourgeois drama  
drame épique: epic drama  
drame liturgique: liturgical drama  
drame satyrique: satyr play  
droit d'auteur: copyright  
duodrame: duologue  
durée: duration  

E

écho: echo  
: echo verse  
école sicilienne: Sicilian school  
écoles silésiennes: Silesian schools  
écrivaillon: penny-a-liner  
édition ne varietur: definitive edition  
édition polyglotte: polyglot  
édition triglotte: triglot  
églogue: eclogue  
: pastoral poetry  
élégie: elegy  
élision: elision  
ellipse: ellipsis  
éloge: eulogy  
éloquence: eloquence  
emblème: emblem  
énallage: enallage  
enclitique: enclitic  
encomion: encomium  
enjambement: enjambment  
enthymème: enthymeme  
envoi: envoi  
épanadiplose: epanadiplosis  
épanalepse: epanalepsis  
épanode: epanodos  
épicédion: epicedium  
épigones: epigonism  
épigramme: epigram  
épigraphe: epigraph  
épilogue: epilogue  
épiphore: epiphora  
épirrhème: epirrhema  
épisode: episode  
épistrophe: complexio  
épitaphe: epitaph  
épitase: epitasis  
: initial incident  
épithalame: epithalamium  
épithète: epithet  
épitomé: epitome  
épître: epistle  
épitrite: epitrite  
épizeuxe: epizeuxis  

épode: epode  
épopée: epic  
: epos  
: epopee  
épopée animale: beast epic  
épopée badine: mock epic  
épopée chrétienne: Christian epic  
épopée courtoise: courtly epic  
épopée galante: metrical romance  
épopée historique: historic epic  
épopée nationale: national epic  
épopée primitive: folk epic  
épopée savante: art epic  
époque de la reine Anne: Augustan period  
époque médiévale: medieval period  
équilibre: balance  
équivalence: equivalence  
expurger: bowdlerize  
erreur tragique: hamartia  
ésotérique: esoteric  
esprit: wit  
esquisse dramatique: sketch  
essai: essay  
esthétisme: aestheticism  
euphémisme: euphemism  
euphonie: euphony  
euphuisme: euphuism  
événement initial: initial incident  
excursus: excursus  
exégèse: exegesis  
exemplum: exemplum  
existentialisme: existentialism  
exode: exodus  
exodos: exodus  
exorde: exordium  
exotérique: exoteric  
exotisme: exoticism  
explétif: expletive  
explication: explication  
exposition: exposition  
: protasis  
expressionisme: expressionism

fable: fable
fabliau: fabliau
fabula atellana: Atellan fables
faible: slack
farce: droll
: farce
: slapstick
fatras: fatras
Félibrige: Félibrige
feuilleton: feuilleton
feuilleton à gros effets: penny dreadful
fiction: fiction

figuré: figurative
figures de rhétorique: figures of speech
: rhetorical figures
fin de siècle: fin de siècle
fin du vers: line endings
flashback: flashback
formalisme: formalism
forme: form
forme lâche: open form
formule: formula
fragment: fragment
futurisme: futurism

galliambe: galliamb
gallicisme: Gallicism
genre: genre
géorgique: georgic
geste: gest

ghazel: ghazel
glose: gloss
glyconique: Glyconic
gongorisme: Gongorism
grotesque: grotesque

hagiographie: hagiography
harangue: harangue
haute comédie: high comedy
hemiepes: hemiepes
hémistiche: hemistich
hémistichomythie: hemistichomythia
hendécasyllabe: hendecasyllable
hendiadys: hendiadys
heptamètre: heptameter
heptasyllabe: heptasyllable
hepthémimère: hephthemimeral
hermétisme: Hermeticism
héros: hero
hexamètre: hexameter
hiatus: hiatus
histoire: story
: yarn
histoire abracadabrante: extravaganza
histoire de pure invention: cock-and-bull story
histoire extraordinaire: tall tale
homélie: homily
homilétique: homiletics

homoeomère: homoeomeral
homoeotéleute: homoeoteleuton
homéoptote: homoioptoton
homogrammes: homographs
homographes: homographs
homonymes: homonyms
homophones: homophones
homophone équivoque: homophones
huitain: huitain
: octastich
: octet
humanisme: Humanism
humour: humor
hybris: hybris
hymne: hymn
hypallage: hypallage
hyperbate: hyperbaton
hyperbole: hyperbole
hypermètre: hypermetric
hypobole: procatalepsis
hypotaxe: hypotaxis

iambe: iamb
iambique: iambic
ictus: accent
: beat
: ictus
: stress
idéalisme: idealism
idéogramme lyrique: carmen figuratum
idiome: idiom
idylle: idyll

image: image
image tangentielle: chiffre
imagisme: imagism
imitation: imitation
impressionisme: impressionism
incantation: incantation
incarnation: empathy
incongruité: incongruity
index: index
in-folio: folio

insinuation: innuendo
interlude: intermezzo
intermède: interlude
 : intermezzo
interpolation: interpolation
interprétation: interpretation
interrogation oratoire: rhetorical question
intrigue: intrigue
 : plot
invective: invective

jargon: cant
 : jargon
jeu de mots: wordplay
 : pun
jeu de rime: nonsense verse
jeune-Allemagne: Junges Deutschland

kommos: commus

lai: courtly song
 : lai
lamentation: plaint
langage des halles: billingsgate
langage imagé: figurative language
 : imagery
langue vernaculaire: vernacularism
l'art pour l'art: aestheticism
légende: legend
légende populaire: folk tale
leitmotiv: leitmotif
lettrisme: letterism
lever de rideau: curtain raiser
libelle: lampoon
licence poétique: poetic licence
lignard: penny-a-liner
ligne: line
limerick: limerick
linguistique: linguistics
lipogramme: lipogram

madrigal: madrigal
maniérisme: mannerism
manifestation: epiphany
mansion: pageant
manuel de savoir-vivre: book of manners
marinisme: Marinism
marque de longueur: macron
mascarade: mummery
masque: masque
maxime: maxim
mélodrame: drame
 : melodrama

inversion: inversion
invocation: invocation
ionique: Ionic
ironie: irony
ironie d'opposition: verbal irony
ironie du sort: irony of fate
ironie romanesque: romantic irony
ironie socratique: Socratic irony
ironie tragique: dramatic irony
irrationalisme: irrationalism

## J

jeune-Vienne: Jung-Wien
jeu parti: partimen
journal intime: diary
journal particulier: diary
justice poétique: poetic justice
juxtaposes: pageant

## K

## L

litanie: litany
litote: litotes
 : meiosis
littérature: literature
littérature alimentaire: potboiler
littérature amérindienne: Amerind literature
littérature didactique: didactic literature
littérature marginale: paraliterature
littérature populaire: trivial literature
littérature provençale: Provençal literature
livre blanc: Blue Book
livre de colportage: chapbook
livret: libretto
logaédique: logaoedic
logogriphe: logogriph
logomachie: logomachy
logorrhée: logorrhoea
longue nouvelle: long-short story
longueur: longueur

## M

mélopée: chant
mémoires: memoirs
ménestrel: minstrel
merveilleux, le: machinery
mésode: mesode
mésostiche: mesostich
message: message
mesure: foot
métalepse: metalepsis
métaphore: metaphor
métaphore disparate: mixed metaphor
métaphore incohérente: mixed metaphor

métaphore vieillie: dead metaphor
métaplasme: metaplasm
métathèse: metathesis
métonymie: metonymy
mètre: meter
 : metron
mètre binaire: duple meter
métrique: metrics
mime: mime
mimèse: imitation
 : mimesis
miracle: miracle play
miracle de Notre-Dame: virgin play
mise-en-scène: mise-en-scène
modulation: modulation
molosse: molossus
moment de l'action: fable time
monodie: monody
monologue: monologue
monologue dramatique: dramatic monologue
monologue intérieur: interior monologue
monomètre: monometer
monopodie: monopody
monorime: monorhyme

narrateur omniscient: omniscient narrator
naturalisme: naturalism
némésis: nemesis
néo-classicisme: neoclassicism
néo-gongorisme: Neo-Gongorism
néologisme: neologism
néo-romantisme: neoromanticism
Nô: Nô
nombre: number

objectivisme: objectivism
objectivité: objectivity
octamètre: octameter
octave: octave
octomètre: octapody
octonaire: octonarius
octosyllabique: octosyllabic
ode: ode
ode horatienne: Horatian ode
ode pindarique: Pindaric ode
oeuvre à sensation: thriller
oeuvre à tiroirs: episodic structure

paean: paean
palimbacchée: palimbacchius
palindrome: palindrome
palinlogie: palilogy
palinodie: palinode
 : palinodic
pamphlet: tract

monostique: monostich
monosyllabique: monosyllabic
montage: montage
morale: message
 : moral
moralité: morality play
morceau de bravoure: purple passage
more: mora
mot de circonstance: nonce word
mot piquant: quip
mot télescopé: blend
motif: motif
motif central: central motif
motif récurrent: central motif
motivation: motivation
moyen âge: medieval period
multisonance à l'initiale: homoiarcton
mystère: Corpus Christi play
 : mystery play
mystère de la Passion: passion play
mysticisme: mysticism
mythe: myth
mythologie: mythology
narrateur: voice

**N**

nom de guerre: pseudonym
nom de plume: pseudonym
nouveau roman: experimental novel
nouveau nouveau roman: experimental novel
nouvelle: nouvella
 : novelette
 : short story
nouvelle critique: new criticism

**O**

oeuvre de fiction: fiction
oeuvre fantaisiste: extravaganza
oeuvre palpitante: thriller
onomatopée: onomatopoeia
opéra: opera
opérette: ballad opera
 : operetta
oratorio: oratorio
orgueil fatal: hybris
ottava rima: ottava rima
oxymoron: oxymoron

**P**

panégyrique: panegyric
pantomime: dumb show
 : pantomime
pantoum: pantoum
parabase: parabasis
parabole: parable
paradoxe: paradox

paragoge: paragoge
paralittérature: paraliterature
parallélisme: parallelism
paraphrase: paraphrase
parataxe: parataxis
parémiaque: paroemiac
Parnassiens: Parnassians
parodie: parody
　　　: travesty
parodos: parodos
paronomase: paronomasia
pasquin: pasquinade
pasquinade: lampoon
Passion: Corpus Christi play
pastiche: pastiche
pastorale: pastoral poetry
pastourelle: pastourelle
pathos: pathos
pathos outrancier: bathos
pause: break
　　　: rest
péan: paean
peinture de genre: genre picture
pentamètre: pentameter
pentapodie: pentapody
penthémimère: penthemimer
pénultième: penult
péon: paeon
période: period
période élisabéthaine: Elizabethan age
période poétique: verse paragraph
péripétie: peripeteia
périphrase: periphrasis
péroraison: peroration
persiflage: persiflage
personnage: character
　　　: persona
personnage complexe: round character
personnage conventionnel: stock character
personnage du répertoire: stock character
personnage énigmatique: round character
personnification: personification
　　　　　: poetic fallacy
pétrarquisme: Petrarchism
petit roman à bon marché: novelette
petit rondel: rondelet
phalécien: Phalaecean
phérécratéen: Pherecratean
philippique: philippic
phraséologie: phraseology
pièce à un personnage: monodrama
pièce à thèse: problem play
　　　: thesis play
pièce dans la pièce: play within a play
pièce de salon: conversation piece
pièce de mardi gras: carnival comedy

pièce destinée à la télévision: television play
pièce didactique expérimentale: living newspaper
pièce en un acte: one-act play
pièce historique: chronicle play
　　　: historical play
pièce populaire: folk play
pièce radiophonique: radio play
pièce satirique: skit
pied: foot
pied à rythme descendant: falling meter
pied trisyllabique: triple meter
piétisme: Pietism
plagiat: plagiarism
plainte: plaint
platitude: platitude
Pléiade: Pléiade
pléonasme: pleonasm
pochade: vignette
poème: carmen
　　　: poem
poème alexandrin: epyllion
poème amébée: amoebean verse
poème en prose: prose poem
poème héroï-comique: mock epic
poème idéogrammatique: carmen figuratum
poème idéogrammatique en forme d'autel:
　　　altar poem
poème nuptial: epithalamium
poésie: poesie
　　　: poetry
poésie abstraite: abstract poetry
poésie animale: animal poetry
poésie bucolique: bucolic poetry
poésie d'amour: love poetry
poésie de circonstance: light verse
　　　　　: occasional verse
poésie de l'aube: aubade
poésie dramatique: dramatic poetry
poésie épique: narrative poetry
poésie érotique: erotic poetry
poésie gnomique: gnomic poetry
poésie goliardique: Goliardic verse
poésie héroïque: heroic poetry
poésie légère: light verse
poésie lyrique: lyric poetry
poésie macaronique: macaronic poetry
poésie mélique: melic poetry
poésie objet: Dinggedicht
poésie orale: oral poetry
poésie ossianique: Ossianic poems
poésie populaire: folk poetry
poète lauréat: poet laureate
poètes métaphysiques: metaphysical poets
poétique, la: poetics
point de vue: point of view
pòlémique: polemic

polyptote: polyptoton
polysyllabique: polysyllabic
polysyndéton: polysyndeton
poncif: hackneyed expression
pornographie: pornography
préambule: preamble
préciosité: preciosity
préface: preface
prélude: prelude
préraphaélites: Pre-Raphaelite Brotherhood
préromantisme: Preromanticism
présent historique: historical present
présent narratif: historical present
primitivisme: primitivism
procatalepse: procatalepsis
procéleusmatique: proceleusmatic
prochronisme: prochronism
proclitique: proclitic
proème: proem
prolepse: prolepsis
prolixité: verbosity
prologue: prologue

proöde: proode
propriété littéraire: copyright
prose: prose
prose polyphonique: polyphonic prose
prosodiaque: prosodiac
prosodie: prosody
prosopopée: poetic fallacy
prosopopée: prosopopoeia
prosthèse: prothesis
protagoniste: protagonist
protase: protasis
prothalame: prothalamion
prothèse: prothesis
proverbe: adage
: proverb
provincialisme: provincialism
psaume: psalm
pseudonyme: pseudonym
purisme: purism
pyramide de Freytag: Freytag's pyramid
pyrrhique: pyrrhic
pythiambique: Pythiambic

Q

qasida: qasida
quarto: quarto
quatorzain: quatorzain
quatrain: quatrain
: tetrastich

quatrain de pentamètres iambiques: heroic stanza
quatrain de tétramètres iambiques: long meter
quatrain héroïque: heroic stanza
quatrain hymnique: common meter
quintil: pentastich

R

ralentissement: retardation
rationalisme: rationalism
réalisme: realism
réalisme magique: magical realism
réalisme socialiste: socialist realism
rébus: rebus
recension: recension
récit: folk tale
: tale
récit à la première personne: first person narrative
récit à la troisième personne: third person narrative
récit à tiroir: frame story
récit fantastique: fantasy fiction
récit humoristique: humoresque
réforme: Reformation
refrain: burden
: incremental repetition
: refrain
: repetend
refrain de mer: shanty
réfutation: refutation
régionalisme: regionalism
règle des trois unités: unities, the three
reizianum: reizianum
Renaissance: Renaissance
renaissance celtique: Celtic Renaissance

renaissance irlandaise: Celtic Renaissance
repartie: repartee
: wit
répétition: ploce
: repetition
reportage: reportage
repoussoir: foil
requiem: requiem
restauration: Restoration
résumé: brief
retour en arrière: flashback
révélation: epiphany
revue: revue
rhapsode: rhapsodist
rhapsodie: rhapsody
rhèse: end-stopped line
rhétorique: rhetoric
Rhétoriqueurs: Rhétoriqueurs
rhythmus tripertitus caudatus: cauda
rime: rhyme
rime alternée: alternate rhyme
rime apocopée: apocopated rhyme
rime apophonique: analyzed rhyme
: imperfect rhyme
rime brisée: broken rhyme
rime couée: tail rhyme

rime défectueuse: imperfect rhyme
rime double: double rhyme
rime féminine: feminine rhyme
rime finale: end rhyme
rime intérieure: internal rhyme
rime interne: Leonine rhyme
rime légère: light rhyme
rime léonine: double rhyme
       : Leonine rhyme
rime masculine: masculine rhyme
rime pour l'oeil: eye rhyme
rime riche: rime riche
rimes annexées: chain rhyme
rimes concaténées: chain rhyme
rime sénées: alliteration
rime serpentine: serpentine verse
rimes couronnées: mosaic rhyme
       : polysyllabic rhyme
rimes croisées: cross rhyme
       : alternate rhyme
rimes embrassées: embracing rhyme
       : enclosing rhyme
rimes empérières: mosaic rhyme
       : polysyllabic rhyme
rimes enchaînées: chain rhyme
rimes fratrisées: chain rhyme
rimes identiques: identical rhyme
rimes polysyllabiques: polysyllabic rhyme
rime riche: perfect rhyme
rimes-tierces: terza rima
ritournelle: ritornello
rococo: rococo
roman: novel
roman à clef: key novel
       : roman à clef
roman à deux sous: penny dreadful
roman arthurien: Arthurian romance
roman à sensation: penny dreadful
roman à thèse: novel of ideas
romance: romance
romancer: romanticization
romancero: cantar
roman chevaleresque: chivalric romance
roman courtois: chivalric romance

roman d'action: event-novel
roman d'anticipation: science fiction
roman d'apprentissage: apprenticeship novel
roman d'aventures: adventure novel
roman de caractères: man-novel
roman de formation éducative:
    novel of educational formation
roman de la table ronde: Arthurian romance
roman de moeurs: novel of manners
roman de science-fiction: science fiction
roman d'évolution psychologique: novel of
    development
roman d'un artiste: novel of the artist
roman d'une époque: time-novel
roman épistolaire: epistolary novel
roman fleuve: roman-fleuve
roman gothique: Gothic novel
roman hétérodoxe: heterodox novel
roman historique: historical novel
roman humanitaire: humanitarian novel
roman paysan: novel of the soil
roman pédagogique: novel of educational formation
roman philosophique: novel of ideas
roman picaresque: picaresque
roman policier; detective story
roman politique: political novel
roman pour concierges: penny dreadful
roman psychologique: psychological novel
roman régionaliste: novel of the soil
roman rustique: novel of the soil
roman sentimental: sentimental novel
romantisme: Romanticism
rondeau: rondeau
rondeau à la façon de Swinburne: roundel
rythme: rhythm
rythme ascendant: ascending rhythm
       : rising meter
rythme balance: rocking rhythm
rythme binaire: duple rhythm
rythme cadencé: running rhythm
rythme coulant: running rhythm
rythme de berceuse: rocking rhythm
rythme descendant: descending rhythm

S

saga: saga
sarcasme: quip
       : sarcasm
satire: lampoon
     : satire
     : skit
satire burlesque: folly literature
satyre: satyr play
saynète: sketch
       : vignette

scalde: skald
scansion: scansion
scénario: scenario
scène: scene
scolastique: Scholasticism
scolie: scolion
scop: scop
sémantique: semantics
sénaire: senarius
sens: meaning

sensibilité: sensibility
sensiblerie: sentimentality
sens littéral: literal meaning
sentence: sentence
sentimentalité: sentimentality
septain: heptastich
: septet
septénaire: septenarius
: septenary
sérénade: serenade
serventois: sirvente
sextine: sestina
sicilienne: Sicilian octave
siècle d'Auguste: Augustan period
siècle des lumières: Enlightenment
signification: meaning
sille: silloi
sillographe: sillographer
similé: simile
sincérité: sincerity
sirventois: sirvente
situation conventionnelle: stock situation
sixain: hexastich
: sestet
sizain: sestet
sketch: sketch
solécisme: solecism
soliloque: soliloquy
songe: dream allegory
sonnet: sonnet
sonnet à codas: tailed sonnet
sonnet à refrains: tailed sonnet
sonnet double: tailed sonnet
sonnet écourté: curtal sonnet
sonnet irrégulier: tailed sonnet
sonnet miltonien: Miltonic sonnet
sonnet quinzain: tailed sonnet
sonnet seizain: tailed sonnet
sonnet spenserien: Spenserian sonnet
sotadée: Sotadean verse
sotie: folly literature
: sotie
source de première main: primary source
sources secondaires: secondary sources
spondée: spondee
stichomythie: stichomythia
strophe: stanza
: strophe
strophe à enjambement: open couplet

strophe alcaïque: Alcaic strophe
strophe asclépiade: Asclepiadic strophe
strophe chaucerienne: rhyme royal
strophe couée: cauda
strophe de ballade: ballad stanza
strophe élégiaque: elegiac stanza
strophe saphique: Sapphic stanza
strophe spenserienne: Spenserian stanza
structure: structure
structure extrinsèque: extrinsic structure
structure intrinsèque: intrinsic structure
style: style
style ampoulé: orotund style
style emphatique: orotund style
style imagé: imagery
style indirect libre: indirect interior monologue
style naturel: middle style
style noble: high style
style simple: low style
stylistique: stylistics
subjectivité: subjectivity
substitution: substitution
sujet: subject matter
: topic
surfiction: surfiction
suspense: suspense
surréalisme: surrealism
syllabe: syllable
syllabe accentuée: accented syllable
syllabe brève: short syllable
syllabe longue: long syllable
syllepse: syllepsis
syllogisme: syllogism
symbole: symbol
symbole à valeur psychologique:
    objective correlative
symbolisme: symbolism
symploque: symploce
symposium: symposium
synalèphe: synaloepha
syncope: syncope
synecdoque: synecdoche
synérèse: synaeresis
synesthésie: synaesthesia
synonyme: synonym
synopsis: brief
    : synopsis
syntaxe: syntax
syzygie: syzygy

T

tableau vivant: tableau
tautologie: tautology
technique de composition et d'analyse: strategy

technique du flux de conscience:
    stream of consciousness technique
teichoscopie: teichoscopy

télestiche: telestich
tempête et assaut: Sturm und Drang
temps de lecture: narrative time
tenson: flyting
: tenzone
tercet: tercet
: tristich
tercet à rimes triplées: triplet
terminaison féminine: feminine ending
: weak ending
terminaison masculine: masculine ending
terza-rima: terza rima
terzines: terza rima
tétralogie: tetralogy
tétramètre: tetrameter
tétrapodié: tetrapody
texte révisé: recension
texture: texture
théâtre de boulevard: boulevard drama
théâtre de l'absurde: drama of the absurd
: theater of the absurd
théâtre pour la lecture: closet drama
théâtre héroïque: heroic play
thème: theme
: topic
thèse: message
thésis: slack
: thesis
thrénodie: lament
: threnody
tintement de vers: jingle
tirade: tirade
tmèse: tmesis
ton: tone

tonique: down beat
: tonic
tournant: volta
tract: tract
tradition: tradition
traduction interlinéaire: interlinear
tragédie: tragedy
tragédie bourgeoise: bourgeois tragedy
tragicomédie: tragicomedy
tragique: tragic
traité: tract
traître: villain
trame: plot
tranche de vie: slice-of-life
travestissement: travesty
triade épodique: triad
tribraque: tribrach
trihémimère: trithemimeral
trilogie: trilogy
trimètre: trimeter
triolet: triolet
tripodie: triple meter
: tripody
tristique: tristich
trochaïque: trochaic
trochée: trochee
trois unités, règle des: unities, the three
trope: trope
tropisme: tropisme
troubadour: troubadour
trouble et agitation: Sturm und Drang
trouvère: trouvère
type: stock character

## U

unité organique: organic form
universalité: universality

usage vernaculaire: vernacularism

## V

verbosité: verbosity
vérisme: verism
vernaculaire: vernacularism
vers: verse
vers acatalectique: acatalectic
vers acéphale: headless line
vers à cinq arsis: pentarsic
vers amphigouriques: nonsense verse
vers blancs: blank verse
vers cadencé: alternate verse
vers catalectique: catalectic
vers de méchants: doggerel
vers de mirliton: doggerel
vers de société: vers de société
vers épique: heroic meter
verset: verset
vers fescennins: Fescennine verses

vers héroïque: heroic couplet
: heroic meter
: heroic verse
vers holorimes: mosaic rhyme
vers iambique de sept pieds: fourteener
versification: versification
vers léonins: Leonine verse
vers libre: free verse
: vers libre
vers métrique: quantitative verse
vers pythique: Pythian verse
vers quantitatif: quantitative verse
vers rapportés: correlative verse
vers rhopaliques: rhopalic verse
vers rythmique: accentual verse
vers saphique: Sapphic
vers spondaïque: spondaic verse

vers stichomythiques: amoebean verse
victorien: Victorian
vision allégorique: dream allegory

vorticisme: vorticism
vraisemblance: verisimilitude
vulgarité: vulgarism

W

western: Western

Z

zeugme: zeugma

# INDEX

## German

A

Abecedarien: abecedarian
Abecedarius: abecedarian
Abenteuerroman: adventure novel
Abfall: anticlimax
abgenutzter Ausdruck: hackneyed expression
Abgesang: epode
Abhandlung: tract
Abschweifung: digression
absteigender Rhythmus: descending rhythm
abstrakt: abstract
    : brief
abstrakte Dichtung: abstract poetry
absurdes Drama: drama of the absurd
absurdes Theater: theater of the absurd
Adamismus: acmeism
adonischer Vers: Adonic verse
Adonius: Adonic verse
Adynaton: adynaton
affektiver Trugschluß: affective fallacy
Agitprop-Stücke: agit-prop
    : living newspaper
Agon: agon
akatalektisch: acatalectic
Akephal: acephalous
    : headless line
Akmeismus: acmeism
Akronym: acronym
Akrostichon: acrostic
Akroteleuton: acroteleutic
Akt: act
Akzent: accent
akzentuierender Vers: accentual verse
Alexandriner: Alexandrine
alkäische Strophe: Alcaic strophe
Allegorie: allegory
Alliteration: alliteration
allwissender Erzähler: omniscient narrator
Almanach: almanac
alternierender Vers: alternate verse
altfranzösische Romanze: chanson de toile
Ambiguität: ambiguity
Amoibaia: amoebean verse
Amoibaion: amoebean verse
Amphibolie: amphibology
Amphibrachus: amphibrach
Amphibrachys: amphibrach
Amphimacer: amphimacer
Amphimacus: amphimacer
Amplifikation: amplification

Ana: ana
Anachronismus: anachronism
Anadiplose: anadiplosis
Anagnorisis: anagnorisis
Anagogie: anagoge
Anagramm: anagram
Anaklasis: anaclasis
Anakoluth: anacoluthon
Anakreontik: anacreontic poetry
Anakrusis: anacrusis
Analekten: analects
Analekton: analects
Analogie: analogy
Analyse: analysis
Anapäst: anapaest
Anapher: anaphora
Anaphora: anaphora
Anastrophe: anastrophe
Andeutung: allusion
    : innuendo
Anekdote: anecdote
Anfangsreim: alliteration
Angemessenheit: decorum
Annalen: annals
anonym: anonymous
Anrede: apostrophe
Anrufung: apostrophe
    : invocation
Anspielung: allusion
    : innuendo
Ansprache: oration
Anstandsbuch: book of manners
ansteigende Handlung: epitasis
Antagonist: antagonist
Antanaklasis: antanaclasis
Antepänultima: antepenult
Anthologie: anthology
Anthropomorphism: anthropomorphism
Antibacchius: antibacchius
Antiheld: antihero
Antiklimax: anticlimax
Antimasque: antimasque
Antiphon: antiphon
Antiphonie: antiphon
Antiroman: antinovel
Antispast: antispast
Antistrophe: antistrophe
Antithese: antithesis
Antizipation: anticipation

Antonomasie: antonomasia
Antonym: antonym
Aphärese: aphaeresis
Aphorismus: aphorism
apokalyptisch: apocalyptic
Apokope: apocope
apokopierter Reim: apocopated rhyme
Apokryphen: apocrypha
apollinisch: Apollonian
Apolog: apologue
Apologie: apology
apophonischer Reim: analyzed rhyme
Apophthegma: apophthegm
Aposiopese: aposiopesis
Apostrophe: apostrophe
Archaismus: archaism
Archetyp: archetype
Archetypus: archetype
Architektonik: architectonics
Arie: aria
Arkadien: Arcadia
Arsis: arsis
Arthusroman: Arthurian romance
asklepiadeische Strophe: Asclepiadic strophe

Assonanz: assonance
Ästhetizismus: aestheticism
astrophische Komposition: astrophic composition
Asyndeton: asyndeton
Atellanen: Atellan fables
Atmosphäre: atmosphere
atonisch: atonic
Attitüde: attitude
Aufklärung: Enlightenment
Aufrichtigkeit: sincerity
aufsteigender Rhythmus: ascending rhythm
Auftakt: anacrusis
Auftritt: act
    : scene
Aufzug: act
auktorialer Erzähler: omniscient narrator
Ausgabe letzter Hand: definitive edition
Ausgangsereignis: initial incident
Ausgewogenheit: balance
Ausruf: apostrophe
äußere Form: extrinsic structure
Autobiographie: autobiography
Avantgarde: avant-garde

**B**

Bacchius: bacchius
Balance: balance
Ballade: ballad
Balladenstrophe: ballad stanza
Bänkelsänger: minstrel
Barbarismus: barbarism
Barde: bard
Barock: baroque
Bauernroman: novel of the soil
Begriffstausch: antonomasia
Beiseitesprechen: aside
Belletristik: belletristic literature
Beredsamkeit: eloquence
Beschwörung: incantation
Bestiarium: bestiary
Bestseller: best seller
betone Silbe: accented syllable
Betonung: accent
    : arsis
    : stress
Bewußtseinsstrom-Technik: stream of
  consciousness technique
Bibliographie: bibliography
Bild: image
    : scene
Bilderbogen-Geschichten: comics
Bildergeschichten: comics
Bilderlyrik: carmen figuratum
Bilderrätsel: rebus
Bilderreim: carmen figuratum

bildlich: figurative
bildliche Sprache: figurative language
Bildlichkeit: imagery
Bildungsroman: apprenticeship novel
Binnenpause: medial caesura
Binnenreim: internal rhyme
Biographie: biography
Blankvers: blank verse
blindes Motiv: blind motif
Bombast: bombast
bombastischer Stil: orotund
Bonmot: bon mot
Bösewicht: villain
Boulevardstück: boulevard drama
brachykatalektisch: brachycatalectic
Brachykatalexe: brachycatalexis
Briefgedicht: epistle
Briefroman: epistolary novel
Brotarbeit: potboiler
Buchdrama: closet drama
Buchstabismus: letterism
Bühnenbild: setting
Bühnenwagen: pageant
bukolische Dichtung: bucolic poetry
bürgerliches Drama: bourgeois drama
bürgerliches Trauerspiel: bourgeois tragedy
Burleske: burlesque
    : farce
Burletta: burletta
Byronismus: Byronic

Cantar: cantar
Canticum: canticum
Canzone: canzone
Carmen: carmen
Cento: cento
Chanson: chanson
Chanson de geste: chanson de geste
Chanson de toile: chanson de toile
Charakter: character
       : persona
Charakterisierung: characterization
Charakterkomödie: comedy of character
Chiasmus: chiasmus
Chiffre: chiffre

Dadaismus: Dadaism
Daktylus: dactyl
Dauer: duration
Debatte: débat
Deckname: pseudonym
Dekadenzdichtung: decadence
Dekastichon: decastich
Dekasyllabus: decasyllable
Denotation: denotation
Detektivgeschichte: detective story
Detektivroman: detective story
deus ex machina: deus ex machina
Deuteragonist: deuteragonist
Dialog: dialogue
Diärese: diaeresis
Diatribe: diatribe
dichterische Freiheit: poetic licence
dichterischer Widerruf: palinode
Dichtung: poetry
didaktische Dichtung: didactic literature
Digression: digression
Diiambus: diiamb
Diktion: poetic diction
Dimeter: dimeter
Dinggedicht: Dinggedicht

Einakter: one-act play
Einfühlung: empathy
Einheiten, die drei: unities, the three
Einleitung: preface
einsilbig: monosyllabic
Einstellung: attitude
Einzugslied: parodos
Echo: echo
       : echo verse
Ekloge: eclogue
Elegie: complaint
       : elegy
elegische Strophe: elegiac stanza

## C

Choliambus: choliamb
Chor: chorus
Choriambus: choriamb
Chrestomathie: chrestomathy
christliches Epos: Christian epic
Chronik: chronicle
Chronogramm: chronogram
Cinquain: cinquain
Clerihew: clerihew
Collage: collage
Complexio: complexio
Correctio: correctio
Couplet: couplet
Curtal Sonnet: curtal sonnet

## D

Dingsymbol: central motif
dionysisch: Dionysian
Dipodie: dipody
Dispondäus: dispondee
Dispondeus: dispondee
Dissonanz: dissonance
Distichomythie: distochomythia
Distichon: distich
Dit: dit
Dithyrambe: dithyramb
Dithyrambos: dithyramb
Dithyrambus: dithyramb
Ditrochäus: ditrochee
Diverbium: diverbium
Dixain: dizain
Dizain: dizain
Dochmius: dochmius
Doggerel: doggerel
Doppelreim: double rhyme
Drama: drama
dramatisch: dramatic
dramatische Dichtung: dramatic poetry
Dramaturgie: dramaturgy
Drehbuch: scenario
Dreireim: triplet

## E

Elisabethanisches Zeitalter: Elizabethan age
Elision: elision
Ellipse: ellipsis
Eloquenz: eloquence
Emblem: emblem
empfindsamer Roman: sentimental novel
Empfindsamkeit: Empfindsamkeit
       : sensibility
       : sentimentality
Emphase: emphasis
Enallage: enallage
Endreim: end rhyme
englischer Neuklassizismus: Augustan period

Enjambement: enjambment
Enklise: enclitic
: recessive accent
enklitisch: enclitic
Enthymen: enthymeme
Entwicklungsroman: novel of development
Epanadiplose: epanadiplosis
Epanalepse: epanalepsis
Epanodos: epanodos
Epicedium: epicedium
Epideiktik: epideictic speech
Epigonentum: epigonism
Epigramm: epigram
Epigraph: epigraph
Epik: narrative poetry
Epikedeion: epicedium
Epilog: epilogue
Epiphora: epiphora
Epirrhema: epirrhema
epische Dichtung: fiction
: narrative poetry
episches Theater: epic drama
Episode: episode
episodische Struktur: episodic structure
Epistel: epistle
Epitaph: epitaph
Epitasis: epitasis
Epithalamium: epithalamium
: prothalamion
Epitheton: epithet
Epitome: epitome
Epitrit: epitrite
Epitritus: epitrite
Epizeuxis: epizeuxis
Epode: epode
Epopöe: epopee
Epos: epic
: epos
Epyllion: epyllion

Fabel: fable
: plot
Fablel: fabliau
fabula atellana: Atellan fables
Falkentheorie: Falkentheorie
fallende Handlung: falling action
fallender Rhythmus: descending rhythm
fallendes Metrum: falling meter
Familienroman: roman-fleuve
Farce: farce
: slapstick
Fastnachtsspiel: carnival comedy
Fernsehspiel: television play
Festschrift: Festschrift
Feszenninen: Fescennine verses
Feuilleton: feuilleton

Equivalenz: equivalence
Ereignis-Roman: event-novel
Er-Form: third person narrative
erhabener Stil: high style
Erklärung: explication
Erläuterung: explication
erlebte Rede: indirect interior monologue
erotische Literatur: erotic poetry
Ersatz: compensation
erweiterter Reim: polysyllabic rhyme
Erzähler: voice
erzählerische Dichtung: fiction
erzählte Zeit: fable time
Erzählung: tale
Erzählzeit: narrative time
Erziehungsroman: novel of educational formation
esoterisch: esoteric
Esprit: wit
Essay: essay
Eulogie: eulogy
Euphemismus: euphemism
Euphonie: euphony
Euphuismus: euphuism
Exegese: exegesis
Exempel: exemplum
Existentialismus: existentialism
Exkurs: excursus
Ex-Metapher: dead metaphor
Exodos: exodus
Exordium: exordium
exoterisch: exoteric
Exotismus: exoticism
Experimental-Roman: experimental novel
Expletiv: expletive
Explikation: explication
Exposition: exposition
: protasis
Expressionismus: expressionism

F

Figur: persona
Figurengedicht: carmen figuratum
Figurenlyrik: carmen figuratum
figürlich: figurative
Flugschrift: tract
Folio: folio
Form: form
Formalismus: formalism
Formel: formula
Fragment: fragment
Frauendienst: courtly love
freier Rhythmus: free verse
Freytags Pyramide: Freytag's pyramid
Füllwort: expletive
Futurismus: futurism

Galliamb: galliamb
Galliambus: galliamb
Gallizismus: Gallicism
Garn: yarn
Gasel: ghazel
Gattung: genre
Gedicht: poem
Geflügelhändler-Maß: poulter's measure
Gegenbegriff: antonym
Gegenspieler: antagonist
      : foil
Gegenstrophe: antistrophe
Gegner: foil
Gehalt: meaning
gehäufter Reim: monorhyme
geistliches Drama: liturgical drama
geistreicher Einfall: wit
Gelegenheitsbildung: nonce word
Gelegenheitsdichtung: light verse
      : occasional verse
Geleit: envoi
Gemeinplatz: platitude
gemischte Metapher: mixed mataphor
Generationenroman: roman-fleuve

G
Genre: genre
Genrebild: genre picture
Georgika: georgic
Gesang: canto
Gesellschaftsroman: novel of manners
Geschichte: story
Geschichtsdrama: historical play
geschwänztes Sonett: tailed sonnet
Gesta: gest
Ghasal: ghazel
Ghasel: ghazel
Ghazel: ghazel
Glanzstelle: purple passage
Gleichwertigkeit: equivalence
Glosse: gloss
Glykoneus: Glyconic
Gnome: gnomic poetry
Goliarden: Goliardic verse
Goliardendichtung: Goliardic verse
Gongorismus: Gongorism
Göttinger Hain: Göttinger Hain
Groschenroman: penny dreadful
grotesk: grotesque
Gustav Freytags Pyramide: Freytag's pyramid

hysteron proteron: hysteron proteron
Hagiographie: hagiography
Hamartia: hamartia
Hamartie: hamartia
Handlung: action
      : plot
Handlungshöhepunkt: crisis
Handlungskomödie: comedy of situation
Hanswurst: harlequinade
Hanswurstspiel: harlequinade
Harlekinade: harlequinade
Hauptfigur: protagonist
Hebung: arsis
Held: hero
      : protagonist
Heldendichtung: heroic poetry
Heldendrama: heroic play
Heldenepos: heroic epic
Heimatkunst: regionalism
Heimatroman: novel of the soil
Hemipes: hemiepes
Hemistichomythie: hemistichomythia
Hemistichon: hemistich
Hemistichus: hemistich
Hendekasyllabus: hendecasyllable
Hendiadyoin: hendiadys
Hephthemimeres: hephthemimeral
Heptameter: heptameter
Heptastichon: heptastich

H
Heptasyllabus: heptasyllable
Hermetismus: Hermeticism
heroische Strophe: heroic stanza
heroischer Vers: heroic meter
      : heroic verse
heroisches Reimpaar: heroic couplet
heroisch-galanter Roman: chivalric romance
heroisch-galantes Epos: metrical romance
heterodoxer Roman: heterodox novel
hetzerische Ansprache: harangue
Hexameter: hexameter
Hexastichon: hexastich
Hiat: hiatus
Hiatus: hiatus
Hintergrund: background
      : setting
Hintertreppenroman: penny dreadful
historischer Roman: historical novel
historisches Drama: historical play
historisches Epos: historic epic
historisches Präsens: historical present
Hochzeitslied: epithalamium
höfischer Roman: chivalric romance
höfisches Epos: courtly epic
      : metrical romance
Höhepunkt: climax
Homiletik: homiletics
Homilie: homily
Homographen: homographs

Homoiarkton: homoiarcton
Homoioptoton: homoioptoton
Homöioteleuton: homoeoteleuton
Homonyme: homonyms
Homöoteleuton: homoeoteleuton
Homophone: homophones
horazische Ode: Horatian ode
Hörspiel: radio play
Huitain: huitain
Humanismus: Humanism
Humor: humor

Humoreske: humoresque
Hybris: hybris
Hymne: hymn
Hymnenstrophe: common meter
Hypallage: hypallage
Hyperbasis: hyperbaton
Hyperbaton: hyperbaton
Hyperbel: hyperbole
Hyperkatalektisch: hypermetric
Hypotaxe: hypotaxis

## I

Ich-Form: first person narrative
Idealismus: idealism
Ideenroman: novel of ideas
identischer Reim: identical rhyme
Idiom: idiom
Idylle: idyll
Iktus: ictus
Imagismus: imagism
Imitation: imitation
Impressionismus: impressionism
impressionistische Kritik: impressionistic criticism
Index: index
Indianer, Literatur der: Amerind literature
Individualroman: apprenticeship novel
Inhalt: argument
       : content
in medias res: in medias res
innere Form: intrinsic structure
innerer Monolog: interior monologue
Inszenierung: mise-en-scène

Interlinearversion: interlinear
Interludium: interlude
Intermezzo: intermezzo
Interpolation: interpolation
Interpretation: interpretation
Interversion: interlinear
Intrige: intrigue
Intrigenstück: comedy of intrigue
              : intrigue
Invektive: invective
         : lampoon
Inversion: inversion
Invokation: invocation
Ionikus: Ionic
irische Renaissance: Celtic Renaissance
Ironie: irony
Ironie des Schicksals: irony of fate
Irrationalismus: irrationalism
isometrisch: homoeomeral

## J

jambisch: iambic
Jambus: iamb
Jargon: cant
       : jargon

Jugendstil: Jugendstil
Junges Deutschland: Junges Deutschland
Jung-Wien: Jung-Wien

## K

Kabarett: revue
Kadenz: cadence
Kakophonie: cacophony
Kalender: almanac
Kanon: canon
Kantate: cantata
Kanzone: canzone
Kapitel: chapter
Karikatur: caricature
Karikaturstreifen: comics
Kasside: qasida
Katabasis: catabasis
Katachrese: catachresis
katalektisch: catalectic
Katalexe: catalexis
Katastasis: catastasis
Katastrophe: catastrophe

katharsis: catharsis
Kehrreim: refrain
keltische Renaissance: Celtic Renaissance
Kenning: kenning
Kettenreim: chain rhyme
Keulenvers: rhopalic verse
Kinderlied: children's song
Kirchenlied: canticle
Klage: complaint
      : lament
      : plaint
Klagelied: complaint
          : dirge
          : elegy
          : monody
Klangmalerei: onomatopoeia
Klassik: classicism

klassisch: classic
Klassizismus: neoclassicism
Klimax: climax
klingender Reim: feminine rhyme
Klischee: cliché
: hackneyed expression
Knittelvers: Knittelvers
Kolon: colon
Kolportageroman: penny dreadful
Komik: comic
komische Entspannung: comic relief
komisches Epos: mock epic
Komma: comma
Kommos: commus
Komödie: comedy
: high comedy
Kompensation: compensation
Konflikt: plot
konkret: concrete
Konkretismus: concretism
Konnotation: connotation
Konsonanz: consonance
Konstruktivismus: constructivism
Konsumliteratur: paraliterature
Kontrafaktur: contrafacture
Kontraktion: blend
kontrapunktischer Rhythmus: counterpoint rhythm
Kontrast: antithesis

Konvention: convention
konventionalisierte Sprachbilder: dead metaphor
Konversationsstück: conversation piece
Konzeptismus: conceptism
Konzetti: conceit
korrelativer Vers: correlative verse
Krasis: crasis
Kretikus: cretic
Kreuzreim: alternate rhyme
: cross rhyme
Krise: crisis
Kritik: critque
: review
kritischer Apparat: apparatus criticus
Kryptogramm: cryptogram
Kubismus: cubism
Kulteranismus: culteranism
Kultismus: cultism
Kunstballade: art ballad
Kunstepos: art epic
künstlerischer Aufbau: architectonics
Künstlerroman: novel of the artist
Kürze: short syllable
kurzer Roman: novelette
Kurzgeschichte: short story
Kurzvers: hemistich
Kurzzeile: hemistich

**L**

Lai: lai
Länge: long syllable
Längestrich: macron
Langzeile: Nibelungenstrophe
Lautmalerei: onomatopoeia
Legende: legend
Lehre: message
Lehrdichtung: didactic literature
lehrhafte Erzählung: cautionary tale
Lehrstück: living newspaper
: thesis play
leichter Stil: low style
Leipogramm: lipogram
Leitmotiv: leitmotif
Leitsymbol: central motif
Leoninischer Reim: Leonine rhyme
Leoninischer Vers: Leonine verse
Lesedrama: closet drama
Lettrismus: letterism
Liebesdichtung: love poetry
Lied: song

Liedchen: ditty
Limerick: limerick
Linguistik: linguistics
Lipogramm: lipogram
Litanei: litany
Literatur: literature
Literatur der Indianer: Amerind literature
Litotes: litotes
Lobgedicht: eulogy
logaödische Verse: logaoedic
Logograph: logogriph
Logomachie: logomachy
Logorrhöe: logorrhoea
Lokalkolorit: local color
Lösung: denouement
: resolution
Lügendichtung: tall tale
Lustspiel: low comedy
Lyrik: lyric poetry
lyrische Dichtung: lyric poetry

**M**

Madrigal: madrigal
magischer Realismus: magical realism
makkaronische Dichtung: macaronic poetry

Manierismus: mannerism
männlicher Reim: masculine rhyme
männlicher Versausgang: masculine ending

männliche Zäsur: masculine caesura
Märchen: fairy tale
Marienspiel: virgin play
Marinismus: Marinism
Maschinerie: machinery
Maskenspiel: masque
            : mummery
Masque: masque
Maß: beat
Matrosenlied: shanty
Mauerschau: teichoskopia
Maxime: maxim
Meiosis: meiosis
Meistergesang: Meistergesang
Melik: melic poetry
Melodrama: melodrama
Memoiren: memoirs
Menschen-Roman: man-novel
Merker: Meistergesang
Mesodos: mesode
Mesostichon: mesostich
Metalepsis: metalepsis
Metapher: metaphor
metaphysische Dichter: metaphysical poets
metaphysische Konzetti: metaphysical conceits
Metaplasmus: metaplasm
Metathese: metathesis
Methode: strategy
Metonymie: metonymy
Metrik: metrics
        : prosody
Metron: metron
Metrum: beat
        : meter
Milton Sonett: Miltonic sonnet
Mimesis: imitation
        : mimesis

Nachahmung: imitation
Nachbildungsrecht: copyright
Nachdruck: emphasis
Nachwort: epilogue
Narrendichtung: folly literature
Nationalepos: national epic
Naturalismus: naturalism
Nebenbedeutung: connotation
Nebenhandlung: subplot
Nemesis: nemesis

objektives Korrelat: objective correlative
Objektivismus: objectivism
Objektivität: objectivity
Ode: ode
Offenbarung: epiphany
offene Form: open form

Mimus: mime
Minne: courtly love
Minnedienst: courtly love
Minnesang: minnesong
Minnesänger: minnesinger
Mirakelspiel: miracle play
Mißverhältnis: incongruity
Mittelalter: medieval period
Mittelreim: internal rhyme
mittlerer Stil: middle style
Modulation: modulation
Molossus: molossus
Monodie: monody
Monodrama: monodrama
Monolog: monologue
Monometer: monometer
Monopodie: monopody
Monostichon: monostich
Montage: montage
Mora: mora
Moral: message
        : moral
Moralität: morality play
More: mora
Moritat: broadside ballad
Motiv: motif
Motivation: motivation
Münchner Dichterkreis: Münchner Dichterkreis
Münchhauseniade: cock-and-bull story
mundartlicher Ausdruck: vernacularism
mündlich überlieferte Dichtung: oral poetry
Musikdrama: musical drama
Mysterienspiel: mystery play
Mystik: mysticism
Mythologie: mythology
Mythos: myth

N

Neogongorismus: Neo-Gongorism
Neologismus: neologism
Neue Sachlichkeit: new objectivity
Neuromantik: neoromanticism
Nibelungenstrophe: long line
                    : Nibelungenstrophe
Novelle: novella
Nō-Spiel: Nō
Numerus: number

O

Oktameter: octameter
Oktapodie: octapody
Oktastichon: octastich
Oktave: octave
Oktett: octet
Oktonar: octonarius

oktosyllabische Zeile: octosyllabic
Onomatopoesie: onomatopoeia
Onomatopöie: onomatopoeia
Oper: opera
Operette: operetta
organische Einheit: organic form

organische Form: organic form
Oratorium: oratorio
Ossianische Dichtung: Ossianic poems
Ottaverime: ottava rima
Oxymoron: oxymoron

## P

Päan: paean
Paarreim: couplet
Paean: paean
Paeonicus: paeon
Paian: paean
Palillogie: palilogy
Palilogia: palilogy
Palimbacchius: palimbacchius
Palindrom: palindrome
Palinode: palinode
Palinodie: palinode
palinodisch: palinodic
Panegyrikos: panegyric
Panegyrikus: panegyric
Pantomime: dumb show
          : pantomime
Pantum: pantoum
Pantun: pantoum
Pänultima: penult
Päon: paeon
Parabase: parabasis
Parabel: parable
Paradox: paradox
Paradoxon: paradox
Paragoge: paragoge
Parallelismus: parallelism
Paraphrase: paraphrase
Parataxe: parataxis
Parnassiens: Parnassians
Parodie: parody
parodistisches Epos: mock epic
Parodos: parodos
Parömiakos: paroemiac
Paronomasie: paronomasia
Partimen: partimen
Pasquill: pasquinade
Pasquinade: pasquinade
Passionsspiel: Corpus Christi play
          : passion play
Pastiche: pastiche
Pastorale: pastoral
Pastorelle: pastourelle
Pastourella: pastourelle
Pathos: pathos
Pathos, lächerlich übertriebenes: bathos
Pause: break
          : rest
Pentameter: pentameter

Pentapodie: pentapody
Pentarsik: pentarsic
Pentastichon: pentastich
Penthemimeres: penthemimer
          : penthemimeral
Periode: period
Peripetie: peripeteia
Periphrase: periphrasis
Peroration: peroration
Persiflage: persiflage
Personifikation: personification
          : poetic fallacy
Perspektive: point of view
Petrarkische Konzetti: Petrarchan conceits
Petrarkismus: Petrarchism
phaläkischer Vers: Phalaecean
phantastische Erzählung: fantasy fiction
phantastisches Werk: extravaganza
Pherekrateus: Pherecratean
Philippika: philippic
Phraseologie: phraseology
Picareske: picaresque
picarischer Roman: picaresque
Pietismus: Pietism
pindarische Ode: Pindaric ode
Plagiat: plagiarism
Platitüde: platitude
Plattheit: platitude
Pleonasmus: pleonasm
Poesie: poesie
Poeta laureatus: poet laureate
Poetik: poetics
poetische Freiheit: poetic licence
poetische Gerechtigkeit: poetic justice
poetische Lizenz: poetic licence
Polemik: polemic
politischer Roman: political novel
Polyglotte: polyglot
polyphonische Prosa: polyphonic prose
Polyptoton: polyptoton
Polysyndeton: polysyndeton
Pöbelsprache: billingsgate
Pornographie: pornography
Portmanteau Wort: blend
Posse: droll
          : farce
          : slapstick
Präambel: preamble

**130**

Präludium: prelude
Präraffaeliten: Pre-Raphaelite Brotherhood
Predigtlehre: homiletics
Preziösität: preciosity
Primärliteratur: primary source
Primitivismus: primitivism
Problemstück: drame
: problem play
Prochronismus: prochronism
Prokatalepsis: procatalepsis
Prokeleusmatikos: proceleusmatic
Proklise: proclitic
Proklisis: proclitic
Prolepse: prolepsis
Prolog: prologue
Proodos: proode
Proömium: proem
Prosa: prose
Prosagedicht: prose poem

quantitierende Dichtung: quantitative verse
Quartett: quatrain
Quartformat: quarto

Rahmenerzählung: frame story
Rahmenstruktur: enveloping structure
Rationalismus: rationalism
Rätsel: charade
: riddle
Realismus: realism
Rebus: rebus
Redefiguren: figures of speech
Redegewandtheit: eloquence
Redeschwulst: bombast
Redewendung: idiom
Reformation: Reformation
Refrain: burden
: incremental repetition
: refrain
: repetend
Refutation: refutation
Regionalismus: regionalism
reicher Reim: polysyllabic rhyme
: rime riche
Reim: rhyme
Reimbrechung: broken rhyme
Reimgeklingel: jingle
Reimpaar: couplet
Reimschema: rhyme scheme
reiner Reim: perfect rhyme
reinigen: bowdlerize
Reisebericht: travelogue
Reisebeschreibung: travelogue
Reißer: thriller
Reizianum: reizianum
Renaissance: Renaissance

Prosodiakos: prosodiac
Prosodie: prosody
Prosopopöe: poetic fallacy
: prosopopoeia
Prosopopöie: prosopopoeia
Protagonist: protagonist
Protasis: protasis
Prothalamion: prothalamion
Prothese: prothesis
provenzalische Literatur: Provençal literature
Provinzialismus: provincialism
Psalm: psalm
Pseudonym: pseudonym
psychologischer Roman: psychological novel
Purismus: purism
Pyrrhichius: pyrrhic
pythiambisches Maß: Pythiambic
pythischer Vers: Pythian verse

Q
Quatrain: heroic stanza
: quatrain

R
Reportage: reportage
Restauration: Restoration
Retardation: retardation
retardierendes Moment: retardation
Revue: revue
Rezension: recension
: review
Rhapsode: rhapsodist
Rhapsodie: rhapsody
Rhetorik: rhetoric
rhetorische Figuren: rhetorical figures
rhetorische Frage: rhetorical question
Rhopalikos: rhopalic verse
Rhythmus: rhythm
rime riche: rime riche
Ritornell: ritornello
Ritterroman: chivalric romance
Rokoko: rococo
Rollengedicht: dramatic monologue
Roman: novel
Romannovelle: long-short story
: novelette
Romantik: Romanticism
romantische Ironie: romantic irony
Romantisierung: romanticization
Romanze: romance
Rondeau: rondeau
Rotwelsch: cant
Rückblende: flashback
Rührstück: comedy of tears
: drame
Rundschau: review

Saga: roman-fleuve
   : saga
Sage: tradition
Sapphische Strophe: Sapphic stanza
Sapphische Zeile: Sapphic
Sarkasmus: sarcasm
Satire: satire
Satyrspiel: satyr play
Satzgefüge: period
Schäferdichtung: pastoral
Scharade: charade
   : conundrum
Schauerroman: Gothic novel
   : penny dreadful
Schaukel-Rhythmus: rocking rhythm
Schauplatz: setting
Schauspiel: drame
Schelmenroman: picaresque
Scherzbuch: jestbook
Schlagfertigkeit: repartee
Schlagreim: internal rhyme
Schlesische Dichterschulen: Silesian schools
Schlüsselroman: key novel
Schluβrede: epilogue
Schluβstrophe: envoi
Schmärede: invective
Schmäschrift: invective
   : lampoon
Scholastik: Scholasticism
schöne Literatur: belletristic literature
Schreiberling: penny-a-liner
Schundroman: penny dreadful
Schüttelreim: mosaic rhyme
schwach: weak ending
Schwank: farce
   : fabliau
   : slapstick
schwebende Betonung: distributed stress
Schweifreim: cauda
   : tail rhyme
Schweifsonett: tailed sonnet
Seemannslied: shanty
Sekundärliteratur: secondary sources
Sekundenstil: slice-of-life
Selbstbiographie: autobiography
Selbstgespräch: soliloquy
Semantik: semantics
Senar: senarius
Senkung: slack
   : thesis
Sensibilität: sensibility
Sentenz: sentence
Sentimentalismus: sentimentality
Sentimentalität: sentimentality

Septenar: septenarius
   : septenary
Septett: septet
Serenade: serenade
Serpentinenvers: serpentine verse
Sestine: sestina
Sextett: sestet
Sextine: sestina
Shanty: Shanty
Silbe: syllable
Silbenrätsel: charade
Sillen: silloi
Sillograph: sillographer
Singsang: chant
Singspiel: ballad opera
sinnlose Verse: nonsense verse
Sittenkomödie: comedy of manners
Sittenroman: novel of manners
Sittenstück: comedy of manners
Situationskomödie: comedy of situation
Siziliane: Sicilian octave
Sizilianische Schule: Sicilian school
Skald: scald
Skansion: scansion
Sketch: sketch
Skizze: sketch
   : vignette
Skob: scop
Skolion: scolion
Skop: scop
sokratische Ironie: Socratic irony
Soliloquium: soliloquy
Solözismus: solecism
Sonett: sonnet
Sonettenkranz: crown of sonnets
Sonettenzyklus: sonnet cycle
Sotadeus: Sotadean verse
sozialistischer Realismus: socialist realism
sozialkritischer Roman: humanitarian novel
Spiel im Spiel: play within a play
spanisches Heldenepos: cantar
Spannung: suspense
Sperrung: hyperbaton
Spondäus: spondee
Spondeus: spondee
Spondiacus: spondaic verse
Spottgedicht: clerihew
Sprachwissenschaft: linguistics
Sprichwort: adage
   : proverb
Spruch: adage
   : gnomic poetry
Stabreim: alliteration
Standpunkt: point of view

Stanze: octave
steigend: rising meter
Stichelei: skit
Stichomythie: stichomythia
Stil: style
Stilistik: stylistics
Stimmung: atmosphere
    : mood
Stoff: subject matter
Streich: farce
Streitgedicht: débat
    : flyting
    : tenzone
Streitgespräch: débat
Strategie: strategy
Strophe: stanza
    : stave
    : strophe
Struktur: structure
Sturm und Drang: storm and stress
    : Sturm und Drang

Subjektivität: subjectivity
Substitution: substitution
Surrealismus: surrealism
Syllepse: syllepsis
Syllogismus: syllogism
Symbol: symbol
Symbolismus: symbolism
Symploke: symploce
Symposion: symposium
Synalöphe: synaloepha
Synärese: synaeresis
Synästhesie: synaesthesia
Synekdoche: synecdoche
Synkope: syncope
Synonym: synonym
Synopsis: brief
    : synopsis
Syntax: syntax
Syzygie: syzygy
Szene: scene

T

Tableau: tableau
Tagebuch: diary
Tagelied: aubade
    : Tagelied
Tautologie: tautology
Technopägnion: carmen figuratum
Teichoskopie: teichoscopy
Telestichon: telestich
Tenzone: tenzone
tertium comparationis: tertium comparationis
Terzett: tercet
Terzine: 'terza rima
Tetralogie: tetralogy
Tetrameter: tetrameter
Tetrapodie: tetrapody
Tetrastichon: tetrastich
textimmanente Interpretation: new criticism
Textur: texture
Thema: theme
    : topic
Threnodie: threnody
Tierdichtung: animal poetry
Tierepos: beast epic
Tirade: tirade
Tmesis: tmesis
Ton: tone
tonisch: down beat
    : tonic
Topik: topic
Tragikomödie: tragicomedy

tragisch: tragic
tragische Ironie: dramatic irony
Tragödie: tragedy
Traktat: tract
Trauergesang: dirge
Traumallegorie: dream allegory
Traumdichtung: dream allegory
Travestie: travesty
Triade: triad
Tribrachys: tribrach
Triglotte: triglot
Trilogie: trilogy
Trimeter: trimeter
Trinklied: drinking song
Triolett: triolet
Tripodie: triple meter
    : tripody
Tristichon: tristich
Trithemimeres: trithemimeral
Trivialliteratur: trivial literature
trochäisch: trochaic
Trochäus: trochee
Trope: trope
Tropus: trope
Troubadourlyrik: courtly song
Trouverelyrik: courtly song
Typ: flat character
    : stock character
typische Situation: stock situation

U

Überheblichkeit: hybris
übertragen: figurative
ubi sunt Motiv: ubi sunt motif

umarmender Reim: embracing rhyme
    : enclosing rhyme

Umgangssprache: vernacularism
umschließender Reim: embracing rhyme
: enclosing rhyme
umschlungener Reim: embracing rhyme
Universalität: universality

unreiner Reim: eye rhyme
: imperfect rhyme
utopische Literatur: Utopian fiction
ut pictura poesis: ut pictura poesis

## V

Vagantendichtung: Goliardic verse
Venus und Adonis Strophe: Venus and Adonis stanza
verbale Ironie: verbal irony
verbla/te Metapher: dead metaphor
Verfremdungseffekt: epic drama
: estrangement effect
Vergleich: simile
verharmlosen: bowdlerize
Verlagsrecht: copyright
Verismus: verism
Vermenschlichung: anthropomorphism
Vers: line
: verse
Versausgang: line endings
Versbau: versification
Versbrechung: enjambment
Versfu/: foot
Verskunst: versification
Verslehre: prosody
Vers-Paragraph: verse paragraph
Verteidigung: apology
Vertrauter: confidant
victorianer: Victorian
victorianisch: Victorian
vielsilbig: polysyllabic
Vierzehnsilber: fourteener
Vierzehnzeiler: quatorzain

Vierzeiler: quatrain
Volksballade: folk ballad
Volksbuch: chapbook
Volksdichtung: folk poetry
Volksepos: folk epic
Volkserzählung: folk tale
Volkslied: folk song
Volkssage: folk tale
Volksschauspiel: folk play
Volksstück: folk play
voller Charakter: round character
Volta: volta
Vorausdeutung: anticipation
Vordeutung: anticipation
Vorrede: prologue
Vorromantik: Preromanticism
Vorspiel: curtain raiser
: preamble
: prelude
: prologue
Vortizismus: vorticism
Vorwort: foreword
: preamble
: preface
: prologue
: prelude
Vulgarismus: vulgarism

## W

Wagenbühne: pageant
Wahrscheinlichkeit: verisimilitude
Wechselgesang: antiphon
weiblich: weak ending
weibliche Zäsur: feminine caesura
weiblicher Reim: feminine rhyme
weiblicher Versausgang: feminine ending
Weihnachtslied: carol
weinerliches Lustspiel: comedy of tears
Weinlied: wine song
Wei/buch: Blue Book
Weitschweifigkeit: circumlocution
Weltanschauung: Weltanschauung
Weltschmerz: Weltschmerz

Wiederholung: repetition
Widersinnigkeit: incongruity
Wildwestgeschichte: Western
Wildwestroman: Western
Witz: wit
Witzbuch: jestbook
wörtlich: literal meaning
Wortspiel: pun
: quip
: wordplay
Wortschwall: verbosity
Wortwahl: poetic diction
Wortwitz: pun
: quip

## Z

Zäsur: caesura
: rest
Zehnsilber: decasyllable

Zauberformel: incantation
Zauberspruch: charm
: incantation

Zeile: line
Zeilenschinder: penny-a-liner
Zeilenschreiber: penny-a-liner
Zeilensprung: enjambment
Zeilenstil: end-stopped line
Zeitgeist: Zeitgeist
Zeit-Roman: time-novel
Zentralmotiv: central motif
Zeugma: zeugma
Zitat: quotation

Zukunftsroman: science fiction
Zusammenfassung: epitome
: brief
zweisilbig: disyllabic
zweisilbiger Endreim: double rhyme
zweizeilige Strophe: couplet
Zwiegespräch: duologue
Zwischenreim: cauda
Zwischenspiel: interlude
Zynismus: cynicism

# INDEX

## Spanish

### A

abstracto: abstract
acataléctico: acatalectic
acción: action
acción decreciente: falling action
acéfalo: acephalous
acento: accent
acento móvil: distributed stress
acento agudo: masculine ending
acento enclítico: recessive accent
acento expresivo: logical stress
acento móviv: distributed stress
acento tónico: stress
acertijo: riddle
acmeísma: acmeism
acontecimiento inicial: initial incident
acroteléutico: acroteleutic
acróstico: abecedarian
    : acrostic
acto: act
adagio: adage
adivinanza: conundrum
    : riddle
adynaton: adynaton
aféresis: aphaeresis
aforismo: aphorism
agono: agon
agudeza: bon mot
    : quip
    : repartee
    : wit
alborada: aubade
alegoría: allegory
    : rebus
alejandrino: Alexandrine
alienación: estrangement effect
aliteración: alliteration
almanaque: almanac
alta comedia: high comedy
alusión: allusion
ambiente: atmosphere
    : mood
ambigiedad: ambiguity
amebeo: amoebean verse
amor cortés: courtly love
amplificación: amplification
ana: ana
anaclasis: anaclasis
anacoluto: anacoluthon
anacreóntica: anacreontic poetry
anacronismo: anachronism

anacrusis: anacrusis
anadiplosis: anadiplosis
anáfora: anaphora
anagnórisis: anagnorisis
anagogía: anagoge
anagrama: anagram
analectas: analects
anales: annals
análisis: analysis
analogía: analogy
anapesto: anapaest
anástrofe: anastrophe
anécdota: anecdote
anecdotario: ana
anfibología: amphibology
anfíbraco: amphibrach
animización: empathy
anónimo: anonymous
antagonista: antagonist
    : foil
    : villain
antanaclasis: antanaclasis
antepenúltimo: antepenult
antibaquio: antibacchius
    : palimbacchius
anticipación: anticipation
anticlímax: anticlimax
    : bathos
antífona: antiphon
antihéroe: antihero
antimascarada: antimasque
antinovela: antinovel
antispasto: antispast
antístrofa: antistrophe
antítesis: antithesis
antología: anthology
átonas: slack
antónimo: antonym
antonomasia: antonomasia
antropomorfismo: anthropomorphism
aparte: aside
aparato crítico: apparatus criticus
apocalíptico: apocalyptic
apócope: apocope
apócrifo: apocrypha
apolíneo: Apollonian
apología: apology
apólogo: apologue
aposiopesis: aposiopesis
apóstrofe: apostrophe

**136**

apotegma: apophthegm
Arcadia: Arcadia
arcaísmo: archaism
arenga: harangue
argot: billingsgate
argumento: argument
aria: aria
arlequinada: harlequinade
arquetipo: archetype
arquitectónico: architectonics
arsis: arsis
arte mayor: arte mayor

arte menor: arte menor
arte nuevo: Jugendstil
asíndeton: asyndeton
asonancia: assonance
asunto: subject matter
atónico: up beat
átono: atonic
autobiografía: autobiography
auto sacramental: Corpus Christi play
: passion play
: virgin play

## B

baja comedia: low comedy
balada: ballad
baquio: bacchius
barbarismo: barbarism
bardo: bard
: scop
: skald
barroco: baroque
bellas letras: belletristic literature
bestiario: animal poetry
: beast epic
: bestiary

best seller: best seller
bibliografía: bibliography
bimembre: duple meter
biografía: biography
boceto: sketch
boceto burlesco: skit
bufonada: folly literature
burlesco: burlesque
byroniano: Byronic

## C

cacofonía: cacophony
cadencia: cadence
canción: canción
: canzone
: chanson
: song
canción a lo divino: contrafacture
canción anacreóntica: drinking song
: wine song
canción de gesta: chanson de geste
canción marinera: shanty
canción popular: folk song
canción trobadoresca: courtly song
canon: canon
cantar: cantar
cantar de gesta: cantar
cantata: cantata
cántico: canticle
: canticum
cantiga: courtly song
cantilena: ditty
canto: canto
: chant
canto fúnebre: dirge
capa y espada: comedia de capa y espada
capítulo: chapter
caracterización: characterization

caricatura: caricature
carmen: carmen
carro: pageant
casida: qasida
catabasis: catabasis
catacresis: catachresis
cataléctico: catalectic
catalecto: catalexis
catarsis: catharsis
catastasis: catastasis
catástrofe: catastrophe
censurar: bowdlerize
centón: cento
: collage
cesura: caesura
: medial caesura
cesura femenina: feminine caesura
cesura masculina: masculine caesura
charada: charade
chanson de toile: chanson de toile
ciclo de sonetos: crown of sonnets
: sonnet cycle
ciencia ficción: science fiction
cifra: chiffre
cinismo: cynicism
circunlocución: circumlocution
cita: quotation

clásico: classic
cliché: cliché
clímax: climax
clisé: cliché
coda: cauda
coliambo: choliamb
colon: colon
color local: local color
coma: comma
combinación métrica: rhyme scheme
comedia: comedy
: drama
comedia burguesa: burgeois drama
comedia burlesca: carnival comedy
comedia de capa y espada:
  comedia de capa y espada
comedia de enredo: comedy of intrigue
: comedy of situation
comedia de figurón: comedy of character
comedia de los bulevars: boulevard drama
comedia de costumbres: comedy of manners
comedia dentro de una comedia: play within a play
comedia de tesis social: thesis play
comedia histórica: chronicle play
: historical play
comedia lacrimosa: comedy of tears
comedia mariana: virgin play
comedia mitológica: masque
comedia musical: musical drama
comedia sentimental: comedy of tears
comedias populares: folk play
comedias tradicionales: folk play
comedia televisada: television play
cómico: comic
comics: comics
compás: beat
compensación: compensation
complexión: complexio
compuesto elíptico: blend
conceptismo: conceptism
concepto: conceit
: quip
conceptos metafísicos: metaphysical conceits
conceptos petrarquistas: Petrarchan coneits
concretismo: concretism
concreto: concrete
conduplicación: conduplicatio

confidente: confidant
connotación: connotation
consonancia: consonance
constructivismo: constructivism
contenido: content
contrapunto poético: partimen
convención: convention
copla: copla
copla de arte mayor: copla de arte mayor
copla humorística de cinco verso: limerick
coriambo: choriamb
coro: chorus
corona de sonetos: crown of sonnets
corrección: correctio
corriente de conciencia: stream of
  consciousness technique
crasis: crasis
creacionismo: blend
Creacionismo: Creacionismo
crestomatía: chrestomathy
crético: amphimacer
: cretic
criptograma: cryptogram
crisis: crisis
crítica: critique
crítica impresionista: impressionistic criticism
crítica intencionada: intentional fallacy
crítica interna: new criticism
crónica: chronicle
cronograma: chronogram
cuadro costumbrista: genre picture
cuadro vivo: tableau vivant
cuarteto: quatrain
cuarteto iámbico: long meter
cubismo: cubism
cuento: novella
: short story
: tale
cuento de niños: children's song
cuento exagerado: cock-and-bull story
cuento de hadas: fairy tale
cuento inverosímil: tall tale
cuento moral: cautionary tale
cuento popular: folk tale
: yarn
culteranismo: culteranism
cultismo: cultism

## D

dáctilo: dactyl
dadaísmo: Dadaism
debate: débat
decadentismo: decadence
decasílabo: decasyllable

décima: decastich
decoro: decorum
denotación: denotation
desenlace: denouement
: resolution

deuteragonista: deuteragonist
diálogo: dialogue
: duologue
diálogo en dísticos: distichomythia
diario: diary
diatriba: diatribe
: tirade
dicción poética: poetic diction
dicho: dit
diéresis: diaeresis
digresión: digression
: excursus
dímetro: dimeter
dionisiaco: Dionysian
dipodia: dipody
disilábico: disyllabic
disonancia: dissonance
disparate: extravaganza
dispondeo: dispondee

eco: echo
: echo verse
: ploce
edición definitiva: definitive edition
égloga: eclogue
ejemplo: exemplum
elegía: elegy
elipsis: ellipsis
elisión: elision
elocuencia: eloquence
emblema: emblem
enálage: enallage
encabalgamiento: enjambment
encantación: incantation
encanto: charm
enclítico: enclitic
encomio: encomium
endecasílabo: hendecasyllable
endecha: endecha
énfasis: emphasis
enfoque crítico: strategy
ensayo: essay
entimema: enthymeme
entremés: droll
: interlude
epanadiplosis: epanadiplosis
epanalepsis: epanalepsis
epanodos: epanodos
épica: epic
épica artística: art epic
épica burlesca: mock epic
épica cristiana: Christian epic
épica heroica: heroic epic
épica histórica: historic epic
épica primitiva: folk epic

dístico: couplet
dístico con encabalgamiento: open couplet
dístico elegíaco: distich
dístico heroico: heroic couplet
dístico irregular: poulter's measure
dístico octosilábico: octosyllabic couplet
ditirambo: dithyramb
ditroqueo: ditrochee
diyambo: diiamb
dizain: dizain
doble sentido: double entendre
drama: drama
drama épico: epic drama
drama heroico: heroic play
drama litúrgico: liturgical drama
dramática: dramatics
dramático: dramatic
dramaturgia: dramaturgy
duración: duration

E

epicedio: epicedium
epideíctico: epideictic speech
epifanía: epiphany
epífora: epiphora
epígono: epigonism
epígrafe: epigraph
epigrama: epigram
epílogo: epilogue
epirrema: epirrhema
episodio: episode
epístola: epistle
epitafio: epitaph
epitalamio: epithalamium
: prothalamion
epítasis: epitasis
: initial incident
epíteto: epithet
epítome: epitome
epizeuxis: epizeuxis
época clásica: classicism
época de Augusto: Augustan period
época isabelina: Elizabethan age
época medieval: medieval period
epodo: epode
epopeya: epopee
: epos
epopeya nacional: national epic
equilibrio: balance
equivalencia: equivalence
equívoco: pun
error trágico: hamartia
escansión: scansion
escazonte: choliamb
escena: scene
escenario: setting

escolasticismo: Scholasticism
escolio: scolion
escuela siciliana: Sicilian school
escuelas silesianas: Silesian schools
esotérico: esoteric
espondeo: spondee
estancia: stave
esticomitia: end-stopped line
    : stichomythia
estilística: stylistics
estilo: style
estilo alto: high style
estilo bombástico: bombast
estilo indirecto libre: indirect interior monologue
estilo medio: middle style
estilo sencillo: low style
estribillo: burden
    : estribillo
    : refrain
estrofa: stanza
    : stave
    : strophe
estrofa alcaica: Alcaic strophe
estrofa al estilo de Spenser: Spenserian stanza
estrofa asclepiádica: Asclepiadic strophe

estrofa chauceriana: rhyme royal
estrofa de balada: ballad stanza
estrofa de himno: common meter
estrofa elegíaca: elegiac stanza
estrofa heroica: heroic stanza
estrofa palinódica: palinodic
estrofa sáfica: Sapphic stanza
estructura: structure
estructura expisódica: episodic structure
estructura extrínsica: extrinsic structure
estructura intrínsica: intrinsic structure
eufemismo: euphemism
eufonía: euphony
eufuismo: euphuism
exégesis: exegesis
existencialismo: existentialism
éxodo: exodus
exordio: exordium
exotérico: exoteric
exotismo: exoticism
expletivo: expletive
explicación: explication
exposición: exposition
expresión gastada: hackneyed expression
expresionismo: expressionism

**F**

fabliau: fabliau
fábula: fable
fábula atellana: Atellan fables
farsa: burletta
    : farce
    : slapstick
ficción: fiction
figuras retóricas: figures of speech
       : rhetorical figures
figurativo: figurative
filípica: philippic
final del verso: line endings
flashback: flashback
flat character: flat character

folio: folio
folletín: feuilleton
    : penny dreadful
fondo: background
forma: form
forma abierta: open form
formalismo: formalism
forma orgánica: organic form
fórmula: formula
fragmento: fragment
fraseología: phraseology
fuente primaria: primary source
fuentes secundarias: secondary sources
futurismo: futurism

**G**

gacetillero: penny-a-liner
galiambo: galliamb
galicismo: Gallicism
género: genre
geórgica: georgic
germanía: cant

gesta: gest
gliconio: Glyconic
glosa: gloss
gongorismo: Gongorism
grotesco: grotesque
guión: scenario

**H**

hagiografía: hagiography
hemiepes: hemiepes
hemistecomitia: hemistichomythia
hemistiquio: hemistich
hendíadis: hendiadys

hechizo: charm
heptámetro: heptameter
heptemímeris: hephthemimeral
heptasílabo: heptasyllable
hermetismo: Hermeticism

héroe: hero
hexámetro: hexameter
hexámetro dactílico: Pythian verse
hexastiquio: hexastich
hiato: hiatus
himno: hymn
hipálage: hypallage
hipérbaton: hyperbaton
hipérbole: hyperbole
hipérmetro: hypermetric
hipotaxis: hypotaxis

ictus: ictus
idealismo: idealism
idilio: idyll
ilustración: Enlightenment
imagen: image
imágenes: imagery
imagismo: imagism
imitación: imitation
impresionismo: impressionism
incongruencia: incongruity
índice: index
insinuación: innuendo
intermedio: intermezzo
interpolación: interpolation
interpolación cómica: comic relief

jerga: jargon
jónico: Ionic
jornada: scene
joven Alemania, la: Junges Deutschland

komos: commus

lai: lai
lamento: complaint
      : lament
      : plaint
leitmotiv: leitmotif
lenguaje figurado: figurative language
letanía: litany
letraísmo: letterism
letrilla: letrilla
leyenda: legend
libro de chistes: jestbook
libro de etiqueta: book of manners
libro del ciclo artúrico: Arthurian romance
libro de tesis: autotelic
libro de viaje: travelogue

historia: story
homeoteleuton: homoeoteleuton
homilía: homily
homófonos: homophones
homógrafos: homographs
homoioptoton: homoioptoton
homónimos: homonyms
humanismo: Humanism
humor: humor
humorada: humoresque

I

interpretación: interpretation
intriga: intrigue
intriga secundaria: subplot
invectiva: invective
inversión: inversion
invocación: invocation
ironía: irony
ironía del destino: irony of fate
ironía dramática: dramatic irony
ironía poética: romantic irony
ironía socrática: Socratic irony
ironía verbal: verbal irony
irracionalismo: irrationalism
isométrico: homoeomeral

J

joven Viena, la: Jung-Wien
juego: nonsense verse
juego de palabras: wordplay
juglar: minstrel

K

L

libro en cuarto: quarto
libro oficial: blue book
licencia poética: poetic licence
lingüística: linguistics
lipograma: lipogram
lira: lira
literatura: literature
literatura comercial: pot boiler
liberatura de Provenza: Provençal literature
literatura didáctica: didactic literature
literatura indigenista: Amerind literature
literatura utópica: Utopian fiction
lítote: litotes
logogrifo: logograph
logomaquia: logomachy

macron: macron
madrigal: madrigal
manierismo: mannerism
máquina: machinery
marinismo: Marinism
mascarada: masque
: mummery
máxima: maxim
medida anárquica: modulation
meiosis: meiosis
melodrama: drame
: melodrama
memorias: memoirs
mensaje: message
mesode: mesode
mesosticha: mesostich
metáfora: metaphor
metáfora disparatada: mixed metaphor
metáfora fósil: dead metaphor
metáfora léxica: dead metaphor
metalepsis: metalepsis
metaplasmo: metaplasm
metátesis: metathesis
metonimia: metonymy
métrica: metrics
metro: meter
: metron
milagro: miracle play
mimesis: imitation
: mimesis

mimo: mime
misterio: mystery play
misticismo: mysticism
mito: myth
mitología: mythology
modismo: idiom
moloso: molossus
momería: mummery
monodia: monody
monodrama: monodrama
monólogo: dramatic monologue
: monologue
monólogo interior: interior monologue
monométrico: monopody
monometro: monometer
monopodia: monopody
monorrima: monorhyme
monosilábico: monosyllabic
montaje: montage
mora: mora
moral: message
: moral
moralidad: morality play
motivación: motivation
motivo: motif
motivo central: central motif
motivo ciego: blind motif
motivo principal: central motif
movimiento estético: aestheticism

nana: children's song
narración dentro de un marco: enveloping structure
narración en primera persona: first person narrative
narración en tercera persona: third person narrative
narración fantástica: fantasy fiction
narrador omnisciente: omniscient narrator
naturalismo: naturalism
némesis: nemesis
: poetic justice
neoclasicismo: neoclassicism
neoclasicismo inglés: Augustan period
neogongorismo: Neo-Gongorism
neologismo: blend
: neologism
neologismo circunstancial: nonce word
neorromanticismo: neoromanticism
no-gaku: nõ
novela: novel
novela de aprendizaje: apprenticeship novel
novela de aventuras: adventure novel
novela de caballería: chivalric romance
: courtly epic
novela corta: long-short story
: novelette

nouvela de acontecimientos: event-novel
novela de costumbres: novel of manners
novela de época: time-novel
novela de formacíon: novel of development
: novel of educational
formation
novela de ideas: novel of ideas
novela del artista: novel of the artist
novela de la tierra: novel of the soil
novela del Oeste: Western
novela de personajes: man-novel
novela en clave: key novel
novela en verso: metrical romance
novela epistolar: epistolary novel
novela experimental: experimental novel
novela gótica: Gothic novel
novela heterodoxa: heterodox novel
novela histórica: historical novel
novela humanitaria: humanitarian novel
novela intelectual: novel of ideas
novela picaresca: picaresque
novela policíaca: detective story
novela política: political novel
novela psicológica: psychological novel

novela sensacionalista: thriller
novela sentimental: sentimental novel

objetividad: objectivity
objetivismo: objectivism
objetos simbólicos: objective correlative
obra de tesis social: problem play
obra didáctica experimental: living newspaper
obra en un acto: one-act play
octámetro: octameter
octapodia: octapody
octava: huitain
: octastich
: octave
: octet
octava rima: ottava rima
octava siciliana: Sicilian octave
octómetro: octapody

palilogia: palilogy
palíndromo: palindrome
palinodia: palinode
panegírico: eulogy
: panegyric
pantomima: dumb show
: pantomime
pantoum: pantoum
parábasis: parabasis
parábola: parable
paradoja: paradox
paráfrasis: paraphrase
paragoge: paragoge
paralelismo: parallelism
paraliteratura: paraliterature
parataxis: parataxis
pareado: closed couplet
paremia: paroemiac
parnasianos: Parnassians
parodia: parody
: skit
parodos: parodos
paronomasia: paronomasia
pasaje exagerado: purple passage
pasaje preciocista: purple passage
paso: curtain raiser
pasquín: lampoon
: pasquinade
pastiche: pastiche
pastorela: pastourelle
pathos: pathos
pausa: rest
pausa rítmica: break
peán: paean
pentámetro: pentameter
: pentapody

novela social: humanitarian novel
número: number

O

octonario: octonarius
octosilábica: octosyllabic
oda: ode
oda horaciana: Horatian ode
oda pindárica: Pindaric ode
onomatopeya: onomatopoeia
ópera: opera
opereta: ballad opera
: operetta
opúsculo: tract
oración: oration
oratoria sagrada: homiletics
oratorio: oratorio
orgullo fatal: hybris
oxímoron: oxymoron

P

pentemímeris: penthemimeral
penúltimo: penult
peón: paeon
perífrasis: periphrasis
período: period
período: period
período poético: verse paragraph
peripecia: peripeteia
peroración: peroration
personaje: character
: persona
personaje bidimensional: flat character
personaje completo: round character
personaje convencional: stock character
personificación: empathy
: personification
petrarquismo: Petrarchism
picaresco: picaresque
pie: foot
pie docmio: dochmius
pie epítrito: epitrite
pietismo: Pietism
pirámide de Freytag: Freytag's pyramid
pirriquio: pyrrhic
pitiyambo: Pythiambic
plagio: plagiarism
pleonasmo: pleonasm
pliego suelto: chapbook
poema: poem
poema de una línea: monostich
poema en prosa: prose poem
poema épico al estilo alejandrino: epyllion
poema ideográfico: carmen figuratum
poema ideográfico en forma de cruz: altar poem
poemas siloicos: silloi

**143**

poesía: poesie
: poetry
poesía abstracta: abstract poetry
poesía amorosa: love poetry
poesía bucólica: bucolic poetry
poesía dramática: dramatic poetry
poesía épica: narrative poetry
poesía erótica: erotic poetry
poesía gnómica: gnomic poetry
poesía goliardesca: Goliardic verse
poesía heroica: heroic poetry
poesía lírica: lyric poetry
poesía macarrónica: macaronic poetry
poesía mélica: melic poetry
poesía ocasional: light verse
: occasional verse
poesía oral: oral poetry
poesía osiánica: Ossianic poems
poesía pastoril: pastoral poetry
poesía tradicional: folk poetry
poeta laureado: poet laureate
poetas metafísicos: metaphysical poets
poética: poetics
polémica: polemic
polémica satírica en verso: flyting
polígloto: polyglot
poliptoton: polyptoton
polisilábico: polysyllabic
polisílabo: polysyllabic
polisíndeton: polysyndeton
pornografía: pornography
preámbulo: preamble

preciosismo: preciosity
prefacio: foreword
: preface
pregunta retórica: rhetorical question
preludio: prelude
prerrafaelistas: Pre-Raphaelite Brotherhood
prerromanticismo: Preromanticism
presente histórico: historical present
primitivismo: primitivism
procacidad: vulgarism
proceleusmático: proceleusmatic
proclítico: proclitic
procronismo: prochronism
proemio: proem
prolepsis: prolepsis
prólogo: prologue
propiedad literaria: copyright
prosa: prose
prosa poética: verset
prosa polifónica: polyphonic prose
prosodia: prosody
prosodion: prosodic
prosopopeya: poetic fallacy
: prosopopoeia
protagonista: protagonist
prótasis: protasis
prótesis: prothesis
proverbio: proverb
provincialismo: provincialism
punto de vista: point of view
purismo: purism

## Q

quiasmo: chiasmus

quintilla: pentastich

## R

racionalismo: rationalism
radio teatro: radio play
rapsoda: rhapsodist
rapsodia: rhapsody
realismo: realism
realismo mágico: magical realism
realismo socialista: socialist realism
recensión: recension
redondilla: redondilla
Reforma: Reformation
refrán: refrán
: repetend
refutación: refutation
regionalismo: regionalism
: vernacularism
reizianismo: reizianum
Renacimiento: Renaissance
Renacimiento céltico: Celtic Renaissance
réquiem: requiem

repetición: incremental repetition
: ploce
: repetition
reportaje: reportage
representación: mise-en-scène
reseña: review
Restauración: Restoration
retardación: retardation
retórica: rhetoric
retrospección: flashback
revista: revue
rima: rhyme
rima abrazada: embracing rhyme
: enclosing rhyme
rima aguda: masculine rhyme
rima alternada: alternate rhyme
rima alternante: cross rhyme
rima apocopada: apocopated rhyme
rima apofónica: analyzed rhyme

rima átona: light rhyme
rima doble: double rhyme
rima encadenada: chain rhyme
rima femenina: feminine rhyme
rima final: end rhyme
rima homónima: rime riche
rima idéntica: identical rhyme
rima imperfecta: imperfect rhyme
rima imperial: mosaic rhyme
rima interna: internal rhyme
rima leonina: Leonine rhyme
rima masculina: masculine rhyme
rima perfecta: perfect rhyme
rima polisilábica: polysyllabic rhyme
rima pueril: jingle
rima quebrada: broken rhyme
rima visual: eye rhyme
ritmo: beat
    : rhythm
ritmo anfíbraco: rocking rhythm
ritmo ascendente: ascending rhythm
    : rising meter

ritmo cadencioso: running rhythm
ritmo de contrapunto: counterpoint rhythm
ritmo descendente: descending rhythm
    : falling meter
ritmo de vaivén: rocking rhythm
ritmo logaédico: logaoedic
ritornelo: ritornello
romance: romance
romance artístico: art ballad
romance folklórico: folk ballad
romance popular: folk ballad
romance publicado en pliego suelto:
    broadside ballad
romancero: romancero
romance satírico: fabliau
romance tradicional: folk ballad
romanticismo: Romanticism
romantización: romanticization
rococó: rococo
rondó: rondeau
rondó al estilo de Swinburne: roundel
rotundo: orotund style

## S

sáfico: Sapphic
saga: roman-fleuve
    : saga
salmo: psalm
sarcasmo: sarcasm
sátira: satire
    : satyr play
semántica: semantics
senario: senarius
sensibilidad: sensibility
sentencia: sentence
sentido: meaning
sentido literal: literal meaning
sentimentalidad: sentimentality
septenario: septenarius
    : septenary
septeto: septet
séptima: heptastich
serenata: serenade
serie indeterminada de versos: astrophic
    composition
seudoliteratura: trivial literature
seudónimo: pseudonym
sextina: sestet
    : sestina
sigla: acronym
sílaba: syllable
sílaba acentuada: accented syllable
sílaba breve: short syllable
sílaba larga: long syllable
silepsis: syllepsis

silogismo: syllogism
silógrafo: sillographer
silva: silva
simbolismo: symbolism
símbolo: symbol
símil: simile
simposio: symposium
sinalefa: synaloepha
sinceridad: sincerity
síncope: syncope
sinécdoque: synecdoche
sinéresis: synaeresis
sinestesia: synaesthesia
sinónimo: synonym
sinopsis: brief
    : synopsis
sintaxis: syntax
situación convencional: stock situation
sizigio: syzygy
solecismo: solecism
soliloquio: soliloquy
soneto: sonnet
soneto al estilo de Spenser: Spenserian sonnet
soneto inconcluso: curtal sonnet
soneto irregular: quatorzaine
    : tailed sonnet
soneto miltoniano: Miltonic sonnet
Sturm und Drang: Sturm und Drang
subjetividad: subjectivity
surrealismo: surrealism
suspenso: suspense

tautología: tautology
teatro de cámara: closet drama
teatro del absurdo: theater of the absurd
             : drama of the absurd
teichoscopía: teichoscopy
telesticha: telestich
teleteatro: television play
tema: subject matter
    : theme
tensón: tenzone
terceto: tercet
    : tristich
terceto monorrimo: triplet
tercetos encadenados: terza rima
terminación débil: weak ending
terminación femenina: feminine ending
             : weak ending
terminación masculina: masculine ending
tesis: message
    : thesis
tetralogía: tetralogy
tetrámetro: tetrameter
    : tetrapody
tetrapodia: tetrapody
tetrástico: tetrastich
textura: texture
tiempo de la obra literaria: fable time
tiempo narrativo: narrative time
tiras cómicas: comics
tmesis: tmesis
tónico: down beat
    : tonic

tono: tone
tópico: topic
tornada: envoi
tradición: tradition
traducción interlineal: interlinear
tragedia: tragedy
tragedia burguesa: burgeois tragedy
trágico: tragic
tragicomedia: tragicomedy
trama: plot
    : story
tramoya: machinery
travestía: travesty
treno: threnody
tres unidades, las: unities, the three
tríada: triad
tribraquio: tribrach
triemímeris: trithemimeral
trilingüe: triglot
trilogía: trilogy
trímetro: trimeter
triolet: triolet
tripodia: tripody
trisilábico: triple meter
trocaico: trochaic
tropo: trope
troqueo: trochee
trova: fabliau
trovador: minstrel
trozo de vida: slice-of-life

U

Ultraismo: Ultraismo

universalidad: universality

V

vanguardia: avant-garde
verborragia: logorrhoea
verbosidad: verbosity
verismo: verism
verosimilitud: verisimilitude
versificación: rhyme scheme
    : versification
verso: line
    : verse
verso acéfalo: headless line
verso adónico: Adonic verse
verso alternado: alternate verse
verso blanco: blank verse
verso braquicatalectico: brachycatalectic
verso cadencioso: alternate verse
verso cataléctico: substitution
verso correlativo: correlative verse
verso cuantitativo: quantitative verse

verso de cinco arsis: pentarsic
verso épico: heroic meter
verso espondaico: spondaic verse
verso faleuco: Phalaecean
verso ferecracio: Pherecratean
verso heroico: heroic verse
verso incoherente: nonsense verse
verso leonino: Leonine verse
verso octosilábico: octosyllabic verse
verso pentamímero: penthemimer
verso rítmico: accentual verse
verso ropálico: rhopalic verse
versos burlescos: doggerel
versos fesceninos: Fescennine verses
versos serpentinos: serpentine verse
verso sotádico: soteadean verse
verso suelto: free verse
victoriano: Victorian

villancico: carol
      : villancico
viñeta: vignette
visión alegórica: dream allegory

western: Western

yámbico: iambic

zejel: ghazel

vorticismo: vorticism
voz: voice
vuelta: volta

W

Y

yambo: iamb

Z

zeugma: zeugma

# Index of Names

| | |
|---|---|
| Abélard, Pierre | Scholasticism |
| Alberti, Rafael | Neo-Gongorism |
| Albertus Magnus | Scholasticism |
| Alcaeus | Alcaic strophe |
| Alexander the Great | Alexandrine |
| Anacreon | anacreontic poetry |
| Apollinaire, Guillaume | cubism |
| Aquinas, Saint Thomas | Scholasticism |
| Aristotle | anagnorisis |
| | catharsis |
| | unities, the three |
| Arp, Hans | Dadaism |
| d'Arrezzo, Guiton | dolce stil nuovo |
| Asclepiad | Asclepiadic strophe |
| Augustus, Emperor of Rome | Augustan period |
| | classicism |
| Babbitt, Irving | neo-humanism |
| Bagricki, Eduard | constructivism |
| Bahr, Hermann | Jung-Wien |
| Baïf, Jean Antoine | Pléiade |
| Bailey, Philip James | spasmodic school |
| Balzac, Honoré de | realism |
| Barocci, Federigo | baroque |
| Baudelaire, Charles | decadence |
| Beckett, Samuel | one-act play |
| | theater of the absurd |
| Bellay, Joachim du | Pléiade |
| Bentley, Edmond Clerihew | clerihew |
| Bely, Andrey | symbolism |
| Blair, Robert | Graveyard School |
| Boccaccio, Giovanni | Falkentheorie |
| Borges, Jorge Luis | Ultraismo |
| Bowdler, Thomas | bowdlerize |
| Braque, Gerorges | cubism |
| Brecht, Bertold | epic drama |
| Brentano, Clemens | Romanticism |
| Breton, André | surrealism |
| Brooke, Rupert | Georgian poets |
| Burns, Robert | Burns stanza |
| Butler, Samuel | Hudibrastic verse |
| Byron, George Noel Gordon, Lord | Byronic |
| | Romanticism |
| | Satanic school |
| Cavalcanti, Guido | dolce stil nuovo |
| Cézanne, Paul | cubism |
| Charles I of England | Caroline period |
| | Cavalier poets |
| Charles II of England | Restoration |
| Chartier, Alain | Rhétoriqueurs |
| Chekhov, Anton Pavlovich | decadence |
| Clerihew, Edmond . . . Bentley | clerihew |

| | |
|---|---|
| Coleridge, Samuel Taylor | Lake Poets |
| Coward, Noël | boulevard drama |
| Crapsey, Adelaide | cinquain |
| Crashaw, Richard | metaphysical poets |
| | |
| Dach, Simon | Silesian schools |
| Dante Alighieri | dolce stil nuovo |
| Davies, William Henry | Georgian poets |
| Delaney, Shelagh | Angry Young Men |
| Demosthenes | philippic |
| Descartes, René | Enlightenment |
| Deyssel, Lodewijk van | Tachtigers |
| Dickens, Charles | realism |
| Diego Cendoya, Gerardo | Creacionismo |
| | Neo-Gongorism |
| | Ultraismo |
| Dilthey, Wilhelm | apprenticeship novel |
| Döblin, Alfred | Neue Sachlichkeit |
| Donne, John | metaphysical poets |
| Doolittle, Hilda | imagism |
| Dorat, Jean | Pléiade |
| Dostoevski, Feodor | realism |
| Drinkwater, John | Georgian poets |
| Droste-Hülshoff, Annette F. von | Biedermeier poets |
| du Bellay, Joachim | Pléiade |
| Dujardin, Edouard | stream of consciousness |
| Dumas, Alexandre | conversation piece |
| | |
| Edward VII of England | Edwardian |
| Eichenbaum, Boris | formalism |
| Eichendorff, Joseph von | Romanticism |
| Eliot, Thomas Stearns | objective correlative |
| | symbolism |
| | vorticism |
| Elizabeth I of England | Elizabethan age |
| Eluard, Paul | surrealism |
| Erasmus, Desiderius | Humanism |
| | |
| Fielding, Henry | Empfindsamkeit |
| | Preromanticism |
| Fleming, Paul | Silesian schools |
| Fontane, Theodor | realism |
| Forster, Edward Morgan | Bloomsbury Group |
| Freytag, Gustav | Freytag's pyramid |
| Friedrich II of Sicily | Sicilian school |
| | |
| Gautier, Théophile | Parnassians |
| Geibel, Emanuel | Münchner Dichterkreis |
| Gellert, Christian F. | Empfindsamkeit |
| George V of England | Georgian poets |
| George, Stefan | symbolism |
| Glycon | Glyconic |

| | |
|---|---|
| Goethe, Johann Wolfgang von | Empfindsamkeit |
| | Knittelvers |
| | Münchner Dichterkreis |
| | Pietism |
| | Sturm und Drang |
| Goldsmith, Oliver | Empfindsamkeit |
| | sensibility |
| Góngora, Luis de | Gongorism |
| Gorky, Maxim | socialist realism |
| Gorodetsky, Sergei M | acmeism |
| Govoni, Corrado | futurism |
| Greene, Robert | University Wits |
| Grillparzer, Franz | Biedermeier poets |
| Gryphius, Andreas | Silesian schools |
| Guitry, Sacha | boulevard drama |
| Gumilyov, Nikolai S. | acmeism |
| Gutzkow, Karl | Junges Deutschland |
| | |
| Hagedorn, Friedrich von | rococo |
| Hauptmann, Gerhart | naturalism |
| Heidegger, Martin | existentialism |
| Herbert, George | metaphysical poets |
| Herder, Johann Gottfried | Pietism |
| Hesse, Hermann | surrealism |
| Heyse, Paul | Falkentheorie |
| | Münchner Dichterkreis |
| Hoffmann, Ernst Theodor Amadeus | Satanic school |
| Hofmannsthal, Hugo von | Jugendstil |
| | Jung-Wien |
| Hofmannswaldau, Hofmann von | Silesian schools |
| Hölty, Ludwig Ch. H. | Göttinger Hain |
| Hopkins, Gerard Manley | sprung rhythm |
| Horace (Quintus Horatius Flaccus) | Augustan period |
| | carpe diem |
| | Horatian ode |
| | ut pictura poesis |
| Hugo, Victor | Romanticism |
| | Satanic school |
| Huidobro, Vicente | Creacionismo |
| Hulme, Thomas Ernest | imagism |
| | vorticism |
| Hume, David | Enlightenment |
| Hunt, James | Cockney School of Poetry |
| Hyde, Douglas | Celtic Renaissance |
| | |
| Ibsen, Henrik | naturalism |
| Inber, Vera | constructivism |
| Ionesco, Eugène | theater of the absurd |
| Isou, Isidore | letterism |
| | |
| Jacobi, Friedrich H. | Empfindsamkeit |
| Jacobson, Roman | formalism |
| James I of England | Jacobean |

James, William — stream of consciousness  
Jodelle, Étienne — Pléiade  
Jonson, Ben — Elizabethan age  
Joyce, James — surrealism  

Kafka, Franz — surrealism  
Kant, Immanuel — Enlightenment  
Kästner, Erich — Neue Sachlichkeit  
Keats, John — Cockney School of Poetry  
Romanticism  
Satanic school  
Khayyam, Omar — Ruba'i  
Kierkegaard, Søren — existentialism  
Kleist, Heinrich von — Satanic School  
Klinger, Maximilian — Sturm und Drang  
Kloos, Willem J. Th. — Tachtigers  
Klopstock, Friedrich G. — Göttinger Hain  
Pietism  
Kingsley, Charles — spasmodic school  

Lamartine, Alphonse de — Romanticism  
Larrera, Juan — Creacionismo  
Laube, Heinrich — Junges Deutschland  
Leconte de Lisle — Parnassians  
Leibniz, Gottfried W. F. von — Enlightenment  
Lemaire, Jean — Rhétoriqueurs  
Lemaître, Maurice — letterism  
Leoninus — Leonine verse  
Lewis, Wyndham — vorticism  
Locke, John — Enlightenment  
Logau, Friedrich F. von — Silesian schools  
Lohenstein, Daniel Casper von — Silesian schools  
Lorca, Federico García — one-act play  
Lovelace, Richard — Cavalier poets  
Lowell, Amy — imagism  
polyphonic prose  
Luther, Martin — Reformation  
Lyly, John — euphuism  
University Wits  

Macpherson, James — Ossianic poems  
Magnus, Albertus — Scholasticism  
Mallarmé, Stéphane — impressionism  
symbolism  
Manfred of Sicily — Sicilian school  
Marinetti, Filippo Tommaso — futurism  
Marino, Giambattista — Marinism  
Marvell, Andrew — metaphysical poets  
Maximilian II of Bavaria — Münchner Dichterkreis  
Milton, John — Miltonic sonnet  
Mistral, Frédéric — Félibrige  
Monet, Claude — impressionism  
Montale, Eugenio — Hermeticism  
More, Paul Elmer — neo-humanism

| More, Thomas | Humanism |
| | Utopian fiction |
| Mörike, Eduard | Biedermeier poets |
| Morris, William | Fleshly School of Poetry |
| | Pre-Raphaelite Brotherhood |
| Musset, Alfred de | Satanic school |
| | |
| Nashe, Thomas | University Wits |
| Nietzsche, Fiedrich | decadence |
| Novalis (Friedrich von Hardenberg) | Romanticism |
| | |
| O'Casey, Sean | Celtic Renaissance |
| Opitz, Martin | Silesian schools |
| Osborne, John | Angry Young Men |
| Ossian | Preromanticism |
| | Ossianic poems |
| Ovid (Publius Ovidius Naso) | Augustan period |
| | |
| Papini, Giovanni | futurism |
| Peele, George | University Wits |
| Pericles | classicism |
| Petrarch, Francesco | Petrarchan conceits |
| | Petrarchism |
| | sonnet |
| Phalaecus | Phalaecean |
| Pherecrates | Pherecratean |
| Philip II of Macedon | philippic |
| Picasso, Pablo | cubism |
| Pindar | Pindaric ode |
| Pissaro, Camille | impressionism |
| Pope, Alexander | Augustan period |
| Pound, Ezra | imagism |
| | vorticism |
| Prévost d'Exiles, A.-F. | rococo |
| | |
| Quasimodo, Salvatore | Hermeticism |
| | |
| Raimund, Ferdinand | Biedermeier poets |
| Raphael (Raffaello Santi) | Pre-Raphaelite Brotherhood |
| Reiz, J. W. | reizianum |
| Renoir, Auguste | impressionism |
| Reuchlin, Johann | Humanism |
| Reverdy, Pierre | cubism |
| Richards, Ivor Armstrong | metaphor |
| Richardson, Samuel | sensibility |
| Rilke, Rainer Maria | Jugendstil |
| | symbolism |
| Rimbaud, Arthur | impressionism |
| | symbolism |
| Robbe-Grillet, Alain | chosisme |
| Roh, Franz | magical realism |

Ronsard, Pierre de — Pléiade
Rossetti, Christina — Pre-Raphaelite Brotherhood
Rossetti, Dante Gabriel — Fleshly School of Poetry
Pre-Raphaelite Brotherhood
Roumanille, Joseph — Félibrige
Ruskin, John — poetic fallacy

Sachs, Hans — Knittelvers
Sappho — Sapphic
Sarraute, Nathalie — antinovel
tropisme
Sartre, Jean-Paul — antinovel
existentialism
Schiller, Friedrich — Sturm und Drang
Schnitzler, Arthur — decadence
Jugendstil
Jung-Wien
Selvinski, Ilya — constructivism
Shakespeare, William — Elizabethan age
sonnet
Venus and Adonis stanza
Shaw, George Bernard — one-act play
Shelley, Percy Bysshe — Romanticism
Satanic school
Sheridan, Richard Brinsley — malapropism
Slovskij, V — formalism
Smith, Alexander — spasmodic school
Socrates — Socratic irony
Sologub, Fedor — symbolism
Sotades — Sotadean verse
Southey, Robert — Lake poets
Satanic school
Spener, Philipp Jakob — Pietism
Spenser, Edmund — Elizabethan age
Spenserian sonnet
Spenserian stanza
Spooner, William A. — spoonerism
Sterne, Laurence — Empfindsamkeit
Preromanticism
Stifter, Adalbert — Biedermeier poets
Strachey, Lytton — Bloomsbury Group
Strindberg, August — one-act play
Suckling, John — Cavalier poets
Swift, Jonathan — Augustan period
Swinburne, Algernon Charles — Fleshly School of Poetry
roundel

Torre, Guillermo de — Ultraismo
Tyard, Pontus de — Pléiade
Tzara, Tristan — Dadaism

Ungaretti, Giuseppe — Hermeticism

**153**

| | |
|---|---|
| Vallejo, César | Ultraismo |
| Vergil (Publius Vergilius Maro) | Augustan period |
| | georgic |
| Verlaine, Paul | impressionism |
| | symbolism |
| Verwey, Albert | Tachtigers |
| Victoria of England | Victorian |
| Voltaire (François Marie Arouet) | rococo |
| Voß, Johann Heinrich | Göttinger Hain |
| | |
| Walther von der Vogelweide | minnesinger |
| Wieland, Christoph Martin | rococo |
| Wienbarg, Ludolf | Junges Deutschland |
| Wilde, Oscar | conversation piece |
| | decadence |
| | one-act play |
| Woolf, Leonard | Bloomsbury Group |
| Woolf, Virginia | Bloomsbury Group |
| Wordsworth, William | Lake Poets |
| | Romanticism |
| | |
| Yeats, William Butler | Celtic Renaissance |
| | symbolism |
| | |
| Zelinski, K. L. | constructivism |
| Zigler, Heinrich Anselm von | Silesian schools |
| Zola, Émile | naturalism |
| Zuckmayer, Carl | Neue Sachlichkeit |